Victorian Studies in Scarlet

BY RICHARD D. ALTICK

Preface to Critical Reading
The Cowden Clarkes
The Scholar Adventurers
The English Common Reader
The Art of Literary Research
Lives and Letters
Browning's Roman Murder Story (with James F. Loucks II)
To Be in England
Victorian Studies in Scarlet

NEW YORK

Richard D. Altick

Victorian Studies

in Scarlet

W · W · NORTON & COMPANY · INC ·

Acknowledgment is made to the following for their kind permission to use copyrighted material in this book: Charles Scribner's Sons, for a quotation from *Letters of Henry James,* edited by Percy Lubbock; and Yale University Press, for quotations from *The George Eliot Letters,* edited by Gordon S. Haight.

FIRST EDITION

Copyright © 1970 by W. W. Norton & Company, Inc. All rights reserved. Published simultaneously in Canada by George J. McLeod Limited, Toronto. Printed in the United States of America.

Library of Congress Catalog Card No. 70-103962

SBN 393 08605 4

1 2 3 4 5 6 7 8 9 0

Contents

Illustrations appear between pages 160 and 161.

Author's Note

ANYONE acquainted with the voluminous litera-
ture of Victorian murder will recognize at once how much I owe
to the volumes of the Notable British Trials series, bound in
cloth of a suitably sanguine hue and published during the first
half of this century by Messrs. William Hodge of Edinburgh. Although I have used many other sources (and left untouched
even more), these full transcripts of the judicial proceedings subsequent to certain famous Victorian murders, so compact of
circumstantial detail, have been most indispensable. In fact, if
they did not exist, neither could this book.

Equally obvious, no doubt, will be my debt to the greatest
British historian of true crime, William Roughead. As Roughead
once remarked, a principal value of printed murder trials (several of which he himself edited) "resides in the light they cast
upon the social history of our race in its darker and less admirable aspects." Thanks to his sage example, more than anyone
else's, the modern chronicler is relieved of any obligation to be
censorious as he reviews the homicidal conduct of certain of his
fellow-creatures, all long since removed from the world, whether
by noose or by nature. The historian's task, fortunately, is to
record, not to rebuke. Here are the facts; let the moralizing
reader make of them what he will.

For valuable assistance in supplying the illustrations for this volume I am indebted to E. V. Gatacre and Laura Dru of Madame Tussaud's Ltd., London; Lord Gretton, O. B. E., Stapleford Park, Melton Mowbray, Leicestershire; and Thomas M. McDade, Scotland Yard, Purchase, New York. And I owe particular thanks to my editor, Carol Houck Smith, for her tireless expertise and resourcefulness in converting the manuscript into a printed book.

It is a pleasure to note that this book is, in effect, a product of the spirit of intellectual ecumenism which, in the face of numerous distractions, still manages to enrich the less publicized part of American academic life. Its subject is a blend of criminology and social history; its author is, by trade, a teacher of English literature; many of the books vital to its composition were supplied by the well-stocked and hospitable library of a College of Law; and the final typescript was prepared with the aid of a grant from a College of Humanities. To those divisions of the Ohio State University go my grateful acknowledgments.

R. D. A.

Introduction

THE FASCINATION murder has had for mankind dates as far back as Old Testament days. Can we not believe that the initial popularity of the Book of Genesis owed as much to the pioneering exploit recorded in the fourth chapter as to the earlier proceedings in the Garden of Eden? Weaponry has become much more sophisticated since Cain, according to an old tradition echoed by Hamlet, slew his brother with the jawbone of an ass. But the hold murder has exercised over men's primitive emotions and imagination has been renewed from society to society and age to age. Never was it stronger than in the Victorian era, which formed the longer part of what George Orwell called "our great period in murder, our Elizabethan period, so to speak."

My purpose is to trace, in not too uniformly solemn a spirit, the crimson thread that runs through the fabric of Victorian social history. My approach is not that of the technician, for which I can claim no qualifications in either practice or theory, but instead that of an amateur social historian who for many years has had a special interest in the Victorian scene. It is chiefly as period pieces rather than as remarkable individual examples of criminous art that the murders of the period have recommended themselves to study. But by "period pieces" I do not mean to imply the mere quaintness associated with bonnets and shawls, mutton-chop whiskers, pre-Morrisian wall hangings, and colonies of stuffed little birds in bell jars. Not much that is picturesque is to be found in the story of bloody Victorian deeds. On the contrary, the prevalence of murder and of an absorbing popular interest in murder is part of the sober, authentic chronicle of the age, a reality that demands realistic treatment.

It was in, or just before, the early Victorian era that homicide first became institutionalized as a popular entertainment, a spectator sport. The millions of men and women in our own time who devoured every grisly detail of the Rillington Place, A6, and Moor murders—to select only three sensations of the years since the Second World War—had their forebears in the Victorian generations who responded to macabre events with what on the surface appears to have been due horror but proves, on closer examination, to have been something nearer to the festival spirit. The emotions of pity and terror, as my epigraph from Sir Walter Scott suggests and much of my evidence will show—we can take for granted Aristotle's venerable statements on the theme—are not far removed from the springs of enjoyment.

I will steer clear of the perilous waters of socio-historical psychoanalysis, a branch of speculative learning for which I entertain a profound distrust. But it does seem likely that the Victorian masses' sustained enthusiasm for murder was in part a product of their intellectually empty and emotionally stunted lives, so tightly confined by economic and social circumstance. In current murder they found a ready channel both for the release of such rudimentary passions as horror, morbid sympathy, and vicarious aggression and for the sheer occupation of minds otherwise rendered blank or dull by the absence of anything more pleasing or intellectually more elevated. The recurrent presence of murder, delivered to their firesides by broadsheets, newspapers, and even Staffordshire figurines, and to their hours of outside entertainment by means reaching from gaslit melodrama to peep shows and waxworks, gave the Victorians something to think about, something for their emotions to respond to in however crude a fashion. Their typical response was, if one can make the distinction, a delicious *frisson* rather than a shudder.

In the total Victorian social temper, this tireless absorption

in murder was an element of considerable and colorful significance. In Chapters 1–5 I try to describe its remarkably broad
scope and the various ways by which it was cultivated. Here, as
throughout the book, I am less interested in the murderous act itself than in the waves it created and the often distant and unexpected shores they washed.

Moreover, the historian who is more concerned with the way
people lived than with the precise manner of their death finds in
the annals of Victorian murder a wealth of authentic social detail which is extracted with difficulty, if at all, from other sources.
This is particularly true of the published transcripts of actual
trials, whose existence has mainly determined the selection of
cases to be discussed in Chapters 6–18. In the past, these transcripts have been used primarily by amateur and professional
criminologists and by students of forensics and (often) of medical
jurisprudence. Of the various kinds of printed evidence generated
by Victorian murders, these are richest in the concrete particulars
of everyday life that the social historian values most highly; and
they have the additional virtue of being composed of testimony
sworn before a court of law and subject to cross-examination, although, since this is not a perfect world, one who uses them must
constantly allow for the possibility of perjury.

No doubt other cases than the ones dealt with in these pages
would serve the same purposes. Readers already acquainted with
the history of Victorian crime will inevitably discover some regrettable omissions; the vintage cases of Constance Kent and
Charles Bravo, for instance, are referred to only in passing because neither resulted in a formal trial and therefore did not
produce the kind of records I have preferred. In general, I have
confined myself to those cases on which the most extensive and
authentic data are readily available, without laborious recourse to
the files of contemporary newspapers and hastily compiled books,
where the risk of unreliability is higher anyway.

The value of these murder records to the social historian is
equaled only by the so-called "blue books" (the voluminous
records of evidence received by the many select committees of
inquiry of the House of Commons and the royal commissions
which investigated a wide range of social problems in the course

of the Victorian period) and by the photographs which began their visual documentation of the contemporary scene in the middle of the century. But the blue books, indispensable though they are, tend toward evidence that on the one hand is either generalized or impressionistic and on the other, statistical; and it is, in any event, often biased. As social documentation Victorian photographs, for their part, are inferior to the testimony of witnesses in a murder trial because they are—the cinematograph having not yet been invented—stop-action pictures, whereas most testimony in trials took the form of narrative. From the mouths of witnesses in the box we receive, not a single arrested view of a street scene or a painfully immobile group of people, but a running and totally unstudied account of people in action—attending to their daily business, pub crawling, quarreling in the dubious security of their homes, going on journeys, being violently and repeatedly and fatally ill. . . . We read of their diet (as reconstructed in the analytical chemist's laboratory), the contents of their pockets, their habits, their amusements, their attitudes and prejudices. Murder trials, if held to the light at the proper angle, are an almost unexcelled mirror of an epoch's mores.

We see the prevailing class bias afresh: in the preliminary hearing of Dr. Smethurst, accused of poisoning his second wife while still wedded to his first, the Crown counsel tells the magistrates that "the lady about whose death they were inquiring was a lady who moved in very respectable society, and her friends were highly respectable"—the assumption being that respectability or its converse somehow qualifies the abstract consideration of guilt or innocence, a crime being more heinous and punishment more urgent if the victim was "respectable" and therefore less deserving of being murdered.

Sometimes, too, we meet characters and situations compressed into a tiny vignette which the most skillful of artists would be hard pressed to equal. The "Rugeley sensation" of 1856 —the trial of another doctor, William Palmer—contains two such brief passages that are pregnant with implicit drama. A Manchester woman, one Anne Brookes, swears to having seen Dr. Palmer in a hotel corridor, holding up a glass of some kind of liquid to the light and shaking it. "I am a married woman," she says upon cross-examination, "and am in the habit of attending race meetings, but my husband does not sanction my going when he knows about it." No Victorian novelist, so far as I know, ever dealt with the theme of a wife who was a compulsive horse-player, but there she is, ready to be limned. Again, what a tragic story from common life is embedded in this almost casual testimony:

CHARLES BLOCKSOME, examined by Mr. Huddleston.—I was apprentice to Mr. Jones, the chemist, at Romsey in 1848. My master made a mistake in preparing a prescription for Mrs. Smith. The mistake was the substitution of strychnine for salacine (bark of willow). He destroyed himself afterwards.

Here, then, in the superficially unlikely realm of criminal records, we are brought face to face with the everyday personality of an age. Ordinary people go about their routine, lawful (or in some instances unlawful) activities, understandably unconscious that history, in the form of a court of law, will have the slightest interest in their prosaic diurnal rounds. Then, by sheer accident as far as they are concerned, a man or woman among them, acting from motives of passion or pique, violently ends another human being's life, and the interests of justice require that the antecedent and surrounding events be exhaustively canvassed; a spotlight of inquiry is turned on all those hitherto unremarkable comings and goings, the normally insignificant transactions of everyday existence. Witnesses, abruptly snatched from the usual obscurity of their lives, must recollect trivial circumstances which, had it not been for the fortuitous intrusion of a murder, would never again have figured in their memories. The actors in a once private play, a mere fragment of human existence to which the accident of murder has suddenly lent crucial meaning, in effect repeat the performance in the theater of English justice, for the uninvited but rapt entertainment of their contemporaries and, though they do not know it, for us.

The cast of characters in this book, therefore, is a double one. There are the participants in a series of celebrated real-life murder dramas, the walk-ons as well as the stars; and there are the spectators, the millions of readers throughout Britain who avidly follow the proceedings day by day, from the discovery of the corpse to the hanging of the murderer, and will remember the high points of character and episode to the end of their lives. The records they have together left behind afford us a most vivid and faithful additional perspective on the way things were in the age of Queen Victoria.

This is the progress of human passion. We ejaculate, exclaim, hold up to heaven our hand[s], like the rustic Phidele—next morning the mood changes, and we dance a jig to the tune which moved us to tears.

—Sir Walter Scott, on the popular mood when Burke was hanged

I

Early Murders for the Million

WHO CAN SAY which was more responsible for the heightened appreciation of murder in Victorian times: an early cluster of sensational cases, or the accident that they occurred during a brief passage in English history—between 1823 and 1837, the year the Queen came to the throne—when journalism was ready and eager to exploit crime, even ordinary crime, as it had never been exploited before? Certainly it was a fortunate and fateful coincidence. Thurtell, Corder, Burke and Hare, and Greenacre performed their felonious deeds, and might, under ordinary circumstances, have had their moment in the spotlight and then been forgotten, as a thousand murderers had been forgotten before them. Perhaps, except for Burke and Hare's, there was nothing extraordinary about these murders, in and of themselves. But the balladmongers and the newspapers turned them into immediate classics, the delectably horrible memory of which affected a whole generation.

A series of murders, and a nascent popular press: it was, in retrospect, a fated combination. Far from disappearing from mind after the trap had been sprung and the last drunken remnants of the crowd had staggered and sung their way from the execution site back to their filthy tenements, these cases became

household words as familiar as Sam Weller and the Duke of
Wellington, material ready to the pens of such writers as Scott,
Lamb, Hazlitt, De Quincey, Borrow, Bulwer-Lytton, and Carlyle. They were part of the early Victorian mentality. And aside
from their powerful intrinsic attraction, they conditioned the
Victorian mind to respond to later murders. In their respective
ways, they served as archetypes, paradigms of the homicidal art.
It was they which first lent murder the popularity it was to enjoy
throughout the Victorian era.

i

Sir Walter Scott, though he died five years before the
Queen's reign began, typified by anticipation the Victorian engagement with murder. In July 1826, he recorded in his journal
that he "slumbered for three or four hours over a variorum edition of the Gill's-Hill tragedy. Admirable recipe for low spirits—
for, not to mention the brutality of so extraordinary a murther, it
led John Bull into one of his most uncommon set of gambols,
until at last he became so maudlin as to weep for the pitiless
assassin, Thurtell, and treasure up the leaves and twigs of the
hedge and shrubs in the fatal garden as valuable reliques—nay,
thronged the minor theatres to see the very roan horse and yellow gigg in which his victim was transported." Scott may, at the
moment, have felt himself superior to all such vulgar fuss over a
killing, but two years later, on his way back to Edinburgh from
London, he took the trouble to make a side trip to a site at Gill's
Hill, Hertfordshire, not far from St. Albans.

The place [he wrote] has the strongest title to the description of
Wordsworth:—

> "A merry spot, 'tis said, in days of yore,
> But something ails it now—the place is cursed."

The principal part of the house has been destroyed, and only the
kitchen remains standing. The garden has been dismantled, though a
few laurels and garden shrubs run wild continue to mark the spot.
. . . The dirt of the present habitation equald its wretched desola-
tion, and a truculent-looking hag who showd us the place and received half-a-crown looked not unlike the natural inmate of such a
mansion. She indicated as much herself, saying the landlord had dis-

mantled the place because no respectable person would live there. She seems to live entirely alone, and fears no ghosts, she says.

Scott's half-crown seems to have been preceded into the hag's grubby palm by many another, because this cottage, where the murderers had stayed overnight after their deed, had become a shrine to which thousands of pilgrims made their way, and the landlord, to whom the lessee had owed considerable rent, found levying a toll a natural means of making up his deficit. The English inquisitiveness which in the later eighteenth century had persuaded a number of noble lords to open their mansions to visitors upon payment of a fee now was extended to places associated with famous murders. It was a sign of the times. True, pilgrimages to Burns's haunts had already begun, and in a decade or two Shakespeare's birthplace would be refurbished into a well-attended national monument, but on a short-term basis, at least, murder scenes consistently outdrew literary sites.

The occurrence that had won Gill's Hill its profitable notoriety was neither complicated nor very romantic. It was the murderer's superficially appealing character, as Scott recognized, which initially engaged the popular imagination. John Thurtell, the son of a prosperous Norwich merchant, having served in the Royal Marines during the closing years of the Napoleonic Wars without hearing a shot fired in anger, had after his discharge fallen in with the London "fancy"—the world of gamblers, mercenary sportsmen, and operators of dubious business enterprises, a race known in the aftermath of the Second World War as "spivs." Thurtell was especially involved with the prizefighting set as trainer and manager, and it was in this connection that he figured, as "Tom Turtle," in William Hazlitt's famous essay "The Fight," which celebrated the epic encounter between Tom Hickman, the "Gas Man," and Bill Neate on Hungerford Down, December 11, 1821. Hazlitt and Thurtell rode to the scene together in a mail coach. The latter was taciturn except when the talk got around to "fighting dogs and men, to bears and badgers" and the way to prepare prizefighters for the ring:

The whole art of training . . . consists in two things, exercise and abstinence, abstinence and exercise, repeated alternately and without end. A yolk of an egg with a spoonful of rum in it is the first thing in a morning, and then a walk of six miles till breakfast. This meal consists of a plentiful supply of tea and toast and beef-steaks. Then another six or seven miles till dinner-time, and another supply of solid beef or mutton with a pint of porter, and perhaps, at the utmost, a couple of glasses of sherry.

Later on the trip, when night had fallen and the passengers were wrapped in their great-coats,

Turtle, starting out of his sleep, swore he knew how the fight would go, for he had had a dream about it. Sure enough the rascal told us how the three first rounds went off, but "his dream," like others, "denoted a foregone conclusion." He knew his men. The moon now rose in silver state, and I ventured, with some hesitation, to point out this object of placid beauty, with the blue serene beyond, to the man of science, to which his ear he "seriously inclined," the more as it gave promise *d'un beau jour* for the morrow, and showed the ring undrenched by envious showers, arrayed in sunny smiles.

It was about the same time that George Borrow saw Thurtell, once at a gypsy camp and again at the home of a wealthy rural magistrate on whose acres Thurtell and a pugilist companion were seeking (unavailingly) permission to stage a fight. The second of Borrow's two descriptions of Thurtell in *Lavengro* supplements Hazlitt's sketchy portrait with numerous physical details:

. . . he was a man somewhat under thirty, and nearly six feet in height. He was dressed in a blue coat, white corduroy breeches, fastened below the knee with small golden buttons; on his legs he wore white lamb's-wool stockings, and on his feet shoes reaching to the ankles; round his neck was a handkerchief of the blue and bird's eye pattern; he wore neither whiskers nor moustaches, and appeared not to delight in hair, that of his head, which was of a light brown, being closely cropped; the forehead was rather high, but somewhat narrow; the face neither broad nor sharp, perhaps rather sharp than broad; the nose was almost delicate; the eyes were gray, with an expression in which there was sternness blended with something approaching to feline; his complexion was exceedingly pale, relieved, however, by certain pock-marks [in the earlier description, Borrow had called them "carbuncles"], which here and there studded his countenance; his form was athletic, but lean; his arms long. In the whole appearance of the man there was a blending of the bluff and the sharp. You might have supposed him a bruiser; his dress was that of one in all its minutiae; something was wanting, however, in his manner—the quietness of the professional man; he rather looked like one performing the part—well—very well—but still performing a part.*

Thurtell's appearance and manner, it is clear, made a deep impression on those of his acquaintances who were best able to transfer it to paper. When he posed, all unknowing, for Hazlitt's and Borrow's pens, he was not yet a criminal, except insofar as the routine career of a Regency low-life sportsman almost by definition involved an occasional flouting of the law. But in the year and a half following his appearance in Hazlitt's essay (in the *New Monthly Magazine,* February 1822), Thurtell got himself into deeper and deeper hot water. A "bombasine warehouse" he and his brother conducted had been burned out, not by accident, and they were being bothered by the insurance company. They had also contracted additional gambling debts. In order to recoup his losses, John Thurtell bethought himself of William Weare, whom the folklore generated by the ensuing tragedy credits with having been a lawyer, but who in actuality had been a waiter in a Fleet Street tavern and then in a gambling hell. In late years he had risen in the world, acquiring a fair amount of wealth as an all-around gambler, billiard shark, and promoter of crooked fights. Thurtell recruited, to assist him in his project, one Joseph Hunt, the bankrupt owner of a pub favored by the fancy, and William Probert, a former London spirit merchant who had failed for £14,000 (his wife's) and, during a sojourn in the King's Bench debtors' prison, had been detected robbing

---

* Thurtell appears also in Borrow's *The Romany Rye,* in the story told by a jockey who asked the sportsman how he could repay him for his kindness in lending him—the jockey—£200. He "bade me come and see him hanged when his time was come." The jockey did. "I arrived at H[ertford] just in the nick of time. There was the ugly jail—the scaffold—and there upon it stood the only friend I ever had in the world. Driving my Punch, which was all in a foam, into the midst of the crowd, which made way for me as if it knew what I came for, I stood up in my gig, took off my hat, and shouted, 'God Almighty bless you, Jack!' The dying man turned his pale grim face towards me—for his face was always somewhat grim, do you see— nodded and said, or I thought I heard him say, 'All right, old chap.' The next moment—my eyes water. . . ." This is one of several anecdotes told of Thurtell's last moments. Another, repeated in Alexander Smith's *Dreamthorp,* has it that his greatest anxiety as he prepared to be hanged was to hear the results of the day's championship fight.

the coffee-room till of that establishment, a venture which cost him six months in the House of Correction at Brixton.

On Friday, October 24, 1823, Thurtell and Weare drove out of London on their way to Probert's cottage at Gill's Hill, to which Weare had been invited for a relaxing weekend of shooting. Save that Weare went voluntarily, it could be said that he was taken for a ride in the Al Capone sense of the term. For the conspirators, assuming that he would be carrying money to the amount of £2,000 on his person, planned to murder him in a sequestered spot. By mistake, Hunt missed connections with the fatal gig and, in the upshot, Thurtell had to kill Weare unaided, in a lane not far from Probert's cottage. He could have used some help, to say nothing of moral support, because things did not go nearly as smoothly as he desired. Thurtell had bought a pair of pistols at a London pawnshop for £1 15s., but they proved to be a poor bargain. They were, as he later said, "no better than pop guns," because when he fired them into Weare's face, they merely had the effect of impelling Weare out of the chaise in a frantic attempt to run away. His assailant therefore had to convert one of his firearms into a bludgeon; he plunged the barrel into Weare's skull and, to adopt the blunt language of a contemporary narrative, "turned it through his brains." The rest of the bloody details need not be specified; suffice it to say that as an afterthought Thurtell also slit his victim's throat.

He then proceeded to Probert's cottage nearby, where his accomplices awaited him. While supper was on the fire, the three went to the murder scene and put Weare, stuffed into a sack, under a hedge. On their return, all partook of the Proberts' meal, except for Thurtell, who, as we shall see in a moment, was off his feed. Afterwards they drank and sang, and Thurtell, taking out Weare's gold watch and chain, gallantly hung the latter, which he said was "more fit for a lady than a gentleman," about Mrs. Probert's neck. The watch he returned to his pocket, and it was never seen again; its fate constituted the intriguing minor mystery of the case. Later the same night the conspirators went out once more, thrust Weare's body over a horse, and brought it to Probert's pond, where they dumped it. They then crowned a busy day's and night's work by dividing the booty.

At six o'clock the next morning Thurtell and Hunt returned to the scene of the murder, to "grabble" in the grass and hedge for whatever incriminating evidence might be there. When a road mender asked what they were looking for, Thurtell said that he had been pitched out of his gig at this spot the night before and had lost a penknife and a handkerchief. Their search thus having become inconveniently public, he and Hunt went off, leaving the laborer and his mate to conduct their own inquiry, which resulted in the discovery of a suspicious reddish dew on the vegetation and a bloody knife and a pistol in the cart ruts. They took the latter treasure trove to the district road surveyor, whose failure to observe that the barrel of the pistol was choked with a substance resembling brains delayed for several days the detection of the crime.

Meanwhile Thurtell and Hunt, returning to Probert's pond, took the much-traveled Weare on yet another journey, this time to a pond at Elstree, and then went their separate ways to London. On the following Wednesday, five days after the murder, they were arrested. Probert escaped indictment by turning Crown evidence—he would reach the scaffold by another route in 1825, for stealing a horse—but Thurtell and Hunt were tried and convicted. Hunt, who was proved to have been only an accessory, was reprieved and shipped to Botany Bay; Thurtell was executed.

The case caused a tremendous sensation throughout the kingdom. During the trial, the county town of Hertford was packed with sightseers, including a numerous company of "the fancy" on their way back from an open-air fight at Worcester. While Thurtell's body was being dissected, in conformity with the court's sentence, at St. Bartholomew's Hospital in London—a leisurely process which occupied some weeks—thousands of morbid curiosity-seekers passed through the dissecting room. Daily accounts of the deteriorating condition of the remains appeared in *The Times* and the *Morning Chronicle* for the benefit of those who were prevented from seeing the body in person.

The excitement the murder caused has never ceased to baffle the expert, because, apart from the specious glamor of the chief protagonist, it was actually a run-of-the-mill affair. De Quincey, writing in *Blackwood's Magazine* four years later, depicted the initial joy of the select club called the Connoisseurs of Murder when news of the murder in Gill's Hill Lane arrived in London.

I admit that at first I was myself carried away by the general enthusiasm. On the morning when the murder was made known in London, there was the fullest meeting of amateurs that I have ever known since the days of Williams [the Ratcliffe Highway murderer, 1811]; old bed-ridden connoisseurs, who had got into a peevish way of sneering and complaining "that there was nothing doing," now hobbled down to our club-room: such hilarity, such benign expression of general satisfaction, I have rarely witnessed. On every side you saw people shaking hands, congratulating each other, and forming dinner-parties for the evening; and nothing was to be heard but triumphant challenges of—"Well! will *this* do?" "Is *this* the right thing?" "Are you satisfied at last?"

But a crusty old cynic, stumping into the room on his wooden leg, threw cold water on the celebration as he growled:

"Not an original idea in the whole piece—mere plagiarism,—base plagiarism from hints that I threw out! Besides, his style is as hard as Albert Dürer, and as coarse as Fuseli." Many [continues De Quincey] thought that this was mere jealousy, and general waspishness; but I confess that, when the first glow of enthusiasm had subsided, I have found most judicious critics to agree that there was something *falsetto* in the style of Thurtell.

One of those judicious critics was Sir Walter Scott, who complained, somewhat more than a year after De Quincey's criticism, that the Thurtell affair was characterized by sheer stupidity rather than brilliance.

Indeed [he wrote] the whole history of the murder and the scenes which ensued are strange pictures of desperate and short-sighted wickedness. The feasting—the singing—the murderer with his hands still bloody hanging round the neck of one of the females the watch-chain of the murderd man, argue the utmost apathy. Even Probert, the most frightend of the party, fled no further for relief than to the brandy bottle, and is found in the very lane and at the spot of the murder seeking for the murderous weapon and exposing himself to the view of the passengers. Another singular mark of stupid audacity was their venturing to wear the clothes of their victim. There was a want of foresight in the whole arrangement of the deed and the attempts to conceal it which argued a strange inconsideration, which a professed robber would not have exhibited.

The fruits of his hectic but not uniformly intelligent labors were considerably below Thurtell's expectations. Instead of the £2,000 Weare was supposed to have been carrying with him, he proved, on posthumous inspection, to have had only three five-pound notes and some silver. The size of the loot therefore did nothing to elevate the crime above the generally mean level which Scott rightly deplored.

Perhaps its unprecedented appeal to contemporaries resided instead in the very circumstance which still commends the crime to our attention: namely, the insight it allowed into the life and characters of the world of Regency fast-buck operators, with Thurtell cast as a kind of latter-day Macheath. The murder is memorable chiefly as a violent incident in the sporting low-life of the period; and it was no accident, but only fitting, that the best-known journalist to cover the subsequent developments was Pierce Egan, whose *Life in London, or the Day and Night Scenes of Jerry Hawthorn, Esq. and Corinthian Tom,* with its thirty-six "scenes from real life" by the brothers Cruikshank, had been a famous success, much imitated in print and on the stage, only two years before Thurtell's adventure with Weare cast a garish light upon Regency life from a rather different angle. Egan's "Tom and Jerry" fame had made him a natural to cover the case, just as modern newspapers commission gossip and café-society columnists to report a sensational trial involving sex and what passes for society. His name is prominent on the title pages of two of the many pamphlets which issued hot from the press during the excitement. They are a hodgepodge of material from several sources, but the pages most positively identifiable as Egan's recount two interviews he had with Thurtell. "I have often read many of your sporting accounts with great pleasure," he told Egan. But he complained bitterly of the press's treatment: "I never committed any serious crime in my life."

He had, indeed, much to complain about in this respect, because, as the editor of the Thurtell and Hunt volume in the Notable British Trials series observes, this "was the first trial 'by newspaper,' and the first in which there was any very serious collision between the Bench and the Press as to the duties of the latter in relation to the detection of crime and its investigation."

The newspapers teemed with stories and innuendoes inadmissible in any courtroom, and the publication, before the trial was under way, of what purported to be Thurtell's confession earned the press a severe rebuke from the bench. But not only the newspaper press was guilty of gross misconduct while the case was *sub judice;* equally culpable were the printers of pamphlets, placards, and handbills which fleshed fact out with rumor, speculation, and editorial comment. According to counsel for the defense, "upwards of ten thousand of these wicked publications have been circulated in the county of Hertford. Some were on sale at Probert's cottage."

The trial itself had many points of interest. It was conducted according to the then-prevailing (but soon to be amended) rules which required the proceedings to be carried on without intermission unless the jury, and only the jury, asked for a recess. It began at eight in the morning, and thirteen hours later the judge arranged for the jury to take some refreshment in their places. (Many of the witnesses, it appears, had strengthened themselves for the ordeal of interrogation by taking liquid refreshment before they took the stand.) A little later Thurtell deferentially pointed out to the judge that he, Thurtell, had been up since six o'clock and was no longer in tip-top shape to direct his defense. After a few more witnesses were heard, the jury asked for some rest and the judge thanked them for relieving him "from a great difficulty." Thurtell's and Hunt's speeches in self-defense and the judge's charge to the jury were therefore put over until the second and last day of the trial.*

There is no official stenographic transcript of the trial. The testimony, arguments, and summing-up reproduced in contemporary accounts are from the busy pens and pencils of newspaper reporters, and the standard modern edition is a conflation

---

* Five years later, at the trial of Burke and Hare, an Edinburgh court and jury proved to be made of sterner mettle. They sat from 10 A.M. Christmas eve to 8:30 Christmas morning, the judges "stimulating their jaded nerves" by taking a brief coffee break in the middle of the night. Burke's counsel began his speech at 3 A.M. The whole trial therefore occupied a continuous span of almost twenty-four hours. By 1862 the procedure had become somewhat less rigorous. In the M'Lachlan trial (Chapter 9) the hours of sitting were from 10 A.M. to 9 P.M. Spread over three and a half days, the trial occupied forty working hours.

of these. It is for reasons of pre-Victorian delicacy, therefore, that we are deprived of the full-blooded language which naturally occurred from time to time during the testimony. "He was then driving very hard," said a witness, "at the wrong side of the road, and he called out ['here,' interrupted the reporter or editor, 'the witness used the ejaculation of whipmen who want to avoid contact on the road']." As often happens with remarks which have become part of popular lore, one, at least, was sharpened in transmission. This was the much-admired response of the Proberts' maidservant to the question, "Was the supper postponed?" "No," she is represented as having replied, "it was pork." Alas, the form of the answer in the printed record somewhat dulls its delight: "I don't know. It was pork." (This was the supper at the cottage after Weare's body had been stowed under the hedge. Thurtell, it was brought out in testimony, had no appetite for it. When he committed the murder, "the blood of Mr. Weare . . . came on his face and into his mouth in such quantities that he was nearly choked. It was in consequence of this that he was seized with sickness at supper and could not eat any pork." For Thurtell the supper *was* postponed.)

But the most famous exchange attributed to the trial does not, in fact, appear—at least in its received form—in any account. Several times in later years Thomas Carlyle quoted or referred to a supposed dialogue between counsel and witness. The form it took in a footnote in his famous review of Croker's edition of Boswell's life of Johnson (*Fraser's Magazine*, May 1832) was: "*Q*. 'What do you mean by "respectable"?'—*A*. 'He [Weare] always kept a gig.' (*Thurtell's Trial*.)" The identification of respectability with sufficient affluence to keep a gig tickled Carlyle, and he repeatedly used it in his ironic way, sometimes in the form of his own coinage, *gigmanity*, as Carlylean shorthand for bourgeois social pretension. But the exchange itself, as Carlyle reports it, seems never to have occurred. The closest the trial documents come to it is in a summary remark in the *Morning Chronicle*'s account: "He always maintained an appearance of respectability and kept a gig." The reputed exchange between counsel and witness was the invention of a writer in the *Quarterly Review* (1828) who admitted he was quoting from memory.

The textual point is an insignificant one, but the larger fact of Carlyle's sardonic infatuation with the idea of gigmanity is a sample of the many literary echoes the Thurtell case had on the threshold of the Victorian era and for many years thereafter. Bulwer adopted Thurtell as part model for his character of Tom Thornton in *Pelham.** Another of his novels, this one based on a famous eighteenth-century crime, so moved Pierce Egan that he called upon the author and presented him with a rather disagreeable souvenir, Thurtell's caul. Only the author of *Eugene Aram*, he declared, was worthy of possessing so intimate a relic of a murderer.

Thurtell was memorialized in the whole gamut of literature, appreciation of his character and exploit being expressed in the language appropriate to both high and low. To hundreds of thousands who had never heard Hazlitt's or De Quincey's name, Thurtell was immortalized in the most famous quatrain ever to issue from the press of a ballad manufacturer. The author is reputed to have been one William Webb, otherwise known as "Flare Up" (a brand of cheap gin) or "Hoppy," a former acrobat in a perambulating circus who had fallen to the low estate of linkman before being transported for stealing the jewels of a prima donna as she left the opera house. In old age Robert Browning still recited with relish the lines he had learned as a child:

> His throat they cut from ear to ear,
>   His brains they punchèd in;
> His name was Mr. William Weare,
>   Wot lived in Lyon's Inn.

ii

The second of the great pre-Victorian cases was the Red Barn murder of 1827. The victim was Maria Marten (or Martin),

---

* The name suggests that Bulwer was recalling, perhaps unconsciously, that of Mary Ashford's accused murderer in 1817 (see page 51). The name of the murderer's victim in *Pelham*, Sir John Tyrell, seems to echo "John Thurtell." Clearer evidence of Bulwer's indebtedness to the Thurtell crime is the fact that Tyrell is murdered in a lonely lane for the £2,000 he is

daughter of a mole-catcher resident at Polstead, Suffolk. Contemporary narratives made strenuous efforts to romanticize her—the fullest source, a book by one J. Curtis,* speaks of her as "the innocent nymph of her native village"—but her credentials are tarnished by the fact that she had had three illegitimate children by as many fathers. The last of these rural swains was a farmer's son named William Corder, who, according to the same authority, "appears to have indulged in an ungovernable propensity for forming intimate connexions with females." Shortly after Maria returned to her domestic hearth with the infant consequence of his latest connexion, Corder induced her to leave with him under promise of marriage. She was last seen on May 18, 1827, going (dressed in man's clothing, according to his direction) toward a red barn, rented by the Corder family, which stood half a mile from her cottage. Corder accounted for her subsequent absence by telling her parents, when he dropped in on his way to market or shooting at various times during the summer, that she had gone to Yarmouth. He remained in the vicinity until the harvest was over in mid-September, then went to London, from where he sent her father the news that he and Maria were married at

---

carrying and that the gambler-sportsman Thornton "put one hand to his mouth, and with the other gashed his throat from ear to ear." One additional detail, however, seems to have been Bulwer's own invention: after the deed, Thornton washed his bloody hands, "and, that the water might not lead to detection, *drank* it." The italics are Bulwer's.

* Curtis was one of the amiable eccentrics with whom the period abounded. His compulsive pedestrianism led him to walk several hours every day in London and its environs (the stormier the weather, the better) and to eschew all other means of transportation. He needed so little sleep that in 1834, as a stunt, he sat up for a hundred consecutive nights without once assuming a horizontal position. But his great passion was murder trials and executions. He haunted the Old Bailey, where "for his own special amusement" he took down every case in shorthand. He was a regular attendant at sermons for the condemned and did not miss an execution in the vicinity of the metropolis for a quarter of a century. The authorities rewarded Curtis's devotion by allowing him to spend more than a hundred nights with criminals in the death cell, "conversing with them with all seriousness and with much intelligence, on the great concerns of that eternal world on whose brink they were standing." As soon as news of the Marten murder arrived in London, he hastened to the scene and remained there until the execution of Corder, with whom he contracted a warm friendship. His book on the case was his only literary work. "Nothing," wrote a contemporary, "pleases him better than to be called the biographer of Corder."

last. She was alive and well on the Isle of Wight. A painful infection of the hand prevented her writing, but she sent her love.

In the autumn, her stepmother began to dream about her. In two of these visions Maria appeared to have been slain and buried in the red barn. After a considerable lapse of time, Mrs. Marten brought herself to communicate this intelligence to her husband, who, predictably, scoffed. It was true that Corder's workmen had earlier brought to their employer's attention the disagreeable odor that permeated the barn, but he had attributed it to some dead rats. A full eleven months therefore elapsed from the date of Maria's disappearance before the repeated importunities of the mole-catcher's wife finally induced him to dig up the barn floor. Maria was there, in a dreadfully mutilated and decomposed state. Within a short time Corder was arrested at Brentwood, Middlesex, where he had married the proprietress of a girls' boarding school.*

The Polstead "Cherry Fair," held annually in mid-July, had never before attracted a crowd as large as the one that packed its street and inns this summer, on the eve of Corder's trial at the county town of Bury St. Edmunds. It was estimated that two hundred thousand pilgrims came, some from fifty miles' distance, to inspect the fatal building and cut or pry off a souvenir. Only the installation of a guard prevented total demolition of the barn. Attracted by placards, between five and seven thousand people gathered in the open air within view of the barn to hear a Methodist preacher from London deliver a powerful sermon on the moral lessons to be learned from Maria's "untimely end." Corder's lawyers complained during the trial that "theatrical representations" of the murder were exhibited in the village,

---

* This lady had become Mrs. Corder as a result of his advertisement in the *Morning Herald*, November 13, 1827, that he was an affluent gentleman eager to hear from "any agreeable lady, who feels desirous of meeting with a sociable, tender, kind, and sympathising companion." This advertisement pulled forty-five replies (postpaid, as he had stipulated). A second appeal, in *The Times* twelve days later, attracted fifty-four replies, the texts of which are reprinted in Curtis's book on the case (1828). They are of substantial interest to the historian of manners, not least for their copious illustration of the variety of prose styles adopted by pre-Victorian spinsters and widows wishing to intimate, in a modest but unmistakable way, that they were open to offers.

one within trumpet sound of his mother's cottage. These may have been the puppet shows alluded to at another point in the trial; the term used is rather general. There were also camera obscura displays, one of which "insured to the proprietors a rich harvest" by depicting "the scene in the 'Red Barn' where the mutilated body was lying on a door on the floor, surrounded by the Coroner and the gentlemen of the jury as they appeared on . . . the day after the fatal discovery took place." Another optical arrangement, mounted in a caravan, seems to have been a promotional device rather than a money-maker in itself: a powerful magnifying glass enlarged twentyfold the dimensions of a print showing the Red Barn (its celebrity requires capitalization henceforth), and a placard advised that a "correct likeness of William Corder, price sixpence, might be purchased at a shop near the Abbey-gate, Bury." It was a prosperous season for many local trades, from religion to print-selling. But not only Suffolk profited by Corder's deed. As we shall see in Chapter 4, its beneficent effects were felt in many directions, as far away as the London stage and the Staffordshire potteries.

Corder, emulating Thurtell, conducted his own defense. It is recorded that "he seemed to be vain of a pair of blue French spectacles" through which he smilingly gazed at the witnesses. Whether or not this affectation had an adverse effect upon the jury, he was quickly adjudged guilty. On the day of his execution, August 11, 1828, all the workmen in Bury St. Edmunds and the surrounding countryside left their jobs to attend the ceremony.

iii

What remained of the Red Barn was still being visited when, at the beginning of November, the imagination of all Britain, nourished but not sated by what it fed upon, shifted its attention to Edinburgh. The arrest of the two Irish "resurrectionists," William Burke and William Hare, and the disclosure of their frightful commerce in cadavers generated throughout the nation a hysteria which was seldom equaled during the long remainder of the century. It was due partly to the unusual number of victims attributed to them and partly to the extraordinarily ruthless nature of their activity in behalf of medical education. Their total acknowledged kill over a period of nine months was sixteen hapless men and women—quite sufficient to guarantee their immediate and lasting fame.* Thurtell and Corder claimed but one victim apiece; Burke and Hare, on the other hand, practiced what can only be called miniature genocide.

It is true that there was a certain repetitiousness in the melancholy roll. As "the Ettrick Shepherd," one of the regular symposiasts in the popular *Blackwood's Magazine* feature, "Noctes Ambrosianae," commented, it was "First ae drunk auld wife, and then anither drunk auld wife, and then a third drunk auld wife, and then a drunk auld or sick man or twa. The confession got unco monotonous—the Lights and Shadows o' Scottish Death want relief." The routine, however, as the Shepherd went on to concede, was refreshingly violated on two occasions: first, when the victim was a veteran eighteen-year-old prostitute whose body, when displayed on the dissecting table to which it had been duly consigned, retained the power to please the beholder; and some months later, when Daft Jamie, a harmless Edinburgh street youth of deficient intellect, fell prey to the murderers.

But over against their lack of imagination (imagination can be a positive handicap to businessmen like Burke and Hare, who knew a good thing when they stumbled upon it and saw no reason to vary the pattern) may be placed the horrible efficiency of their method, efficiency so great, in fact, that as applied to them the term "resurrectionist" was a misnomer. They converted what had hitherto been a relatively tolerated trade, however illegal and repulsive to the moral sensibilities it may have been, into a grim racket. That was the gravamen of the charge against them. Earlier body snatchers, such as those who were reputed, on tenuous authority, to have removed Laurence Sterne's body from its

---

* The computation is Burke's own, and on the whole he had no reason to exaggerate. But, as in most such cases of multiple homicide, rumor quickly outran sober factuality. Some estimates of Burke and Hare's toll ran as high as thirty or forty, but these probably were the products of sheer exuberance. The quantitative nineteenth-century English murder record is probably held by one Mary Ann Cotton, executed in 1873 for the poisoning, over a period of a dozen years, of twenty-five people, young and old.

grave near London's Bayswater Road, almost in the shadow of Tyburn Tree, and sold it to the Cambridge University school of medicine, depended on nature to do their initial work for them; their offense lay merely in violating the decencies associated with Christian burial.

Burke and Hare, however, anticipated nature and bypassed the grave completely. Their exclusive customer, Dr. Robert Knox, was a professor of anatomy who, according to his own statement, had under his tutelage over four hundred students eager to learn the things every good doctor should know. So large an enrollment in the dissecting room required a steady flow of classroom supplies, and, with the demand multiplied several times over because of the presence of a half-dozen other teaching anatomists in the city, these supplies were simply not forthcoming in the ordinary course of events. Burke and Hare hit upon the happy solution of manufacturing their own product, with only moderate assistance by way of debilitating disease, alcoholism, meager diet, and the ravages of age. Given raw material in a weakened condition—and there was an inexhaustible fund of it in Scotland—their tried-and-true formula was simply the liberal administration of cheap spirits in order to reduce the prospective cadaver to a state of acquiescence, and then the determined application of hand and knee to the breathing apparatus, a technique now enshrined in the language by the verb "to burke." All that remained was for the Burke & Hare Punctual Delivery Company, which prided itself on the freshness of its merchandise, to deliver the product to Dr. Knox's "museum," they without bothering with even maimèd rites, he without raising any awkward questions. The traffic was conducted on as businesslike a basis as anybody could wish for: at the outset, the standard rate for a subject was £10, with a pound or two knocked off for any serious defects. Later, when the production line was in full operation, the scale allowed for seasonal rates, £10 in winter, £8 in summer.

Edinburgh opinion, once the long series of transactions became public knowledge, could not persuade itself that Knox would not at some time or other have been uneasy about the origin of what Burke and Hare brought to his door jammed in-

side a tea chest. His standing in the community in the months
following the arrest of his valued suppliers was not to be envied.

> Up the close and doun the stair,
> But and ben wi' Burke and Hare.*
> Burke's the butcher, Hare's the thief,
> Knox the boy that buys the beef.

As was to be expected, the voluminous nonce literature inspired by the partners' systematic depletion of the Edinburgh
slum population for mercenary ends—twenty or more books and
pamphlets, twenty-three broadsides, and twenty-two ballads,
according to the fullest bibliography—concentrated on the grisly
narrative, the background being painted in only as it was essential to the full development of the theme.† The authors were
intent solely upon conveying the horror of Burke and Hare's
operations, and they may well have taken for granted that their
readers were sufficiently aware of the fetid conditions in which
the murderers and their victims existed without having to be
reminded of them. But despite their emphasis on events rather
than locale, into all accounts of the West Port atrocities, as they
were called, necessarily crept an appalling sense, still vivid to
us today, of the degradation in which the victims lived—the
sordidness of their surroundings in the festering slums, the filth
and depravity and hopelessness of their personal lives, sodden
with drink and seething with vermin. And the fact that Burke
and Hare chose as their special prey penniless transients, who
it was reasonable to assume never would be missed, implicitly
generalized the Edinburgh conditions into a picture of the state

---

* In the Scots tongue, *but* and *ben* are, respectively, the outer and inner
rooms of a two-room house.

† Burke and Hare inspired later writers as diverse as Robert Louis
Stevenson ("The Body-Snatcher") and Dylan Thomas (the script for an
unproduced motion picture, *The Doctor and the Devils*). One famous writer
in Burke and Hare's own time who did not contribute to the literature,
despite an invitation to do so, was Scott. Two months after Burke was
hanged, Sir Walter received a letter from David Paterson, Knox's purchasing
agent, "suggesting that I should write on the subject of Burke and Hare, and
offering me his invaluable collection of anecdotes. 'Curse him's imperance
and him's damn insurance,' as Mungo says in the farce. 'Did ever one hear
the like?' The scoundrel has been the companion and patron of such atrocious murderers and kidnappers, and he has the impudence to write to any
decent man."

of the poor in Scotland at large. The reason why the Edinburgh streets and tenements abounded with so many derelicts, male and female, of all ages from childhood to senility, was that things were even worse outside the city. These pathetic homeless wanderers would possibly have starved sooner in the country; had it not been for Burke and Hare, the lease of life some of them had in Edinburgh would have been longer, although hardly less miserable.

What effect, one wonders, did the intensive publicity thus given to the conditions of life in Edinburgh's lower depths have upon the social temper of the time? The printed literature on Burke and Hare constituted, in the aggregate, a document of unintended but potentially explosive propaganda value, anticipating by a number of years the shocking reports of the inquiries into social conditions conducted by select committees of Parliament, royal commissions, and private agencies—exposés which would usher in an era when the ruling class would gradually apply its social conscience to the problems of the industrial and urban poor.

The revelations attending the Burke and Hare case, however, seem not to have had any direct and immediate effect, apart from the passage four years later of the Anatomy Act, which successfully regulated the traffic in cadavers. But this was, of course, a specialized enactment applicable to a minuscule portion of the population. Contemporary readers were probably too mesmerized by the cold-blooded villainy of the murderers and by pity for their wretched victims to reflect that those unfortunates were distinguished from countless others only by the chance that they died violently at the hands of a pair of evil flesh peddlers—in the most literal sense—rather than as the slow victims of an equally pitiless social situation. Nobody remarked that the preponderant indictment in the case of Burke and Hare was of a whole neglectful society rather than of two relatively negligible criminals and a woman "paramour." After Burke was executed and Hare, having turned King's evidence, was set free, public passions subsided and, except for the absence of Burke, British society was not an iota improved.

Yet if responsible people in the decade before Victoria's

accession did not consciously follow up their shudders with a firm resolution to do something about the conditions that produced human dregs fit only for extermination by resurrection men, the subliminal effect of Burke and Hare may have been to predispose them to sympathize with and assist the humanitarian movement which slowly gathered momentum in the thirties. In the long chain of events which led finally to a moderate amelioration of life among the poor, it is conceivable that the revulsion aroused by the Burke and Hare case played a significant, if undemonstrable, role.

Valuable though the published trials of later murderers are in other respects as social documents, none approaches that of Burke and Hare in its lurid revelation of life among the destitute and derelict. The London underworld of *Oliver Twist,* for example, is not reflected in any extensive trial record I know of. Throughout the long Victorian era murders occurred with routine frequency in the shadowy criminal neighborhoods of London and the other large cities. But the police, the courts, and the press handled them as a matter of course; few if any were the stuff of which celebrated crimes are made. To this extent, the archives of Victorian murder fail the historian bent upon gaining additional insight into one large and, on the whole, obscure portion of Victorian social life.

Near the end of the era, however, in 1888, occurred a series of murders which evoked in the British public horror of a quality it had not experienced for sixty years, and which may have produced somewhat the same effect upon the contemporary social outlook that I have postulated in the case of Burke and Hare. These were, of course, Jack the Ripper's killing and sexual mutilation of five East End prostitutes. Since the psychopathic murderer was never caught, the case occasioned no trial, and for that reason will not figure, except briefly in two or three connections, in the pages to come. But its records contain a wealth of authentic social detail. Seen a little hazily through the necessarily evasive language of contemporary newspaper reports and now with clinical explicitness in recent books, the East End of London in the late eighties, the haunt of the most degraded prostitutes conceivable, takes its place with the vile Edinburgh tenements of the twenties. Once again there is no evidence that in its fear-filled preoccupation with the mystery of the silent, elusive, maniacal killer, the late Victorian public recognized the wider social implications of the case. It was merely coincidental that only a few months after the last of Jack the Ripper's victims was discovered, the first volume of Charles Booth's great sociological study, *Labour and Life of the People* (later retitled *Life and Labour of the People in London*) appeared. It was only coincidental, too, that this first volume dealt with East London, where more than a third of the people lived in the most desperate poverty, and that another volume, published less than two years later, contained a remarkable "poverty map" which included the very area in which the Ripper had operated.

Booth's revelations, though based upon research on a street-by-street, door-to-door scale never before attempted, were not wholly new; previous journalists and urban missionaries had contributed to an ever-growing literature on life among the poor and outcast of the metropolis. But it may be that the publicity attending Jack the Ripper, like the furor over Burke and Hare, subconsciously prepared the public—which hitherto had been generally apathetic to the sentimentalism, impressionism, and indignation that had characterized the preceding books and pamphlets—to pay greater heed to Booth's infinitely more authoritative seventeen-volume anatomy of London social conditions. If the plight of the lowest of the low eventually was relieved—in part through the growing power of Labour politics—the accident of well-publicized murder, which dramatized the long-existing situation, may have been in part responsible. If so, neither Burke and Hare nor the unknown Ripper committed their ferocious deeds without some ultimate social benefit. An aroused social conscience, as a number of Victorian cases prove in more restricted contexts, is sometimes an unexpected by-product of murder.

iv

This—passing over a number of murders which would merit inclusion in any more ambitious survey—brings us to the very eve of the new Queen's reign. On December 28, 1836, a London

policeman discovered on a building site near the Pine Apple toll
bar, Edgware Road, a sack containing a quantity of bloody
clothing and the torso of a woman, lacking head and legs. Ten
days later, the head was found jammed in the sluice of the Ben
Jonson lock in the Regent's Canal, Stepney; after another interval
a pair of legs, which perfectly fitted the torso, came to light near
Camberwell. The victim thus had been distributed in a roughly
triangular pattern, several miles to a side. Three months after the
first discovery, she was identified as a widow washerwoman
named Hannah Brown, aged between forty and fifty.

Inquiries revealed that several days before Christmas, Hannah had told friends that she was to be married to a Mr. James
Greenacre, a forty-year-old cabinet maker, and Greenacre himself had verified the happy news. The wedding was fixed for St.
Giles's Church on Christmas day. Accompanied by her be-
trothed, Hannah moved out of her lodgings on the afternoon of
Christmas Eve. Late that same evening, Greenacre had made another round of her acquaintances to inform them that the wedding was off, because Hannah had grossly deceived him as to the
amount of property she would bring to their union. Such an explanation seemingly was perfectly understandable and acceptable to persons of their social condition. But nothing more was
seen of Hannah—nothing identifiable, that is—until March 20,
when her brother recognized the head found in the canal lock
as hers.

Greenacre was arrested at his Lambeth lodgings. With him
was his mistress, Sarah Gale, who had in her possession Hannah
Brown's earrings and a blood-stained handkerchief. He made
three separate confessions, partly designed to exculpate Sarah
(she was to be transported for life as an accessory) and partly
in hope of reducing the charge to manslaughter. The confessions
agreed on the main point, that after taking leave of her friends,
he and Hannah had repaired to his rooms, where, already the
worse for liquor, they continued to celebrate Christmas Eve with
tea laced with rum. Deeming this a propitious time to talk
finances, Greenacre raised the question of the three or four
hundred pounds she had assured him were hers. She "made a
laugh of the matter, and said I was as bad as she was, as I had

deceived her as regarded my property. She then began to sneer and laugh. . . ."

It was the familiar case of the cheater cheated; but Greenacre failed to see the humor. A spirited tussle ensued, in the course of which, according to that version of events most favored by the public, Greenacre knocked her eye out with a rolling-pin.* The argument grew rougher and rougher, until Hannah succumbed to her injuries. Greenacre made sure by cutting her throat, then partially dismembered her with a saw he used in his trade.

But it was not this activity, gruesome though it may have been, which most enthralled the buyers of newspapers and broadsides. Rather, it was Greenacre's narrative of his ensuing holiday travels. He wrapped Hannah's head in a silk handkerchief and carried it in an omnibus to Gracechurch Street, City, where he transferred to another bus going to Mile End, Stepney, calmly resting the globular parcel on his knee the whole time. From Mile End he walked to the canal and rid himself of this encumbrance. Then, returning across the river, he disposed of the legs in a Camberwell marsh. Finally he wrapped the torso in sacking and carried it on his back through the streets until he met a carter who compassionately allowed him to rest his burden on the tailboard of the cart. At the Elephant and Castle, where their intended routes diverged, Greenacre, after thanking the carter for the accommodation, hired a cab which took him the rest of the way, to the toll bar in the Edgware Road. Thus, at considerable expense of time and fare, he had disposed of the embarrassments of his deed.

The omnibus rides especially appealed to the popular imagination; this was the first time that this new form of urban transportation—George Shillibeer had put his first buses on the London streets in 1829—figured in a murder case. Inevitably, fancy embellished fact; an apocryphal story which went the rounds

---

* The children in the streets trilled a variant version which had the pleasant effect of an internal rhyme in the third line:

> Oh! Jimmy Greenacre!
> You shouldn't have done it, Greenacre;
> You knocked her head in with the rolling-pin,
> You wicked Jimmy Greenacre.

was that on leaving one of the buses with his parcel, Greenacre had jocosely remarked to the conductor that "by right he ought to pay for two passengers." *

The climax of the Greenacre fever came on May 2, some seven weeks before the young Queen's accession to the throne, when a vast crowd gathered outside Newgate Prison to applaud Greenacre's execution. A number of men and boys perched on lampposts all night, and the newspapers reported that the competition for other places of vantage, in windows commanding the site, was greater than on any previous occasion in the history of Newgate. After the trap was sprung, the women in the crowd were even more ferocious than the men as they fought for a good look at Greenacre's body.

Thurtell—Corder—Burke and Hare—Greenacre: it was an auspicious, indeed (if one may coin a necessary word) gorious prelude to a long reign in which the supply of murder would happily prove adequate to the unremitting demand. Given the spirit of the age, it was but fitting that in the course of forty-two years, the Queen herself was to encounter a would-be assassin no fewer than seven times. She escaped unharmed in all cases; but the immunity that did hedge a queen did not protect some thousands of her subjects.

---

* Another story, this one with a reverse twist, had it that when Greenacre asked the conductor the fare and the conductor replied "Sixpence a head," the murderer nearly fainted. Collecting all the grisly humor that acquired currency in the wake of a great murder would be a rewarding occupation in itself.

2

"A Highly Popular
Murder Had Been
Committed"

THE ENGLISH EXPERIENCE has repeatedly shown
that a common enthusiasm is a great and useful social leveler. A
powerful force in the nineteenth century, one which neutralized
the political radicalism and class struggle that brought revolution to continental countries, was the evangelical religion. Evangelicalism, a spiritual and moral climate rather than a denomina-
tion—for it not only was a vital agent within the Church of England but permeated the nonconformist sects as well—originated
in the middle class. But from the early years of the century onward it exerted great influence upon the upper class (who, after
having entertained a relaxed attitude toward religion and morality during the deistic eighteenth century, now resumed church-
going and the performance of good works) and upon at least the
more receptive and pliable portion of the masses. Whatever the
shortcomings of evangelicalism, it did unite high and low in a
common atmosphere of piety, concern for the souls of one's
brothers, and stringent, self-conscious morality.

It has been observed less often that at the opposite end of

the moral spectrum, the widely shared taste for murder had a similar effect. When gentleman and workingman found a common interest in the most recent sanguinary deed related in the newspapers—as, in the latter part of the century, they joined in singing the latest music hall songs and adulating current music hall stars—this, as much as any pervasive body of spiritual principles, helped ease the social tensions of the time.

Although respectable London families would not themselves be seen buying broadsheets describing the most recent outrage, they would send a footman out to buy half a dozen copies from a street hawker. The passion for real-life murder was most unapologetically manifest among "the million," as the Victorians called the working class, but it prevailed as well by the firesides of the middle class and sometimes, though rather more covertly, in the stately halls of the aristocracy.

At certain trials, the fashionable vied with the unwashed for the few spectator seats available in the ill-ventilated, overheated Old Bailey. And conspicuous among them were women. We are told that in 1877, when the jury returned in the sordid case of the Stauntons,* the benches "were filled even at this dread hour with the bevy of smartly dressed, overjewelled women who had drunk champagne in the luncheon interval and skimmed the pages of *Punch* when the interest flagged." Nine years later, when Adelaide Bartlett's trial came to a rousing conclusion in the same courtroom, the smart set was again well represented.

The interest which genteelly reared women evinced in murder was among the most striking of the innumerable Victorian paradoxes. "It is a noteworthy fact," commented a minor novelist in 1864,

that women of family and position, women who have been brought up in refined society, women who pride themselves upon the delicacy of their sensibilities, who would faint at the sight of a cut finger and go into hysterics if the drowning of a litter of kittens were mentioned in their hearing—such women can sit for hours listening to the details of a cold-blooded murder. They will put aside their costly lace veils

---

* In these earlier chapters, brief allusion sometimes will be made to Victorian murder cases which are described more fully later in the book. To locate the principal discussion of each case, the reader may consult the index.

to catch a glimpse of the man who has hurried his brother man to an untimely death. They will peer through their jewelled eyeglasses at the murderous weapon, the knife, or pistol, or blood-stained club, which is brought into court as mute witness of the deed of wrong.

Repeatedly we find in mid-Victorian fiction women whose candid relish for murder is represented so matter-of-factly as to suggest that it was nothing out of the ordinary, merely an amusing but unreprehensible departure from the feminine stereotype. The elderly Mrs. Hopkinson, in Emily Eden's *The Semi-Detached House* (1859), remarks, "I like a good murder that can't be found out; that is, of course, it is very shocking, but I like to hear about it." And eight years later, in Julia Kavanagh's *Sybil's Second Love*, Mrs. Mush is heard: " 'Well, I do not like accidents,' replied Mrs. Mush, 'there is no meaning in them; but,' she added confidentially, 'I dearly like a murder. Of course I do not wish for murders,' she continued, in a tone of resigned virtue; 'but when there is one, why, I like it. It is human nature.' "

Human nature it was, indeed; and that is why all portions of Victorian society, the poor and the rich, the illiterate and the classically educated, the children and the grandparents, the women as well as the men, welcomed representations of murder in whatever form they took.

i

Murder had been a favorite topic of popular literature in England as early as Elizabethan times. Then, and in the two succeeding centuries, occasional homicides, pathetic or merely horrifying, were recounted in broadsheets, along with such other newsworthy events as military and naval victories, ceremonial observances, fearful calamities, and curiosities such as ghostly apparitions and freak animals, human or barnyard. From Defoe's era in the early eighteenth century, likewise, Grub Street authors scratched for a living by concocting catchpenny biographies, part fact, part pure invention, which narrated the careers of eminent criminals. Collections of such biographies, along with accounts of the malefactors' trials and their ensuing executions, found a ready sale among the literate part of the population. The most

famous was the *Newgate Calendar*, first issued in 1773 and repeatedly enlarged in the early years of the next century. The
name was also used for at least two completely new collections,
in 1809–10 (enlarged 1826–28) and in 1841. A similar compila-
tion, with a title of its own, was *Celebrated Trials, and Remarkable Cases of Criminal Jurisprudence, from the Earliest Records
to the Year 1825* (six volumes, 1825), edited by George Borrow
—a youthful literary chore which he describes in *Lavengro*. The
physical bulk of these collections suggested the format of learned
reference works, but their contents were decidedly more lively.
Their popularity in the pre-Victorian decades was a modest but
unmistakable indication of the increasing and enduring taste for
tales of fatal violence which was about to be so memorably exploited.

In the early nineteenth century, intelligence of the latest
murders was still being brought to the masses chiefly in the form
of halfpenny or penny broadsheets, a form of printed communication that had its origins in the days of Elizabeth I. Of the many
printers in this trade in London and the country, the most famous in retrospect, as he seems also to have been the most
productive, was James (Jemmy) Catnach, who had come to
London from Newcastle-on-Tyne in 1813 and set up shop at
Seven Dials, an unsavory neighborhood just east of the present
Cambridge Circus, at a point where a number of narrow thor-
oughfares converge upon Monmouth Street. Seven Dials was
long notorious as the fount of sensational, often salacious, and
in any event extremely cheap "literature for the people." A
shifting complement of decrepit, gin-thirsty authors, "the Seven
Bards of Seven Dials" as they were called, concocted the texts of
broadsides to order, on any subject Catnach deemed saleable
at the moment. The resultant appeals to laughter, patriotism,
sentiment, scorn, or horror, depending on the news or mood of
the moment, were hawked in London streets and village lanes
by a corps of "paper-workers" who, if their specialty was murder broadsides, were also known as "death-hunters." Those who
vended their wares on the move, with accompanying sales talk,
were known as "running patterers," while their colleagues who,
like Silas Wegg in *Our Mutual Friend*, worked at a fixed location

were "standing patterers." The latter's were sometimes audio-visual operations, the talk being supplemented by pictorial boards illustrating the contents of the merchandise being hawked. Painted in the brightest colors and wholly negligent of perspective and background, each board was divided into compartments, in the manner of present-day comic strips.

This information comes, as does most of what we know about the street sale of Victorian murder literature, from that peerless sociological journalist Henry Mayhew. The board he describes was used to promote the broadsides and pamphlets dealing with the Manning sensation of 1849—an event which will be referred to so often in the following pages that it must be summarized at once. It involved a husband-and-wife team who, when their story unfolded, faintly reminded some observers of Macbeth and his lady. Maria Manning, a Swiss-born lady's maid formerly in the household of the Duchess of Sutherland, was married to a railway guard of criminal tendencies but lived off and on with an Irishman named Patrick O'Connor, a customs officer and petty usurer. On August 9, 1849, the Mannings, having invited O'Connor to dine with them in their lodgings at Bermondsey, did him in, Maria leading off with a pistol and her husband following up with a chisel. They then buried the man who came to dinner in quicklime under the kitchen floor. After helping themselves to his cash and bonds, they went their separate ways. The police eventually caught up with Maria in Edinburgh and with Frederick on the Isle of Jersey. During their trial their demeanor toward each other was distinctly frigid, not least because husband tried to pin all the blame on wife. Maria's histrionic, sometimes hysterical behavior in prison and in the courtroom added dramatic interest to the case. In the prison chapel, half an hour before they were hanged, the couple kissed and made up, asserting that they bore no permanent animosity toward each other; not that they would have had much opportunity to do so. Their execution at Horsemonger Lane Gaol attracted a vast and unruly mob. Maria's choice of a black satin gown for the ceremony is said to have caused Victorian women to relegate such dresses to the farthest recesses of their wardrobes, where they remained for many years until the evil associations had faded.

These, then, were the personages depicted on the street hawker's board Henry Mayhew described:

In the Mannings' board there were . . . compartments . . . showing the circumstances of the murder, the discovery of the body of Connor [*sic*], the trial, &c. One standing patterer, who worked a Mannings' board, told me that the picture of Mrs. Manning, beautifully "dressed for dinner" in black satin, with "a low front," firing a pistol at Connor, who was "washing himself," while Manning, in his shirt sleeves, looked on in evident alarm, was greatly admired, especially out of town. "The people said," observed the patterer, "'O, look at him a-washing hisself; he's a doing it so nattral, and ain't a-thinking he's a-going to be murdered. But was he really so ugly as that? Lor! such a beautiful woman to have to do with him.' You see, sir, Connor wasn't flattered, and perhaps Mrs. Manning was. I have heard the same sort of remarks both in town and country. I patters hard on the women such times, as I points them out on my board in murders or any crimes. I says: 'When there's mischief a woman's always the first. Look at Mrs. Manning there on that werry board—the work of one of the first artists in London—it's a faithful likeness, taken from life at one of her examinations, look at *her*. She fires the pistol, as you can see, and her husband was her tool.' . . . It answers best, sir, in my opinion, going on that patter. The men likes it, and the women doesn't object, for they'll say: 'Well, when a woman is bad, she *is* bad, and is a disgrace to her sex.' There's the board before them when I runs on that line of patter, and when I appeals to the 'lustration, it seems to cooper the thing. They *must* believe their eyes."

Veterans who, like the one quoted, revealed to Mayhew the secrets of their wily trade, agreed that of all the topics dealt with in their broadsides and little books, murder sold best, followed at some distance by really *good* fires.

The sales figures that come down to us have little real value as statistics, because they are nothing more than (possibly) "informed" guesses; but they suggest the order of magnitude in which contemporary observers thought of the murder-broadside trade. Catnach's biographer, Charles Hindley, claims that in 1823 Catnach alone, working four presses day and night, produced a quarter of a million copies of a "Full, True and Particular Account of the Murder of Mr. Weare by John Thurtell and His Companions," a record soon broken when he added two more printers and turned out 500,000 copies of the trial proceedings. According to Mayhew, the Manning murder and the immediately preceding Rush affair of 1848–49 were celebrated by an outpouring of 2,500,000 pieces each, and four other murders, including the earlier Red Barn and Greenacre sensations, sold about 1,650,000 each—figures which presumably include the output of all the printers who joined in keeping the public informed and entertained.

Mayhew's informants pointed out, however, that murders, though incomparably profitable when conditions were right, were chancey things. The popular response to a new murder could not be reliably forecast at the outset. In ideal circumstances, when the great public was hungry for a sensation, it would indeed respond in gratifying numbers. But, said one old hand, "Greenacre didn't sell so well as might have been expected, for such a diabolical out-and-out crime as he committed; but you see he came close after Pegsworth, and that took the beauty off him. Two murderers together is never no good to nobody. Why there was Wilson Gleeson, as great a villain as ever lived—went and murdered a whole family at noon-day—but Rush coopered him—and likewise that girl at Bristol—made it no draw to any one." Still, he added, "There's nothing beats a stunning good murder, after all. . . . When I commenced with Rush, I was 14s. in debt for rent, and in less than fourteen days I astonished the wise men in the east by paying my landlord all I owed him. Since Dan'el Good there had been little or nothing doing in the murder line—no one could cap him—till Rush turned up a regular trump for us." *

The contents of the street literature of murder varied somewhat with the occasion and the period. Sometimes, to cash in

---

* William Pegsworth in 1837 stabbed to death a shopkeeper in the Ratcliffe Highway who had entered judgment against him for 20s. he owed for a jacket he bought for his son.

John Gleeson Wilson (Mayhew erred in transcribing the name) killed a ship captain's wife, her two children, and her servant in their Liverpool house in 1849. No motive was established for the deed, but the judge rejected a plea of insanity and Gleeson was hanged before a crowd of one hundred thousand.

"That girl at Bristol" was Sarah Thomas, a maidservant who in 1849 used a stone to bash in the head of her mistress, a sixty-one-year-old eccentric named Elizabeth Jefferies, who she claimed, probably on good grounds, had grievously mistreated her. She was hanged despite the ferocious resistance she offered; it took half a dozen men to deliver her to the scaffold. The hang-

at the earliest possible moment, the broadside would contain
simply a terse account of the murder itself. Libel laws then
being far less stringent than they are now, if the murderer was
not immediately identified, the author of the sheet suggested
candidates for the distinction. " 'Then,' said one Death-hunter,
'we has our fling, and I've hit the mark a few chances that way.
We had, at the werry least, half-a-dozen coves pulled up in the
slums that we printed for the murder of 'the Beautiful Eliza
Grimwood, in the Waterloo-road.' I did best on Thomas Hopkins, being the guilty man—I think he was Thomas Hopkins—
'cause a strong case was made out again him.' " *

After the scarehead announcement of the crime, usually
contained in a handbill measuring 9½ by 7½ inches, the printer
would, if encouraged by the sale of this initial venture, issue
fresh broadsides, twice the size of the first, recounting new developments in the manner of newspaper extras. These and the
subsequent broadsheets which covered the trial and execution
drew most of their contents from the newspapers. Some broadsheets, perhaps the commonest of all varieties of "gallows literature," were of the comprehensive type. They included a prose
résumé of the murder itself, a confession (if such had been
vouchsafed by the condemned man, or in some instances even
if it had not), perhaps a lugubrious ballad allegedly composed
by him in the death cell, and finally a description of the execution itself, including the sufferer's last dying speech. The ballad

---

man Calcraft said it was the most pathetic scene he had ever witnessed.

Daniel Good, a London coachman, killed his paramour, Jane Jones, in
1842, sawed her body apart, burned the head and limbs in the harness room,
and buried her trunk beneath a pile of hay in the stable. One memorable
feature of this case was that Good remained at large for two weeks, during
which all England was looking for him. He finally turned up at Tunbridge,
working as a builder's helper.

* This was the "Waterloo Road Mystery" of 1838. Eliza Grimwood, a
lady of the evening, was found in her lodgings with throat cut and multiple
stab wounds. She lived with her cousin, a bricklayer named William Hubbard, who shared the proceeds of her vocation when he tired of laying
bricks. Two depressions in the pillow on her bed were strong *prima facie*
evidence that she had done business the night before, while Hubbard, following the protocol adopted at such times, slept upstairs. Whether the
unidentified customer or Hubbard himself killed her was never ascertained.
This was one of the most famous cases handled by Inspector Field, one of
Dickens's favorite Scotland Yard detectives.

conventionally was laden with moral admonitions, a device employed by the printer's hireling lyricists to fend off the persistent complaints of the pious that crime literature of the streets was morally poisonous. And if it happened that the murderer had a surviving wife or sweetheart, the broadside also featured a love letter, beginning in the vein of "Dear ———, Shrink not from receiving a letter from one who is condemned to die as a murderer. Here, in my miserable cell, I write to one whom I have, from my first acquaintanceship, held in the highest esteem. . . ." Gallows literature, in fact, had something for every taste.

In 1836 Parliament revoked the provision in the act of 1752 which required that a condemned criminal be hanged just two days after sentence was passed, unless the day of execution happened to fall on Sunday, in which case it was to be postponed to Monday. The extended interval between conviction and execution gave more time for the Seven Dials poet to cultivate his muse and for the presses to turn out the results. Before 1836, the "sorrowful lamentation" sheet, featuring the criminal's repentance and his moving advice to his survivors ever to tread in the path of virtue, was almost unknown. "There wasn't no time for a Lamentation; sentence o' Friday, and scragging o' Monday. So we had only the Life, Trial, and Execution." On the other hand, the wider spacing of events brought the risk that interest in the case might lapse. This was a peril already built into the earlier phase of a *cause célèbre*, when, after the discovery of the body, the coroner's inquest, and the magistrates' hearing—all of which might occupy but a brief span of time—several weeks or even months might pass before the trial, thus taxing the trade's ability to keep the public appetite alive. "There's so long to wait between the murder and the trial," an old flying stationer complained to Mayhew, "that unless the fiend in human form keeps writing beautiful love-letters, the excitement can't be kept up." But, as he quickly added, it was far from unknown for the broadside-composer to supply what the murderer, lacking "any regard for the interest of art and literature," churlishly failed to provide from his own pen.

The crude woodcut which, *de rigueur*, headed the broadsheet usually showed either the murderous deed itself or the moment of the execution, with the elevated gallows in the background and a rough approximation of many hatted and bonneted spectators silhouetted in the foreground. Like most of the illustrations used in the first centuries of printing—it was in this street-literature trade that the practice lasted longest—these cuts, conveniently generalized, were used over and over again. A frightened female thrown to the ground and being bound hand and foot by a ruffian served for every rape murder, and the gallows block could, and did, represent every execution. Similarly with the cut recommended by the hawker as "an exact likeness of the murderer, taken at the bar of the Old Bailey": the truth was that the same cut had been used for every noted criminal for the past forty years, and what had been vended as a faithful portrait of a Quaker forger one year served for a wife-murderer the next. The purported likeness of a murderer in one case became that of the hangman in another; but what, as the Victorian street loafer would have said, were the odds? Both murderer and hangman, after all, were evil-looking. On great occasions such as the Thurtell, Rush, and Manning murders, however, the printer might go to the expense of having a cut especially made. The hawkers' routine guarantees of authenticity then took on the extra fervor that only unaccustomed sincerity could supply.

One future celebrated artist who did some of his apprentice work in this field was George Cruikshank. In the second decade of the century he provided the frontispieces and other illustrations for a number of catchpenny books on current murders—not bad training for an artist who would later realize some of the most lurid passages in *Oliver Twist* and design the scenery for one stage version of William Harrison Ainsworth's criminal novel, *Jack Sheppard*. These books catered to tastes left unsatisfied by the necessarily abbreviated narratives provided by the broadsides and to pockets a trifle more affluent than those which could afford only the halfpenny or at most the penny that a single sheet cost. An octavo pamphlet or "street book," issued in London or the provinces, might run to as many as 120 double-columned pages. A typical title page, from the press of John Fairbairn, Ludgate Hill, read:

HORRIBLE RAPE AND MURDER!!

The Affecting Case of
M A R Y   A S H F O R D ,

A beautiful young Virgin, Who was diabolically
Ravished, Murdered, and thrown into a Pit, as she
was returning from a Dance; including the Trial of
Abraham Thornton, for the Wilful Murder of the
said Mary Ashford; with the whole of The Evidence, Charge to the Jury, &c.

TRIED AT WARWICK ASSIZES, BEFORE MR. JUSTICE
HOLROYD,

On the 8th of August, 1817.

Taken in Short Hand. To Which is added Copious
Elucidations of this extraordinary Case and Correct
Plan of the Spot Where the Rape and Murder
Were Committed, &c. &c.*

---

* Thornton, a young laborer, was acquitted, but the legal fireworks had
only begun. His victim's eldest brother, seizing upon a law enacted in the
reign of Henry VII, appealed the verdict, thus placing Thornton, with perfect legality, in what we would today regard as double jeopardy. He was
thereupon rearrested and tried in the Court of King's Bench, Westminster
Hall. His counsel, equally learned in antiquarian law, invoked on his behalf
a privilege not used since the reign of Charles I—that of "waging battel,"
i.e., challenging one's accuser to a trial at arms. After the gauntlet was
(literally) thrown down, however, a long legal wrangle ensued, the upshot
of which was that although the judges upheld the continuing availability of
the right to wage battle, the appellant's counsel declined to subject his
client to the ordeal, and Thornton was discharged. He was on his way to
America a few months later, while Parliament was acting to abolish the trial
at arms.

The emotive power of the Thornton title page was outdone, however, by the capacious summary that served as the title of a
similar book, printed at Derby though the murder was, of course,
committed in London:

GREENACRE,

OR THE EDGEWARE-ROAD MURDER.

Presenting an Authentic and Circumstantial Account of This Most Sanguinary Outrage of the
Laws of Humanity; and Showing, upon the Confession of the Culprit, the Means He Resorted to,
in Order to Effect His Bloody Purpose;

Also his Artful and Fiendlike Method of Mutilating
his Murdered Victim,

The Inhuman Manner in which he afterwards Disposed of The Mangled Body and Limbs, and His
Cold-Blooded Disposal of The Head of the Unfortunate Female, on the Eve of Their Intended Marriage;

With a full Account of the Facts which led to the
Discovery of the Atrocious Deed;

His Apprehension, Trial, Behaviour at the Condemned Sermon, and Execution.

From the freedom with which the printers "faithfully" illustrated their productions, as well as from the overwrought language of title page and text, it may be gathered that the multi-
farious products of Catnach and his fellow printers fall short of
being absolutely reliable or objective historical evidence. In dependability they are, of course, poles removed from the sworn
testimony found in the trial transcripts. Catnach's authors and
vendors, hot after the mob's pennies, had no scruples against
embellishing the truth or even, in a pinch, inventing it, as they

often invented "sorrowful lamentations" and confessions. Although the newspapers did fairly well by way of adorning James Rush's history with apocryphal details, their rivals, the patterers, far outshone them, making Rush confess to the murder fourteen years earlier of his old grandmother, whom he buried under the apple tree in the garden; and, more recently, to the murder of his wife.

From the earliest days of the broadsides, their vendors had peddled a variety of "cocks"—accounts of events which had never happened at all or had happened decades, even centuries, earlier, or which were written in such general terms that they could be adapted to any locality in which the hawker happened to be operating. In the case of gallows literature deriving from actual contemporary murders, this immemorial practice of free invention was continued through practical necessity. "The last dying speeches and executions," a specialist in that line told Mayhew, "are all printed the day before. They're always done on the Sunday, if the murderers are to be hung on the Monday. I've been and got them myself on the Sunday night, over and over again. The flying stationers goes with the papers in their pockets, and stand under the drop, and as soon as ever it falls, and long before the breath is out of the body, they begin bawling it out." At a distance from the hanging scene, the vendors observed no "hold for release" precautions, because in the unlikely event of a last-minute reprieve, they would be out of the neighborhood before news of the fiasco, and thus of the broadsides' fraudulence, arrived. And at the scene itself, even if sales did not begin until the murderer was dangling from the halter, the hawkers were still one up on the newspapermen, telegraph lines and express trains notwithstanding. No amount of journalistic speed after the event can match stories prepared and printed in advance. "If the *Times* was cross-examined about it," said one patterer, "he must confess he's outdone, though he's a rich *Times,* and we is poor fellows."

Nevertheless, the future lay with the newspapers, endowed as they were with resources that the hand-to-mouth broadsheet trade could never hope to equal. By the sixties, therefore, the Seven Dials firms were declining. Of the most sensational cases of the 1860s, that of Müller the railway murderer accounted for

only 280,000 broadsheets, and that of Constance Kent, despite
its novel theme of a middle-class teenage girl under grave suspicion of murder, was responsible for the sale of 150,000. A
similar decline in total volume probably was noticeable in Glasgow, where the trial of Dr. Pritchard, assisted by his widespread
personal unpopularity in the city, called forth anonymous poems
in pamphlet form as well as broadsheets with doggerel verse,
all of them reflecting unfavorably on his character.

The hawkers had had their day—their long day—but their
twilight was prolonged into the twentieth century. Although the
street literature of crime had probably disappeared from London
by that time, in the provinces a particularly sensational murder
still made the broadside commercially feasible. From Chelmsford
prison in June 1903, the murderer Samuel Dougal wrote one of
the country girls he had seduced: "I see there were at the Show
at Bishops Stortford two men, one playing a banjo and singing a
ballad on the Moat House, etc., and the other was dispensing of
the copies of the song at 1*d.* each, and doing a good business. I
saw one verse of the song in a local paper, and no doubt you
may see a copy of it in your neighborhood. If you do, see if there
is the Printer's name at the bottom of the page, and if so, make
a note of it for me, please." He did not make clear whether he
wanted to order a quantity or sue the printer.

ii

In 1867 a minor novelist, Joseph Hatton, poring over a file
of an old Bristol weekly newspaper, paused at a typical issue
from the eighteenth or early nineteenth century.

In this Saturday's paper we came across a paragraph of local news,
to the effect that "We hear that a dreadful murder was committed in
Bedminster, on Wednesday evening;" then followed two or three lines
indicating the manner of the murdered man's death; and this was all
the information considered necessary for the reader. Bedminster was
really a portion of the city in which the journal was published, and
in the present day that same paper would, between the time of the
murder and the Saturday publication, have reported the fullest details
of the crime, with a description of the scene of the murder, the antecedents of the dead man, a full report of the inquest and finding of

the jury, and, supposing the criminal captured, a full report of the examination before the magistrates, and committal, occupying in the narration of this one case as much type and paper (to say nothing of writers and printers) as would have published the old journal for several weeks.

There was, said Hatton, "no more startling illustration of the rapid rate at which we live in these times." It also epitomized the revolution that had occurred in English journalism in no more than fifty years. In a momentous development inextricably caught up with certain crucial political and social events, the newspapers, discovering that indignation and sensation were the prime components of successful popular journalism, took over murder from the broadside trade and exploited it on a scale never before approached and never exceeded since.

It is true that so long as there had been newspapers (English journalism had its origins in the late seventeenth century) murders, along with such other evidences of men's depravity or ill-fortune as treason, highway robbery, forgery, piracy, shipwrecks, epidemics, and catastrophic storms, had been news. Occasionally during the eighteenth century a murder of such compelling interest had occurred as to transcend the normal parochialism and sluggish communications of the time and become a national sensation. In 1751–52, for example, the case of Mary ("Molly") Blandy, the "Female Parricide" who was executed at Oxford after a sensational trial, dominated the whole country's newspapers, at the expense even of such concurrent events as the reform of the calendar to compensate for the accumulated inaccuracy of the Julian mode of reckoning. There was a belief abroad in the land that by ordering that September 2, 1752, should be followed by September 14, Parliament was shortening the life of every man, woman, and child in the nation by eleven days. Nonetheless, the question of the life or death of a single girl, especially when she was beautiful, and equipped, as Molly was, with a conspiring lover, loomed greater in people's minds.

But the Blandy case was merely an exception that helped prove the rule. For although the English scene was periodically enlivened by murders and the consequent trials and executions, until early in the nineteenth century the newspaper press ordinarily was neither inclined nor equipped to capitalize on them to the degree which later became routine. The London papers were thin affairs, usually no more than four, or at the most eight, pages. Their editorial contents, emphasizing politics and "foreign intelligence," were designed for a limited upper- and middle-class audience. Working people, even if many of them had been able to read (which was not the case), would have found little to interest them. The treatment of spot news was brief and, on the whole, perfunctory. Such provincial newspapers as existed —outside London there were no dailies at all—were of no greater popular interest. Most of their national and foreign news was copied from the London papers, and coverage of local crime, as Hatton suggested, was meager. Furthermore, at the beginning of the century the London sheets were subsidized by one political party or the other, and this, combined with a fair amount of revenue from advertising, made it unnecessary for them to strive for increased sales. The circulation of all the papers, per thousand of the literate population, was small, although the regular presence of copies in coffeehouses and taverns, and the habit of reading aloud, meant that a single copy served many more persons than would later be the case.

Until after Waterloo, therefore, it was the broadsides and the more detailed pamphlets which almost alone catered to the popular taste for murder in print. But the end of the war, which had supplied the greatest single staple of news since England first became involved in 1793, suddenly left the papers with something of a vacuum. How large it was is indicated by the avidity with which the press fell upon the Thurtell case in 1823–24, "showing," said Sir Walter Scott, "that a bloody murther will do the business of the newspapers when a bloody battle is not to be heard." More importantly, in the inflamed years just after the coming of peace, political radicalism, grimly suppressed since the time of Tom Paine and the native sympathizers with the French Revolution in the early 1790s, revived; and the workers, suffering from widespread unemployment and from the high, artificially maintained price of corn for their bread, turned to the radical press to learn the causes of their present distress and the drastic prescriptions urged for its cure. The threat this unprecedented popular interest in the printed word offered to the nation's internal peace was so grave, in the view of the reactionary government, that in 1819 a whole cluster of repressive laws, including an increased stamp tax, was passed with the avowed purpose of wiping out the radical press.

However, tensions among the thinking portion of the people were so high during the ensuing decade—the period just before the riotous agitation for the passage of the First Reform Bill—that no amount of attempted thought-control could curb their newly discovered voracity for print, above all print that dealt with immediate topics. And after the Reform Bill, as finally enacted, proved not to have brought to the masses any of the political fruits they had expected, their disillusioned fury found two main channels of expression—the formation of political action movements (chief of which was Chartism) and the establishment and distribution, tax or no tax, of radical weekly papers to propagandize for the cause. Year by year, newspapers with their inflammatory contents, which were supremely topical, found their way into the lives of more thousands of common people.

Meanwhile, a revolution was under way in middle-class, "respectable" journalism. With the end of partisan subvention, new sources of revenue had to be found, and these were, of course, the closely associated ones of increased advertising and increased circulation. The proprietors had, therefore, to find ways of adapting the papers' contents to the needs and interests of a larger audience. Those most sensitive and responsive to the demands of an expanded clientele were the London Sunday papers, which in 1829 sold an aggregate of 110,000 copies a week as compared with the seven morning dailies' total circulation of 28,000 and the six evening papers' 11,000. The success of these Sunday sheets, which were duly taxed, pointed the way popular journalism had to go. In politics they were overwhelmingly radical; the conservative papers sold only a tenth as many copies as the others. And—most important for our purposes—their popularity among the middle class demonstrated that the perfect formula for increased circulation included generous helpings of

Establishment scandal and sidewalk sensation. In these weekly papers, murder first received systematic, detailed coverage.

The dailies soon were forced to remodel themselves on the same pattern. The ferocity of their rivalry as early as 1824 is indicated by the fact that every energetic London paper had four to six "horse expresses" carrying the latest news of the Thurtell trial from Hertford to the metropolis; it was said at the time that no fewer than a hundred fresh horses were stationed along the route for that purpose. The Thurtell case, indeed, was a bonanza for London journalists as much as for the broadsheet publishers. No sooner had the murder been discovered than the penny-a-liners got to work, ferreting out, as a contemporary writer on the newspaper press said, "everything connected with the murdered party and the murderer . . . with an alacrity which exceeds all belief." One such free-lance was said to have earned £70 from the Thurtell sensation alone.

By fortunate coincidence, it was at this very moment in history that the mass production of cheap newspapers and other periodicals was becoming technically possible, thanks to the invention of papermaking machines and stereotypes and the application of steam to the printing press. In 1836 a Parliament temporarily liberalized by the Reform Act reduced the newspaper tax to a single penny, and the last substantial obstacle to exploiting a huge potential readership was removed. The most significant result of the reduction of the stamp tax was to make weekly papers available to hundreds of thousands of working-class readers who hitherto, the cost of living being what it was, could not afford them. In the late thirties and the forties the weeklies proliferated, under the guidance of a number of enterprising publishers and editors, preeminent among them Edward Lloyd and G. W. M. Reynolds, the trail blazers of the English yellow press.

This new branch of the Sunday press, designed for the semi-literate audience as contrasted with the superior readership of the old-established weeklies, was the product of the Victorian decade when political passions ran highest, the decade of Chartism and strikes, mass meetings, and riots among the unemployed and disaffected. But, as if to hedge their bets, from the outset the new entrepreneurs included in their lurid sheets as much crime as radical politics. This precaution paid off handsomely when, by the middle of the century, political passions subsided. A psychological need-pattern had been created, and when bitterness against Church and State no longer preoccupied the minds of the million, crime news was ready to fill the void. The focus of sensationalism, in short, moved from politics to crime. And although the mass-circulation Sunday press never lost its radical bias, in the remainder of the Victorian period politics was eclipsed by subjects whose appeal to the great public did not depend on the vagaries of party and Parliament—reliable subjects like sport, sex in high society, and, above all, murder, wherever found.

The commercial profitability of these papers increased with the spread of literacy through the populace. It was not a very high degree of literacy, barely sufficient to enable the man or woman to comprehend the gist of narratives written in a style as plain as it was graphic, but it admitted ever more people to the delights of contemporary murder. And where illiteracy remained, there was always an eager audience for the odd person who could read. In the Three Jolly Bargemen inn, for example (in Chapter 18 of *Great Expectations*), a group "assembled round the fire . . . attentive to Mr. Wopsle as he read the newspaper aloud."

A highly popular murder had been committed, and Mr. Wopsle was imbrued in blood to the eyebrows. He gloated over every abhorrent adjective in the description, and identified himself with every witness at the Inquest. He faintly moaned, "I am done for," as the victim, and he barbarously bellowed, "I'll serve you out," as the murderer. He gave the medical testimony, in pointed imitation of our local practitioner; and he piped and shook, as the aged turnpike-keeper who had heard blows, to an extent so very paralytic as to suggest a doubt regarding the mental competency of that witness. The Coroner, in Mr. Wopsle's hands, became Timon of Athens; the beadle, Coriolanus. He enjoyed himself thoroughly, and we all enjoyed ourselves, and were delightfully comfortable. In this cozy state of mind we came to the verdict Wilful Murder.

Similarly, in another generation (*Our Mutual Friend*, Chapter 16), did the boy Sloppy entertain old Betty Higden: "You

mightn't think it," she told some visitors, "but Sloppy is a beautiful reader of a newspaper. He do the Police in different voices"
—an accomplishment, incidentally, which captivated T. S. Eliot,
who inscribed the latter sentence on the typescript of *The Waste
Land* as an alternate title for the second part, "A Game of Chess."

The development of cheap and comparatively fast techniques for making newspaper engravings, a great improvement
over the crude woodblocks of the Catnach school, increased the
newspapers' advantage. The *Observer,* which for many years
early in the century was in the forefront of the weeklies thriving
on crime, ran five illustrations in one issue—a number then unprecedented—relating to the Thurtell case, and kept its readers
up to date by printing, the following month, a picture of the
courtroom at Hertford when the prisoners were brought up to
plead—an anticipation of the day when newspapers would routinely employ skilled artists to draw courtroom scenes each day
for the duration of a trial. The bold novelty of the *Observer's*
kind of journalism, keeping on top of a continuing story with
pictures as well as text, can be gauged from the fact that it was
widely condemned. But circulation figures argue more eloquently
than conservative criticism, and the *Observer* maintained its
profitable course to the point where, some years later, it was advertising twenty columns of crime per issue, with supplements
when an especially exciting crime called for them. Meanwhile
the *Weekly Chronicle,* a keen competitor in the field, went all
out with eight pictures relating to the Greenacre murder in a
single issue. The energy of its proprietors was well repaid: that
issue sold the immense total (for the time) of 130,000 copies.

Such exploits, and the profits resulting from them, did not
go unnoticed by Herbert Ingram, the former Nottingham news-
agent who founded the middle-class *Illustrated London News* in
1842. On the fiftieth anniversary of the event, a report appeared
in the press that Ingram had initially considered making his
paper "merely a record of crime, inspired thereto by the success
of journals dealing with the Thurtell and Greenacre murders."
This allegation drew a vehement denial from Ingram's widow;
but by this time the paper had long been established as an indispensable amenity in middle-class homes, and its lifelong re-

spectability had to be vindicated. The truth was that, though Ingram probably never intended it to be exclusively a police gazette, from the outset the *News* did cover crime as thoroughly as its intended audience wished—vividly illustrated but written and edited to eliminate "vulgarity."

If longer, day-by-day accounts were desired, the London daily papers could be depended upon for exhaustive coverage. Preeminent among them in this respect, after the middle of the century, was the *Daily Telegraph*, founded as the first penny daily in 1855. This was the year when the last remaining "tax upon knowledge," the paper duty, was abolished. By the early seventies the *Daily Telegraph* was boasting that its circulation, then two hundred thousand, was the largest in the world; and mainly because of the exhaustiveness of its crime coverage. That it, like all other London dailies until the 1880s, was edited for a middle-class clientele rather than for the workers is proof enough that murder sold as well to the substantial shopkeeper, clerk, civil servant, and professional man as it did to the manual laborer who bought it, in his own press, on Sunday alone.

And if the *Daily Telegraph* excelled in murder reporting, it had lively competition. *The Times* in the Victorian era lavished attention on court cases, whether for murder or divorce; and in the large provincial and Scottish towns the principal papers followed the lead of London. In the late forties and the fifties, before special press rates made it practicable for out-of-town newspapers to send extensive dispatches by the new electric telegraph, local papers in a town that was the site of a sensational trial had a decided advantage over their contemporaries in London and elsewhere. Although there were not yet any newspapers published on a regular daily basis outside London, in 1849 the Norwich papers were converted into dailies for the duration of the Rush trial and circulated far beyond their usual area. So great was the national demand for news from the scene that on a single night the postmaster handled twenty-three extra sacks of papers, and one newspaper proprietor alone used £98 worth of postage.

At Trowbridge, when Constance Kent was examined after her confession in 1865, more than thirty newspapermen were present, staff reporters and "special correspondents" from the London press as well as from provincial papers as far away as Manchester, Leeds, and Plymouth. As the years passed, the size of the press corps at any out-of-the-ordinary murder trial steadily increased. The so-called Ardlamont Mystery trial in Edinburgh in December 1893 attracted over a hundred journalists, including twenty feature writers, seventy ordinary reporters, and fifteen artists. The leading local paper, the *Scotsman,* devoted twenty columns a day to the proceedings, and a total of 1,860,000 words were filed for out-of-town papers in the course of the trial.* Although the editors who dispatched the reporters and the proprietors who paid the bills had no notion that they were serving the cause of history, such actually was the case; for, in the absence of official stenographic transcripts of many trials, the newspaper reports are today the fullest available records of what was said and done during those dramatic sittings. Most of the book-length studies of famous Victorian trials are necessarily based on them.

It would be naïve to assume that all the vast wordage which moved across sub-editors' desks in the course of a Victorian murder case could have met the standards either of the scientific historian or of the modern legalist. When the newspapers first began to cut the ground from under the old-fashioned broadsheet trade, they were no more scrupulous than their rivals as to facts or palpable bias. "Lord love you," said one of Mayhew's informants, whose views admittedly were colored by professional jealousy, "there's plenty of 'em [i.e., newspapers] gets more and more into our line. They treads in our footsteps, sir; they follows our bright example. O! isn't there a nice rubbing and polishing up. This here copy won't do. This must be left out, and that put in; 'cause it suits the walk of the paper." Nothing that was put in, we may believe, diminished the effectiveness of the paper's reportage, whatever its possible inadmissibility in a court of law.

Such laws as the books contained governing press coverage of cases that were *sub judice* failed to deter many papers from

---

* By contrast, the trial of Dr. John Bodkin Adams at the Old Bailey in 1957, one of the most sensational English trials of the present century, was covered by a total of eighty press representatives, including foreign correspondents and novelists given briefs for the occasion. The decrease may, of course, have been due to the limited press facilities at the Old Bailey.

behavior almost unbelievable when one considers the circum-
spection with which present-day British and (more recently)
American papers, apprehensive of the court's possible displea-
sure, report crime. William Roughead's description of the way
the Glasgow press increased its circulation fivefold during the
M'Lachlan case in 1862 is applicable to much of the Victorian
journalism inspired by sensational murders: "Reporters dogged
the footsteps of the criminal officers and forestalled in print the
results of their investigations; even the sacred operations of the
Fiscal's *camera segreta* [equivalent to the grand jury] were not
respected—witnesses who had been examined were waylaid, and
full reports of their evidence published with such comments as
editorial bias suggested; some papers treated 'the wretched
woman' already as a convicted murderess. . . . The daily news
sheets rivalled one another in starting fresh theories of the crime,
and advising the authorities on how and how not to conduct the
inquiry."

In general, newspapers felt themselves free to speculate,
theorize, admonish; if they did not accuse outright, they came
as close to it as need be. And in their descriptions of the characters involved in the drama the reporters used abundant colorful—and prejudicial—detail. What with their appropriating the
functions of the police, overseeing and commenting on those of
the court, and employment of slanted language, some portions
of the Victorian press exemplified in its fullest meaning the term
"trial by newspaper."

Victorian journalists sought by various means to repel the
charge, which resounded throughout the era, that they were
pandering to the most morbid tastes of the public. This is a
topic which will be touched upon in the concluding chapter. But
one may note here that the press shared in the attempt sometimes made to hitch the cart of murder to the fashionable steam
engine of popular instruction. When the *Illustrated London
News* ran a picture of Daniel Good in its second issue, the editors were "not quite sure if we ought not to apologize for its
appearance in this paper."

It is not our intention to disfigure the pages of the "Illustrated News"
with engravings, especially connected with crime and its conse-

quences; we do not profess to be of the "raw head and bloody-bones" school, nor do we desire to encourage the tastes of such as are only gratified with pictorial representations of murders and murderers.

Still (they may have murmured among themselves) the new paper had to make its way in a world where "pictorial representations" of murderers were known to bring joy to the ledgers of many a popular journal. And an acceptable rationalization was at hand: "Many of our readers may be disciples of Lavater [the physiognomist], and to them we shall, for once, in such a case, afford an opportunity of exercising their judgment upon the countenance of this man." *

This is not as disingenuous as it may seem, because there was serious scientific interest in the faces and heads of famous criminals. For the devotees of the then-fashionable branches of physiognomy and phrenology, death masks and casts were taken of the heads of executed murderers, including Good, Gleeson Wilson, and the Mannings.† The *doyen* of the phrenologists, George Combe, made a cast of Burke's head, reporting, *inter al.*, that his bump of amativeness was "very large," that of destructiveness "very large," that of benevolence "large," and of conscientiousness "rather large," although that of wit was "deficient." Combe was reported to have tried to reconcile these embarrassingly inconsistent findings by declaring that "the character of this individual . . . *in consequence of his late atrocities, was somewhat obscured from the public eye;* and that it should be remembered that he had, during a considerable portion of his life,

---

* In 1864 Madame Tussaud's Chamber of Horrors was renamed the Chamber of Physiognomy, but the "disciples of Lavater" proved to be less numerous than had been thought, and the chamber soon reverted to its former title.

† Corder's actual head, or what was represented as such, was exhibited at Bartholomew Fair in 1828. I do not know if the showman stressed its phrenological significance—according to scientific opinion his skull proved that Corder's "secretiveness, destructiveness, and philoprogenitiveness were inordinately developed"—but he is reputed to have made £100 from displaying the relic. Corder's death mask and his now-blackened and wrinkled scalp, along with two of his pistols and a knife and sheath found under the stairs of his house, are now in the Moyse's Hall Museum, Bury St. Edmunds. In the same exhibit is a copy of the record of his trial bound in his skin. He was one of the select company of murderers who were hanged, drawn, and quartoed.

refrained from crime . . . *not having committed murder till the thirty-sixth year of his age.* No former theory of philosophy could explain the anomaly of these debasing faculties having remained so long inactive, except Phrenology."

This was too much for William Hazlitt, no admirer of phrenology, who in a pair of articles in the *Atlas* newspaper (February 15 and July 19, 1829) ridiculed Combe and his solemn measurement of cranial bumps. "Your wiseacre," he remarked, "is your only fool." The truth was that "In Burke . . . the organ of destructiveness was in its absolute size smaller than thirty-seven out of fifty crania in Sir William Hamilton's collection; and it was relatively and absolutely below the average, while his organ of benevolence was absolutely and relatively above the average." In Hare's skull—measured before he was freed and had fled from Edinburgh—the best-developed organ was that of ideality, "which was larger than the same organ in one of our most distinguished living poets, as also in the heads of Sheridan, Sterne, Canning, Voltaire, and Edmund Burke. . . . One might as well quote the Koran to a Cossack as truth to a phrenologist."

Despite such attacks phrenology continued to command the enthusiastic respect of some lay scientists—less and less so that of qualified ones—for decades to come. But even if it had been totally discredited by the results obtained from the skulls of murderers, the deletion of this one "educational" feature would have detracted little from the aggregate claimed for murder narratives. Possibly the most comprehensive summary of the alleged instructive and uplifting qualities of the genre is found in the introduction to J. Curtis's *An Authentic and Faithful History of the Mysterious Murder of Maria Marten,* published by Thomas Kelly, Paternoster Row, in 1828: "The Polstead Catastrophe . . . may . . . be called 'a Medley,'—for such it is—as it exhibits the ferocity of man—the frailty and fidelity of woman—the ruin of families—the municipal authority—the power of conscience— the palladium of British liberty—the blessings of a court of judicature, under the jurisprudence of a humane judge—and, finally, that the 'glorious laws, those brightest pearls which gem our monarch's crown,' are not to be violated and the violator go unpunished; that 'he that sheddeth the blood of a fellow-creature (wilfully), by man shall his blood be shed.'

"Furthermore," pursued the indefatigable apologist, "herein will be found mythology, necromancy, biography, topography, history, theology, phrenology, anatomy, legal ingenuity, conjugal correspondence, amatory epistles, poetry, theatrical representations, affecting anecdotes, etc., etc." The "etc., etc." would seem to be almost superfluous.

It is hard to believe that Curtis or anybody else engaged in the true-murder literature trade wrote such extravagant blurbs without tongue in cheek. They had a product to sell in an age which demanded that the printed word be laden with wholesome instruction and moral improvement; and if, on casual inspection, that product seemed to be conspicuously deficient in those qualities, they were determined to discover them on behalf of their large clientele. Probably the clientele did not credit those wild claims, either; but whatever scruples they might have had against reading entertaining books like Curtis's on Maria Marten or the newspapers on any current murder were quieted by such assurances.

What is plain, in any event, is that by the sixties, whether in behalf of the nation's entertainment or of its enlightenment, the newspapers had taken over the proprietorship of English murder. Whereas the broadside-makers had acquired their pittance of news from diverse sources, ranging from newspapers through rumor to sheer invention, the newspapers threw into the preparation of each daily or weekly report the resources and energies of an increasingly professional corps of journalists with expense accounts and open telegraph lines ever at their disposal. And whereas the imprecisely named flying stationers had plodded from village to village, selling curtailed versions of a murder or execution that had happened as many as several weeks earlier, the newspapers, using the railways, could get the latest detailed news to the most remote hamlet within a few hours. The policy of the new aggressive, circulation-hungry journalism was to give the broadening public what it wanted; and high on the list of what it wanted was Murder.

3

Literature with a
Sanguinary Cast

THUS, SPEAKING METAPHORICALLY, blood was an important ingredient in nineteenth-century printers' ink. Not only did the prevalence of real-life murder assist the prosperity of newspapers, helping transform British journalism into a major industry. More than that, murder was a staple of the century's popular fiction.

It had come into prominence in the Gothic novel, which had reached its peak of fashion a generation before the Victorian age began. Horace Walpole's initiatory thriller, *The Castle of Otranto* (1764), had been followed by Clara Reeve's *The Old English Baron* (1777); the several novels of Mrs. Ann Radcliffe, notably *The Romance of the Forest* (1791), *The Mysteries of Udolpho* (1794), and *The Italian* (1797); and Matthew Gregory Lewis's *The Monk* (1796). As the eighteenth century faded into the nineteenth, the romance of terror was all the rage. Murder— Gothic style—along with rape, sadism, incest, ghosts, vampirism, permanent imprisonment, natural and man-made cataclysms, and other such inducements to horror, deliciously stirred the sensibilities of readers who had fed too long on the bland diet of the domestic novel, the polite essay, and the generally placid effusions of the poets Rogers, Crabbe, and Cowper. The age

yearned for madder music, stronger wine, and Mrs. Radcliffe's
many imitators were only too happy to oblige.

So far as educated readers were concerned, the Gothic
vogue had pretty well spent its force by the time Sir Walter
Scott rose to supremacy among early nineteenth-century novelists. But the debased progeny of the genre continued to flourish,
decade after decade, in the ever-widening marketplace which
purveyed cheap thrills to the masses. While Catnach ground
out broadsides and pamphlets of (more or less) true crime, his
colleagues in the street literature trade sold fictional sensations
by the pennyworth to the laborers, factory hands, and domestic
servants of London and the large industrial towns. The most
characteristic product of this branch of the hole-in-the-wall trade
down to the thirties was what might be called the poor man's
Gothic novel, an ill-printed sixpenny pamphlet, bound in blue
covers, which abridged into thirty-six pages or so all the heart-
stopping excitements contrived by Mrs. Radcliffe and her school,
but omitted the lengthy landscape descriptions to which she had
been addicted.

The sole purpose of these crude examples of the Holywell
Street hack's craft was succinctly expressed by Dickens's Fat
Boy: "I wants to make your flesh creep." Such works as *The
Black Monk; or, The Secret of the Gray Turret; Almira's Curse;
or, The Black Tower of Bransdorf; The Ranger of the Tomb; or,
The Gypsy's Prophecy;* and above all *Varney the Vampire; or,
The Feast of Blood* chilled the marrows of countless workingmen
and their families, transporting them from their dingy world
into the dungeons of sinister castles hidden in German forests,
or convents where nuns found entertainment in flogging screaming novices. Life was much easier to endure when one could
read, with mounting horror, of the evil deeds of werewolves and
vampires, specters and hags, in a twilight or midnight world
where murder was the most commonplace of events.*

In time, the supernatural and exotic trappings that had
marked the Gothic novel from its beginnings disintegrated and

---

* I confess to having lifted some of the phraseology here from an earlier
book of mine. In a volume devoted, as this one is, to capital crimes, the
mere misdemeanor of petty larceny is, I hope, forgivable.

vanished; *autres temps, autres goûts.* But the element of murder remained as popular as ever. Now, however, it tended to be (along with the general setting) more realistic. This does not mean that stories of adventure, suspense, and crime set in past epochs declined in popularity; in the cheap trade, sword-and-swagger fiction with criminal themes—the stuff of Jack Sheppard, Dick Turpin, and the rest—sold as well as before, decade after decade. But with the ever-widening market for such reading matter there was also ample room and demand for fiction that appealed to the sharpened sense of contemporaneity. Why confine oneself to ineffably thrilling transactions in far-off places which no reader among this semi-literate clientele had ever visited, when the same fearsome episodes could be portrayed in completely believable English settings? * Murder was all the more dreadful, in a most agreeable sort of way, when the criminal and his victim wore the everyday dress of the present.

And it was all the more credible, because this was the early day of the popular newspaper, whose headlines assisted whatever suspension of disbelief was needed. As the author of a novel called *Gideon Giles the Roper* observed in 1841:

Let an author draw the character of a villain in the blackest colours he can use, such a one lives in the world. Let him paint murder in its most sanguine hues, writhing, brutal and horrible, the next month proves how much he fell short of reaching the actual colouring. Let him break hearts asunder, bleeding and aching with blighted love; draw the curtain and reveal all that is awful in suicide and death—then turn to the everyday world, and with a shudder he may view the selfsame picture. He outrages not nature, for nature is every day outraged; let those who disbelieve us sum up all the unnatural deeds which the last twelve moons have waxed and waned over, and which are recorded in almost every newspaper.

---

* But the Gothic element was not wholly expunged; the tendency was still to enhance the horror of a more or less contemporary English murder by placing it in a ruinous setting, as had been the normal Gothic habit. Compare the titles of four typical thrillers at mid-century: *Ada the Betrayed; or, The Murder at the Old Smithy; Retribution; or, The Murder at the Old Dyke; The Blighted Heart; or, The Murderer in the Old Priory Ruins;* and *The Black Marble; or, The Murder at the Old Ferry.* All of these, with the possible exception of the first, which has also been ascribed to Malcolm J. Rymer, are said to have been the work of one of the most prolific toilers in the Grub Street vineyard, Thomas Peckett (or Preskett) Prest.

In respect to murder, therefore—perhaps less so in connection with such esoteric pursuits and conditions as vampirism and lycanthropy—the events formerly described in Gothic novels were shown to be the gruesome accompaniments of everyday life in William IV's Britain. In their respective ways, the deeds of Burke and Hare and of James Greenacre were forms of Gothic horror domesticated. Murder most foul was now committed in surroundings most familiar. One might say, in fact, that, given the heightened effect provided by imaginative journalism, readers brought up on a diet of spurious Gothicism found in Regency and early Victorian murders a series of instances of life imitating art.

This outpouring of lurid reading matter designed for the lowest level of the populace continued throughout the Victorian period. At mid-century the "penny dreadful" was joined by the "shilling shocker," which in effect embraced the serialized or separate thrills of the dreadful between a single set of covers. These garishly dressed entertainments were written in a style which, even to the loose grammar, was both comprehensible and agreeable to the dullest product of the dismal schools where children of the masses acquired such literacy as they possessed. And they sold in enormous quantities. Apart from contemporary estimates, which are vitiated by palpable bias or simple lack of authority, there is no way of telling how many copies were issued annually, but the figure must run into many millions. Murder and the other standard hazards and excitements favored by the mass imagination had become big business.

Informally but effectively correlated with the popular fiction of the day was the popular drama. It was an axiom of the time that, as Wilkie Collins put it in his preface to *Basil* (1852), "the Novel and the Play are twin-sisters in the family of Fiction; that the one is a drama narrated, as the other is a drama acted; and that all the strong and deep emotions which the Play-writer is privileged to excite, the Novel-writer is privileged to excite also." The existence side by side of two cheap series, Purkess's Penny Library of Romance and (in accidental anticipation of Mrs. General's prunes and prisms) Purkess's Pictorial Penny Plays, aptly symbolized the entirely free trade that governed the literary used-goods market in the era. The former, as Montague Summers, the bibliographer of the genre, wrote, "were merely the story of popular melodrama . . . resolved into fiction. Very often the melodrama itself was the dramatization of a famous novel," as would be true of many specimens in the latter series. Fiction and the stage constituted a common pool from which writers for both genres drew their material. Back and forth, from drama to fiction and from fiction to drama again, shuttled the plots of popular literature. In many instances it would be impossible to establish in which form they originated.

Such probably is the case with the most memorable of the horrific stories that became part of Victorian popular lore—the tale of Sweeney Todd, the mad barber of Fleet Street, whose penny shaving shop was equipped with a trapdoor beside the barber chair. Sweeney's practice, whenever the needs of the adjoining establishment dictated, was to slit his unsuspecting customer's throat with his razor and precipitate him through the trapdoor into the cellar. There he was efficiently converted into the meat which gave the shop next door, a pastry cook's, its enviable reputation for cheap and tasty pork pies.* Countless other tales of spilled gore gratified (or perhaps in some instances spoiled) the appetites of Victorian readers. Charles Dickens spoke not only for himself but for countless thousands of his contemporaries—and their children and even their children's children, down to the very end of the century—when he affectionately recalled his boyhood indulgence in the suspenseful thrills of the penny blood: "I used, when I was at school, to take in the Terrific Register, making myself unspeakably miserable, and frightening my very wits out of my head, for the small charge of a penny weekly; which considering that there was an

---

* This beloved Victorian gorge-raiser is attributed to the above-mentioned T. P. Prest. He may have remembered that in 1818 James Catnach had been sued for libel by a Drury Lane pork butcher about whom he incautiously circulated a similar story. The parallel careers of Sweeney Todd in Victorian fiction and on the stage are a good example of the intimate collaboration of popular fiction and the popular theater. One of the earliest stage versions of the story was by George Dibdin Pitt (1841). The Todd role was long a favorite with the "heavies" in the minor theaters. Its famous catch-phrase, accompanied by the business of stropping a razor, was "I'll polish 'em off!"

illustration to every number, in which there was always a pool of blood, and at least one body, was cheap."

ii

On a higher level of literary interest, but reflecting to a degree the taste of the masses served by the penny dreadful in its manifold forms, was the Newgate novel, which had a brief and controversial vogue in the 1830s and early 1840s. It was, by definition, a narrative dealing with crime (principally murder and robbery) and punishment, most often on the Newgate gallows. Actually, the incidence of crime in English fiction at this period was probably no greater than at any other, but the occurrence of the several famous murders we have noted in the period 1823–40, as well as the coincidental agitation for the reform of the nation's outmoded criminal statutes, made it a peculiarly timely subject. The most prominent examples of the type were Bulwer's *Paul Clifford* (1830) and *Eugene Aram* (1832); Ainsworth's *Rookwood* (1834); Dickens's *Oliver Twist* (1838–39) and *Barnaby Rudge* (conceived at the same time as *Oliver Twist*, but not published until 1841); Ainsworth's *Jack Sheppard* (1839–40), so resounding a success that within a year at least eight stage versions had been produced and the Lord Chamberlain, in the interests of public morality, forbade additional ones; and Bulwer's *Night and Morning* (1841) and *Lucretia* (1846). Several of these novels were based upon famous crimes and criminal careers of the past (Eugene Aram, Dick Turpin in *Rookwood*, Jack Sheppard); others derived from contemporary crime. Thornton in Bulwer's *Pelham* (1828), as we have seen, was modeled after Thurtell, and Varney in *Lucretia*— the author had been hyphenated into Bulwer-Lytton by then— after Thomas Griffiths Wainewright.*

---

* For the latter novel, Bulwer-Lytton went to the length, surely unique in the history of English fiction, of obtaining from the Eagle Insurance Company all the papers it had recovered from the forger-poisoner's French refuge when he was taken into custody at its behest in 1837. Despite Bulwer-Lytton's exertions and the insurance company's surprising cooperation, however, the documents did not, in the end, add to the novel's authenticity; Varney's career differs widely from the career of his real-life model.

At any other time, such novels might have sold well enough—their subject matter, after all, was of persistent interest—but they would not have aroused the immediate and sustained criticism they then encountered. This was a period when England was particularly apprehensive in the face of continual breaches of domestic peace; the radical political activities of the 1820s and 1830s, encouraged if not directly inspired by the popular press which laid so much stress on violence, freshly fed a national unease which could be traced all the way back to the era of the French Revolution. By a sweeping association of robbers and murderers with rioters and strikers, influential critics and moralists found the Newgate novel's romanticizing of criminals a practice that was inimical to public safety. A life of crime, they argued, was being made glamorous, when its consequences should instead be painted in the most monitory colors.

Dickens especially, of the several accused novelists, made a vigorous reply: far from tempting suggestible readers to enter a life of picking pockets, receiving stolen goods, or prostitution—each according to his talents—*Oliver Twist* was intended to strip the false glamor from the criminal life. So he argued in the preface to the third edition (1841), directly replying to Thackeray's indignant strictures a year earlier in his essay "Going to See a Man Hanged" (*Fraser's Magazine*, August 1840).

Whatever the merits of Dickens's defense of his own novel, the Newgate fictionists were put further on the defensive in 1840 by the report that François Bernard Courvoisier, the valet who murdered his master, Lord William Russell, had alleged in one of his several confessions that he had been inspired to the deed by reading Ainsworth's *Jack Sheppard*. This was neither the first time nor the last that a criminal attributed his fall from virtue to ill-chosen reading matter,* but coming at the moment

* Useful light is thrown on this perennial charge by the mid-Victorian journalist James Greenwood ("the Amateur Casual") in his book *The Seven Curses of London* (1869). The governor of a prison in one of London's suburbs, he wrote, "is quite convinced in his own mind that the mainspring of crime is the perusal of the sort of literature herein alluded to [i.e., penny bloods and their ilk]. This is a fact generally known among the juvenile criminal population, and they never fail to make the most of it when the time comes. I went the rounds of his jail with this governor on one occasion, when the 'boy wing' was occupied by about forty tenants, and in each case

it did, Courvoisier's claim powerfully assisted the campaign against sensational fiction. Whether novelists were frightened away from the Newgate theme by such criticism or whether the vein simply dried up, they did abandon it for the time being, and when sensationalism born of murder reappeared conspicuously on the English literary scene, it was, with one exception, under different auspices.

The exception was Dickens himself, whose career spanned the interval between the Newgate novel and the sensation novel of the 1860s. In the light of his many-sided interest in crime and punishment, it was inescapable that criminals should continue to appear in his fiction long after *Oliver Twist* and *Barnaby Rudge* had taken their place on the shelves. The popularity of his novels between the late forties and the early sixties reflected the persistence of the public taste for melodrama, suspense, and murder. In the Dickens canon, murders have a crucial or incidental role in *Oliver Twist, Nicholas Nickleby, Barnaby Rudge, Martin Chuzzlewit, Bleak House, Great Expectations, Little Dorrit, Our Mutual Friend, A Tale of Two Cities,* and *The Mystery of Edwin Drood,* not to mention such shorter fictions as "Hunted Down."

iii

The strength of the popular taste for murder in Dickens's last decade (1860–70) is demonstrated by the great vogue of the sensation novel. Like its forerunner, the Newgate novel, **this**

---

was the important question put, and in the majority of cases it was answered, 'It was them there penny numbers what I used to take in, sir,' or words to that effect; and the little humbug was rewarded by a pat on the head, and an admonition 'always to speak the truth.' " The Victorian juvenile reading public obviously had its share of Uriah Heeps.

In any event, it is hard to see what inspirational value Ainsworth's novel may have had for Courvoisier, apart from the fact that Blueskin, Sheppard's accomplice, slit a woman's throat just as Courvoisier slit his master's. Although there are several murders in the book, they are more or less incidental, Sheppard's great specialty being carceroclasm: he was popular literature's, if not penal history's, most accomplished escape artist. If Courvoisier murdered Lord William Russell so that he could emulate his hero's feats of self-liberation, once in custody he made no gestures in that direction—perhaps because security in Newgate was more stringent in 1840 than it had been in Sheppard's day early in the eighteenth century.

genre—its name dates from 1861—had a life of hardly more than ten or fifteen years, although some of its individual practitioners, such as Mary Elizabeth Braddon and Mrs. Henry Wood, continued for many more years to prosper on the mixture as before. Its beginnings, aside from Dickens's obvious contributions, usually are traced to Wilkie Collins's *The Woman in White,* which sold out seven editions in the first six months after its publication in 1860, and Miss Braddon's *Lady Audley's Secret,* which appeared two years later and was an even greater success. But Collins was working this vein as early as 1852.

If it is true that no other Victorian novelist relied as often as Dickens did upon man's homicidal proclivities, it is also true that no popular or would-be popular novelist of the sixties and early seventies wholly overlooked the possibilities of the subject. There is murder in Mrs. Gaskell's "A Dark Night's Work" (1863) and also in her earlier *Mary Barton* (1848); in Charlotte Yonge's *The Trial* (1864: the sequel to, of all books, *The Daisy Chain!*); in Collins's *The Woman in White, Armadale* (1866), *The Moonstone* (1868), and *The Law and the Lady* (1875); in his brother Charles Allston Collins's *At the Bar* (1866); in Charles Reade's *Griffith Gaunt* (1866) and elsewhere; and in Thomas Adolphus Trollope's *A Siren* (1870: a genuine mystery story).* To cite a few more titles from the vast stock of Victorian circulating-library fiction whose dust only the most occasional reader ever disturbs, murder is central to the plots of Margaret Oliphant's *Salem Chapel* (1863) and *The Minister's Wife* (1869); R. D. Blackmore's first novel, *Clara Vaughan* (1864); Charlotte Riddell's *A Life's Assize* (1868–70); "Ouida's" *Strathmore* (1865); and at least three of Joseph Le Fanu's novels, *The House by the Churchyard* (1863), *Wylder's Hand* (1864), and *Uncle Silas* (1864).

---

* The *modus operandi* here is the killing of a sleeping person with a needle that pierces the heart, the tiny orifice then being covered with wax and rendered virtually invisible. Trollope said that "the facts were related to me by a distinguished man of science at Florence, as having really occurred." Compare the story of a murder told by Dr. Jobling in *Martin Chuzzlewit* (below, page 150). Trollope's brother Anthony had a murder early in *Dr. Thorne* (1858), and an accused murderer standing trial in *Phineas Redux* (1873–74).

The sensation novel had several attractions for the patrons of Mudie's Select Circulating Library, then at the peak of its long and influential career, and for the buyers of the various popular monthly magazines whose development, assisted by the serializing of this very sort of fiction, was another important phenomenon in the literary world of the day. One of its distinctive features—its almost obligatory setting in contemporary fashionable life—recalled the silver fork school of fiction, whose vogue had been almost concurrent with that of the Newgate novel.

Contemporaneity of setting, in this age when newspapers were becoming an ever-more-familiar accessory to daily living, was a necessity. Charles Reade spoke for all of his money-conscious colleagues in the workshop of popular fiction when he said:

I write for the public, and the public don't care about the dead. They are more interested in the living, and in the great tragi-comedy of humanity that is around and about them and environs them in every street, at every crossing, in every hole and corner. An aristocratic divorce suit, the last great social scandal, a sensational suicide from Waterloo Bridge, a woman murdered in Seven Dials, or a baby found strangled in a bonnet-box at Piccadilly Circus interests them much more than Margaret's piety or Gerard's journey to Rome. For one reader who has read "The Cloister and the Hearth," a thousand have read "It Is Never Too Late to Mend." The paying public prefers a live ass to a dead lion.

Persons of wealth and social dignity, the sort of people who figured in the "fashionable intelligence" columns of the London press, would have objected to being classified as asses rather than lions, but for the rest, Reade's remarks were accurate enough. Popular taste required that the plot of the sensation novel, in addition to being set in the present, be complicated by mysteries and studded with "strong" dramatic situations involving adultery, bigamy, misappropriated legacies, unexplained disappearances, mysterious parentage, and—above almost all else—murder achieved, contemplated, or merely suspected.

In the sensation novel, then, as earlier in the penny dreadful and (as we shall see) the popular melodrama, murder was domesticated. In the older Gothic fiction murder had been a "romantic" event, as romantic—that is, as far removed from the experience of the average reader—as the setting in a landscape suggestive of Salvator Rosa. Now the "romantic" event was transferred to a "familiar" setting, and middle-class readers, like their inferiors a generation before, had the best of both worlds. The new sensation novelists in effect followed the lead of Dickens, who had explained in the preface to *Bleak House* (1853) that he had "purposely dwelt upon the romantic side of familiar things," and of Dickens's comrade Wilkie Collins, who the preceding year, in the preface to *Basil*, had insisted that "those extraordinary accidents and events which happen to few men" were "as legitimate materials for fiction to work with . . . as the ordinary accidents and events which may, and do, happen to us all." Sensation novelists transplanted Gothic thrills to the England of the 1860s, revealing terrible secrets behind the majestic fronts of Belgrave Square and desperate murder hidden in cisterns in country-house gardens. These were "those most mysterious of mysteries," as Henry James put it when speaking of Collins, "the mysteries which are at our own doors."

It was this effort to render murder and other crimes plausible in terms of the mid-Victorian reader's own familiar social environment which lent the sensation novel its irresistible fascination. The philosopher Henry L. Mansel wrote in the *Quarterly Review* in 1863:

We read with little emotion, though it comes in the form of history, Livy's narrative of the secret poisonings carried on by nearly two hundred Roman ladies; we feel but a feeble interest in an authentic record of the crimes of a Borgia or a Brinvilliers; but we are thrilled with horror, even in fiction, by the thought that such things may be going on around us and among us. The man who shook our hand with a hearty English grasp half an hour ago—the woman whose beauty and grace were the charm of last night, and whose gentle words sent us home better pleased with the world and with ourselves—how exciting to think that under these pleasing outsides may be concealed some demon in human shape, a Count Fosco or a Lady Audley! He may have assumed all that heartiness to conceal some dark plot against our life and honour, or against the life or honour of one yet dearer; she may have left that gay scene to muffle herself in a thick veil and steal to a midnight meeting with some villanous [sic] accomplice.

There was, however, the problem of credibility. For this was a period in the history of English fiction when a strong realistic tide was setting in. Ainsworth and the other practitioners of the melodramatic historical romance, successors to Scott, had lost the popularity they had once enjoyed among educated readers, although they still retained it among large portions of the mass audience. Instead, fiction generally was becoming increasingly contemporary and domestic in its concerns, dealing more and more with the here and now, with the struggles and anxieties, the defeats and triumphs of ordinary people, especially those of the middle class. In such a setting, the conventional melodramatic recourse to murder as a means of launching or resolving a plot, or conveniently disposing of an unneeded and unloved character, or constituting a mystery whose solution would be revealed in the last chapter, or merely giving an opportune boost of voltage to a faltering story line—this handy device from the past struck the judicious reader as being indefensibly artificial, as indeed it was. The hectic microcosm of the sensation novel seemingly was opposed to the tendency of fiction at large, for in it there was a far higher probability of murder than existed in the macrocosm of the real, everyday, contemporary life which fiction was intended to mirror. The odds against one's personal life or circle ever being touched by murder were quite long. But the very premise of the sensation novel, overruling the statistical evidence, was that they were in fact quite short.

The problem of credibility was made additionally acute by the fact that this was an epoch when, for various reasons lying deep in the Victorian mind, fiction had to rest on sturdy documentary props. The prevailing temper of the time was positivistic, scientific, rationalist: it disdained, indeed distrusted "romance" insofar as the word connoted any imaginative departure from actuality, thus requiring Dickens to cite supposedly true cases of human death by spontaneous combustion in defense of Krook's spectacular manner of passing, George Eliot to fill notebooks with historical facts in order to authenticate the setting of *Middlemarch,* and Collins to have the legal sophistications of *The Woman in White* certified by the proper authorities. Murder, too, had to be documented as a verifiable accompaniment to everyday existence.

And it was—amply, circumstantially, graphically, by the daily papers. For now life, even more than in the era of the penny blood's first prosperity, came to the aid of fiction; it proved itself equal to the new artistic demand for fidelity to common experience. Every good new Victorian murder helped legitimize, and prolong the fashion of, sensational plots. And even more happily, no conflict existed between the homicidal interest and the convention of setting the sensation novel in eminently respectable society, because in the sixties it was an all-too-well attested fact that murder could occur there just as easily as in the realm, unentered by decent people, of a second-generation Bill Sikes and his mob. In 1857 Madeleine Smith, daughter of a prosperous Glasgow architect, was tried for poisoning her lover, and three years later Constance Kent, daughter of a government official who was himself the son of a retired London carpet manufacturer, was thought to have killed her stepbrother. Such real-life murders made it easy to believe that fictional titled ladies like Lady Audley were capable of killing, even though, compared to the Misses Smith and Kent, she was a miserable bungler.

Fiction, therefore, however sensationalized, could be regarded as a faithful transcript of contemporary life: there were the newspapers to prove it. They added verisimilitude to extravagance, and thus made the extravagant credible. The novelist-journalist Albany Fonblanque wrote with somewhat heavy irony:

Husbands never do poison their wives out of novels, and that affair of Dr. Smethurst was a myth. People do not go about and shoot each other in broad mid-day about women, and the Northumberland Street tragedy was a penny-a-liner's hoax. We who write these sort of books take human nature as we think we find it, taking our models out of those confounded newspaper reports, and supposing that what people tell my lords the Queen's Justices on their oaths, and on the strength of which men and women are hanged and transported may, after all, be true—and we have our reward.

Thackeray, too, deserves to be quoted on the subject. He takes his point of departure from the amazing Northumberland Street

business of 1861, mentioned by Fonblanque: a story which re-
minds a twentieth-century reader of nothing so much as one of
the more improbable romances of E. Phillips Oppenheim or,
reaching further back, one of the more fanciful Sherlock Holmes
cases:

Have any novelists of our days a scene and catastrophe more strange
and terrible than this which occurs at noonday within a few yards
of the greatest thoroughfare in Europe? At the theatres they have a
new name for their melodramatic pieces, and call them "Sensation
Dramas." What a sensation drama this is! What have people been
flocking to see at the Adelphi Theatre for the last hundred and fifty
nights? A woman pitched overboard out of a boat, and a certain
Dan taking a tremendous "header," and bringing her to shore?
Bagatelle! What is this compared to the real life drama, of which
a midday representation takes place just opposite the Adelphi in
Northumberland Street? The brave Dumas, the intrepid Ainsworth,
the terrible Eugène Sue, the cold-shudder inspiring "Woman in
White," the astounding author of the "Mysteries of the Court of London," never invented anything more tremendous than this. It might
have happened to you and me. We want to borrow a little money. We
are directed to an agent. We propose a pecuniary transaction at a
short date. He goes into the next room, as we fancy, to get the bank-
notes, and returns with "two very pretty, delicate little ivory-handled
pistols," and blows a portion of our heads off. After this, what is the
use of being squeamish about the probabilities and possibilities in the
writing of fiction? . . . What a cavern of terror was this in Northumberland Street, with its splendid furniture covered with dust, its
empty bottles, in the midst of which sits a grim "agent," amusing himself by firing pistols, aiming at the unconscious mantelpiece, or at
the heads of his customers!

After this, what is not possible? It is possible Hungerford Market
is mined, and will explode some day. Mind how you go in for a penny
ice unawares. "Pray, step this way," says a quiet person at the door.
You enter—into a back room:—a quiet room; rather a dark room.
"Pray, take your place in a chair." And she goes to fetch the penny
ice. *Malheureux!* The chair sinks down with you—sinks, and sinks,
and sinks—a large wet flannel suddenly envelopes your face and
throttles you. Need we say any more? After Northumberland Street,
what is improbable? . . . I protest I have seldom contemplated anything more terribly ludicrous than this "agent" in the dingy splendor
of his den, surrounded by dusty ormolu and piles of empty bottles,
firing pistols for his diversion at the mantelpiece until his clients
come in!

If, then, as a candid consideration of the realities insisted, murder might not touch our own lives, the news of the day assured us that it might well touch the lives of people just like us. It happened in the very streets in which we walked, in the very houses we visited, among the sort of men and women we knew.

It was not merely credibility that real-life murder and its melodramatic circumstances in the sixties supplied to authors serving the popular taste: from it they got the very stuff of their plots. Casting a jaundiced eye over a large assortment of sensation novels not long after the fad began, a writer in the *Quarterly Review* accurately described the process:

From vice to crime, from the divorce-court to the police-court, is but a single step. When fashionable immorality becomes insipid, the materials for sensation may still be found hot and strong in the "Newgate Calendar"; especially if the crime is of recent date, having the merits of personality and proximity to give it a nervous as well as a moral effect. Unhappily, the materials for such excitement are not scanty, and an author who condescends to make use of them need have little difficulty in selecting the most available. Let him only keep an eye on the criminal reports of the daily newspapers, marking the cases which are honoured with the especial notice of a leading article, and become a nine-days' wonder in the mouths of quidnuncs and gossips; and he has the outline of his story not only ready-made, but approved beforehand as of the true sensation cast. Then before the public interest has had time to cool, let him serve up the exciting viands in a *réchauffée* with a proper amount of fictitious seasoning; and there emerges the criminal variety of the Newspaper Novel, a class of fiction having about the same relation to the genuine historical novel that the police reports of "The Times" have to the pages of Thucydides or Clarendon.*

* Did literature, in return, replenish life, providing inspiration for further murders? Whether or not Courvoisier was prompted by *Jack Sheppard,* critics of sensation fiction were fond of alleging that these novels served as handy textbooks for the homicidally inclined. A parody novel by the Rev. Francis Edward Paget, *Lucretia, the Heroine of the Nineteenth Century* (1868), said of them: "Through their teaching, murder has been made easy to the meanest capacity: the choicest and most scientific modes of destroying life have been revealed to us. . . . For the benefit of students in the science of Toxicology . . . the most approved recipes for poisoning have been set forth with medical and surgical minuteness." More than one pretty poisoner in these years seems to have derived useful hints from her reading. On the cognate topic of the newspapers' value to persons contemplating murder, see pages 297–99.

Wilkie Collins's *The Moonstone* is probably the best-known example of a Victorian novel which borrowed some elements from
celebrated contemporary murder cases. The friction between
Superintendent Seegrave and Sergeant Cuff recalls the equally
uneasy relations between the inept country policeman, Superintendent Foley, and the Scotland Yard expert, Inspector Whicher,
in the Constance Kent case. The interest the detectives show
in the household laundry book and in a stain on the night-
dress of one of the characters was suggested by a similar crucial
issue in the Kent mystery. Collins also utilized the Northumberland Street sensation of the following year in the episode in
which Godfrey Ablewhite is attacked in a house (also in Northumberland Street) to which he has been lured.

Mid-Victorian murder headlines, finally, not only helped
make books: they helped sell them. In the spring of 1876 the
whole nation was absorbed in the "Balham mystery," a fresh
chapter in the homicidal annals of the rich. The victim was a
thirty-year-old barrister named Charles Bravo who died of poison at the suburban villa, set in ten acres of grounds, which his
bride had brought him upon their marriage five months earlier.
There were two chief suspects: his wife Florence, who in the
interval between her brief first marriage and this second one
had been the mistress of a well-known elderly hydropathic doctor; and her paid companion, a middle-aged female of somewhat
repellent aspect named Jane Cox. The acutely embarrassed doctor ran a poor third. The mystery remained so, officially at least.
After occupying the headlines from late April to mid-July, when
a second inquest lasted twenty-three working days, the Bravo
murder had to be filed away in the bulging dossier of Victorian
cases in which "evidence to fix the guilt upon any person or
persons," in the usual formula of the coroner's jury, was lacking.
The interesting thing about the jury's verdict in this case, though,
was that it omitted the word "unknown" after "person or persons."

The veteran novelist William Harrison Ainsworth, whose
career reached back to the Newgate novel fad, was quick to
detect the commercial possibilities of the Balham affair. His
latest novel, *Chetwynd Calverley*, which had been running in

the magazine *Bow Bells,* was about to be issued in book form. "There is a poisoning case in *Chetwynd Calverley,*" he wrote William Tinsley, his publisher, "which bears a curious resemblance to the great sensational case now before the public. . . . If you can get an early notice of *Chetwynd Calverley* into some papers, drawing attention to the remarkable resemblance between the poisoning case in that story and 'The Balham Mystery,' you might quote it in your advertisements with effect. . . . A notice just now in *The Daily Telegraph* would sell an edition." If the records of Victorian publishing were closely examined, many such hopeful tie-ins between a newly published book and a newly committed crime might be disclosed.

It was during the brief reign of the sensation novel that George Eliot mastered the art of fiction and Thomas Hardy began his career as novelist. They found themselves in a dilemma as a consequence. Bred, like all their contemporaries, in a literary atmosphere which tolerated and even encouraged the free use of murder as a convenient plot device—a contrivance on the same level as the sudden reappearance of a long-lost son or husband, or the disclosure of a hidden will or birth certificate—the two great Victorian novelists could not help being conditioned toward its use. Not only was murder handy: it was sanctioned, as the newspapers and reviews were constantly reminding them, by the events of the times. Whatever their personal view of melodrama as art, and especially of murder as a melodramatic device, they were, like Lady Macbeth contemplating her unwashable hands, stuck with it.

But their philosophy of life and of literary art transcended their melodramatic leanings. In their hands, serious fiction grew more and more concerned with moral issues and with psychological analysis, and relied less upon episodic excitement, suspense, and surprise. In such fiction, murder—the ultimate expression of human desperation from one cause or another—is an indefensible excrescence, *except* insofar as it can be shown to be the result of credible human passions. Eliot's and Hardy's predecessors, such as Bulwer-Lytton, Dickens, and Collins, had sometimes dignified their use of murder by attempting to depict "the criminal mind," a topic which understandably had a special attraction for the Victorians. But they did so only to the extent of describing that mind's operation as they conceived it to be, not concerning themselves with its origins or development. Normally they did not think it necessary to convince the reader that the murderer was psychologically bent to be a murderer, or that murder would have inexorably ensued from the circumstances described. To them, as to most of their contemporaries, the criminal was a man apart.

Novelists like Eliot and Hardy, however, were concerned with the forces of life that lay behind the criminal act, with the development of the murderer, or would-be murderer, from the ordinary human being under the irresistible pressure of circumstance and passion. They tended to use homicide, meditated or achieved, to probe the psychology of ordinary men and women and illustrate the personal and social forces that caused basically well-disposed human beings to commit criminal acts. Instead of studying the criminal personality, in short, they studied the personality which became criminal.

Inheriting murder as a plot device, therefore, they sought—Hardy especially, in *Desperate Remedies, Far from the Madding Crowd, The Woodlanders, Tess of the D'Urbervilles,* and *Jude the Obscure* *—to convert it into an organic element, to make it a means of exemplifying evil, a symbol, a culmination, a deed somehow to be integrated into the whole moral and artistic pattern. The distinction between their ambition and that of their predecessors was tersely put by a writer in the *Saturday Review* in 1901. "The great murderers of tragedy," he said, "are philosophers and psychologists under pressure of the Nemesis. The murderers of melodrama belong to the Old Bailey: the concealment, the plot, the means, the discovery, the ordinary material of the detective story, are the main sources of interest." Novelists as-

---

* There are more actual murders in Hardy than in George Eliot. In the latter's fiction, only four persons die by another's hand—Hetty's illegitimate baby, Mme. Laure's husband (stabbed on the stage of a theater), Tito in *Romola,* and the constable Felix Holt kills (a case of manslaughter, not murder). George Eliot seems to prefer her characters to accuse themselves of murder they have not really committed (Gwendolen in the case of Grandcourt's accidental drowning) or to harbor murderous intentions (Bertha in "The Lifted Veil" and Caterina in "Mr. Gilfil's Love Story").

piring in the Eliot-Hardy manner to express a profound reading of life aspired, in effect, to do what the French and Russian masters of realism had been doing: to employ murder thematically, as a means of embodying the tragic vision. But one feels that much of the murderous violence so produced has a meretricious air about it, the air of the Old Bailey and the melodramatic stage—the ineradicable curse of its descent from the sensation fiction of the preceding generation. In later Victorian fiction there are many reminiscences of the sensation novelist's facile use of murder as a mechanism; but there is no Raskolnikov.

4

The Blood-Stained Stage and Other Entertainments

THE ENGLISH DRAMA has always been hospitable to murder. Apart from Shakespeare's numerous adaptations of classical and historical murder plots, in Elizabethan times there was strong interest in stage adaptations of domestic cases. *A Yorkshire Tragedy*, printed in 1608 and once attributed to Shakespeare, dealt with an actual case, some three or four years earlier, of a remorseful gambler who killed his wife and two children. A murder at Feversham, Kent, half a century earlier (1551), recorded in Holinshed's *Chronicles of England, Scotland, and Ireland*, had already provided the plot for the anonymous tragedy *Arden of Feversham* (1592), another play once ascribed to Shakespeare. In the eighteenth century the same event was dramatized afresh by George Lillo. Lillo's more famous play, *The London Merchant, or The History of George Barnwell* (1731), also treating of a domestic murder (derived, this time, from an old ballad), remained in the repertory for over a century. Playbills announcing revivals of this old standby exist in great abundance, dating all the way down to early Victorian times; Mr. Wopsle starred in it, in *Great Expectations;* Thackeray grafted the Eugene Aram story onto it, the parody result being "George de Barnwell, by Sir E. L. B. L., Bart," in

Novels by Eminent Hands; and it was part of the allusive equipment of every man in the street. The playgoer Sam Weller, for
example, volunteered that "it's always been my opinion, mind
you, that the young 'ooman deserved scragging a precious sight
more than he did."

Nineteenth-century melodrama was as voracious a consumer
of scripts as is modern television, and no subject was drawn on
more heavily by playwrights with impatient managers at their
door than the incomparably dependable one of murder. Of the several thousand plays produced in England during the century,
only a small proportion of those with murder in their plots had
murder as the leading word in their titles or subtitles. Yet the
fullest list of nineteenth-century plays, that of Allardyce Nicoll,
contains no fewer than seventy of the latter. Typical of them
are:

> *A Dark Night's Work; or, Murder at the Dead Man's Pool*
> *Murder on the Thames*
> *Emma Hardy; or, The Murder of Leyburn Mill*
> *The Murdered Maid; or, The Clock Struck Four* *
> *The Murder on the Cliffs; or, The Smuggler's Dogs*
> *Murder in Hoxton*
> *Murder Near the Old Mill: A Story of Three Christmas
> Nights*
> *Murders of the Round Tower Inn*
> *The Solitary of Lambeth; or, The Murder of St. George's
> Fields*
> *The Thieves' House; or, The Murder Cellar of Fleet Ditch*
> *The Murder House; or, The Cheats of Chick Lane*
> *Pedlar's Acre; or, The Murderess of Seven Husbands . . .*

In addition, there are scores of plays, less accessible through

---

* Seemingly a revival (1819) of a play based on the Abraham Thornton
case, possibly written by the prompter at the Theatre Royal, Birmingham:
*The Mysterious Murder; or, What's the Clock, a Melodrama in Three Acts
Founded on a Tale Too True.* The latter evidently was acted only at fairs
and "halls of a popular character." Another play based on a portion of the
Thornton case was William Barrymore's *Trial by Battle; or, Heaven Defend
the Right,* produced at the newly opened Coburg Theatre in 1818. As the
title indicates, the drama hinged on the curious legal device involved; the
plot itself, however, was set in the Middle Ages and had nothing to do with
the Thornton murder.

alphabetical lists, whose titles contain *murder* in subordinate positions, and hundreds more—such as those whose titles contain such words as *fatal, mystery,* and *death*—which may reasonably be assumed to have at least one murder in the script. A further, even less determinable number provided murder as a side dish mentioned only in the detailed menu of the playbill. Such a one was George Dibdin Pitt's *Susan Hopley; or, The Trials and Vicissitudes of a Servant Girl* (1841), which was advertised as containing, among other sensational episodes, "A Vision of the Double Murder at Upton." *Susan Hopley*, incidentally, might be viewed as almost the archetypal Victorian domestic murder drama. Based on an early novel by the once well-known Mrs. Catherine Crowe—the book had appeared only months before the play—it featured a heroine of the servant class whose adventures fully equaled those of the high-born maidens and wives of Gothic fiction. Not only did she see instructive visions, but she met and held her own with highwaymen, and, in the last act, commanded a posse that captured the villain when he returned to the scene of his crime. The play was kept in the English repertory for decades and captivated audiences in the United States and Australia as well.

That the popular theater faithfully reflected the murder fever of the Thurtell-Corder-Burke/Hare-Greenacre period is indicated by the fact that of the seventy nineteenth-century plays with *murder* prominent in their titles, twenty-five were produced in the two decades 1821–40. One of the most popular plays of the genre at this time was *Jonathan Bradford; or, The Murder at the Roadside Inn,* written by Edward Fitzball and produced at the Surrey Theatre on June 12, 1833. The plot was based on a crime which was said to have occurred in an inn on the Oxford-London road in 1736. Jonathan Bradford, the innkeeper, a man of good reputation, was found standing aghast by the bed of a murdered guest, Christopher Hayes. In one of his bloody hands he held a bloody knife. It seemed, as a later generation would say, an open-and-shut case, and despite his protestations of innocence Bradford was tried, convicted, and executed at Oxford. Just before he was hanged, however, he told the attending clergyman that although he admittedly had gone to his guest's room with the object of murdering him for his money, he found him already dead. "He was struck with amazement, he could not believe his senses, and in turning back the bed-clothes, to assure himself of the fact, he, in his agitation, dropped his knife on the bleeding body, by which means both his hands and the knife became bloody." Some time after Bradford was executed, another person—his ostler according to some, Hayes's footman according to others—confessed to the crime.

Fitzball's melodrama was a landmark in the history of English staging, because it was, except for an uninfluential play some years earlier, the first to use a multi-level set, composed in this instance of four rooms—bedrooms above, back parlor and bar below—the action occurring simultaneously in several rooms or moving from one to another. The novelty of this device, combined with the intrinsic appeal of a murder drama, gave the play a run of 264 consecutive nights, during which, its author reckoned in his memoirs, four hundred thousand people saw it. *

Murder in Gothic castles and Oriental palaces, murder on the high seas, murder everywhere—but, above all, murder on English soil, in or near the present day: although melodrama was extremely eclectic in its adoption of settings of time and place, the acute sense of immediacy which marked so much of the popular art of the period was particularly noteworthy in the theater. When literary and foreign dramatic sources failed—the contemporary German and French drama, being unprotected by

---

* The Jonathan Bradford story was familiar to many before the Surrey staged it. It had appeared in print in a number of places, including the *Percy Anecdotes* (1821) and R. S. Kirby's *Wonderful and Scientific Museum* (1804). In his long, histrionic speech to the court, Thurtell had cited the case to illustrate the danger of convicting an accused murderer on circumstantial evidence alone. After Fitzball successfully dramatized the story, it was borrowed in the usual manner by the manufacturers of cheap fiction. Edward Lloyd issued a novel, *Jonathan Bradford,* in 1851; its author may have been—this cautious form of the verb is always requisite in connection with him—Thomas Peckett Prest. Dickens, in the first section of "The Holly-Tree Inn" (1855), refers to this or another version of the story, "a sixpenny book with a folding plate, representing in a central compartment of oval form the portrait of Jonathan Bradford, and in four corner compartments four incidents of the tragedy with which the name is associated"—the layout thus fortuitously suggesting the play's distinctive stagecraft. Later Joseph Le Fanu used the same theme in *A Lost Name* (1868).

English copyright, was freely pillaged for the London stage—there were always the newspapers to inspire the playwright as they inspired the novelist.

Ten years before he wrote *Jonathan Bradford*, Fitzball, having already made a reputation as an adapter of Scott's novels for the stage, was invited by the new manager of the Surrey Theatre to become the house's resident playwright, receiving six to eight pounds a week to write plays on subjects to be assigned him. The manager's first choice was the Weare murder, which had just occurred and as a consequence of which Thurtell was now in prison. "My blood," Fitzball recorded, "was absolutely chilled at the proposition. . . . Young as I then was, I indignantly threw up my engagement, and quitted the theatre in disgust." But the manager was a shrewd estimator of popular taste, and he got another hand to write a Thurtell play, *The Gamblers; or, The Murderers at the Desolate Cottage*, for the production of which he bought the horse and the "identical chaise" which figured in the murder, as well as the "identical table" around which the group had supper that night, and the "identical sofa" on which Thurtell later rested his uneasy head. The premiere of the play, authenticated as it reputedly was with these props (though Thurtell denounced them to Pierce Egan as "a most infamous falsehood"), attracted a large crowd, but Thurtell's counsel, with the trial still six weeks away, obtained an injunction against further performances, and the Surrey's exertions were, for the moment, wasted. But after the trial the show was revived with expectable success.

The episode generated considerable folklore. There is no question that the manager of the Surrey at the moment was one Williams. According to one account, into which it would be humorless to inquire too closely, this gentleman was otherwise known as Boiled Beef Williams because when he was at liberty he was the proprietor of the Old Bailey Boiled Beef House near Newgate Prison. At the time he took over the Surrey, however, he was at liberty only, if one may put it so, in a restricted sense; legally he was an involuntary inmate of the King's Bench debtors' prison nearby. Such persons, according to old custom and under certain conditions, were entitled to residence and free movement "within the rules" (that is, within a certain adjacent area) of the prison. But despite its proximity the Surrey Theatre, as a playhouse with a raffish clientele and therefore a place unsuitable for the entertainment of detained debtors, was outside the rules. If mere attendance at the Surrey by the inmates of the prison was frowned upon, certainly managing it was infinitely more culpable. And if Williams was, in fact, not a free man at the time *The Gamblers* was staged, it is easy to understand why the authorities took so unsympathetic a view of the production. By his breach of "the rules" he was as much in contempt of the Court of King's Bench as, by the presentation of the Thurtell case on stage while it was still *sub judice*, he was in contempt of the home circuit court preparing to try it at Hertford.

Fitzball's refusal to dramatize Weare's death did not prevent his going on to write dozens of melodramas during his long and prolific career. But his attitude at the time was symptomatic of the disdain with which the more fastidious theater people regarded melodramas drawn not from literary sources, but from the newspapers. In rejecting such themes, however, they proved to be overlooking a lode which kept the so-called minor theaters prosperous for many a year. While the three "patent" theaters (Covent Garden, Drury Lane, and in the summer months the Haymarket) produced the legitimate drama on which they enjoyed a legal monopoly, the minors were the playhouses of the people. Of those which specialized in melodrama, the best-known were the former Royal Coburg (renamed the Victoria in 1833, soon popularly christened "the bleedin' Vic," and subsequently immortalized as "the old Vic"), the Surrey, the Adelphi, the Britannia Saloon, Hoxton ("the old Brit"), the Pavilion in Whitechapel Road, the Royal Standard, Shoreditch, the Marylebone, the Queen's Theatre, Fitzroy Square, and the Olympic before the famed Vestris-Mathews management took over. While other minor houses made a specialty of spectacles—with water shows ("tank dramas") at Sadler's Wells and equestrian performances (literally horse operas) at Astley's Amphitheatre— the Victoria, Surrey, Adelphi, and the rest based their appeal frankly on blood. They, along with the two hundred or more playhouses that existed in the provinces in the 1820s and '30s, made murder melodrama an enduringly favorite entertainment among the masses of playgoers. As the years passed, the social gulf that had existed between the educated audiences at the patent theaters and the unwashed, raucous ones at the minors gradually disappeared; melodrama's unique appeal to a wide social spectrum had a momentous reconciling effect which in the course of time transformed not only the nature of the London playgoing audience but the kind of entertainment provided for it.

Until the Theatres Act of 1843 ended the monopoly of the Big Three, the minors used the device of the burletta—the insertion of incidental music and a few songs in what was otherwise a straight spoken play—to circumvent the law forbidding their presentation of legitimate drama. In melodrama, the murders therefore were necessarily enacted under difficulties. Although the burletta requirement became almost a dead letter in the thirties (managers dutifully included the requisite music in the scripts submitted to the Lord Chamberlain for licensing but then forgot to include it in the actual performances), the grotesque effects it had produced were not easily forgotten. In *Oliver Twist* Dickens describes what happened when the law was observed:

It is the custom on the stage, in all good murderous melodramas, to present the tragic and the comic scenes, in as regular alternation, as the layers of red and white in a side of streaky bacon. The hero sinks upon his straw bed, weighed down by fetters and misfortunes; in the next scene, his faithful but unconscious squire regales the audience with a comic song. We behold, with throbbing bosoms, the heroine in the grasp of a proud and ruthless baron: her virtue and her life alike in danger, drawing forth her dagger to preserve the one at the cost of the other; and just as our expectations are wrought up to the highest pitch, a whistle is heard, and we are straightway transported to the great hall of the castle: where a grey-headed seneschal sings a funny chorus with a funnier body of vassals, who are free of all sorts of places, from church vaults to palaces, and roam about in company, carolling perpetually.

The following of the murder scene in *Macbeth* with the comic drunken porter business is, as De Quincey went to memorable pains to argue, dramatically defensible. But the London theaters, in their legally required *mélange des genres*, would seem to have gone too far.

Nevertheless, the minors did all they could with the rich materials provided them by sudden death in the midst of contemporary life. Probably the most successful of the plays based on the police news was the "Red Barn" drama which, in many versions, held the boards for a full hundred years; there was a revival of it at the Elephant and Castle, London, as late as the 1920s, and in the same period it was still being toured through the industrial parts of the provinces in the form of a "portable theatre" (peep show). This drama had the great theatrical advantage of a supernatural element, Mrs. Marten's dreams which led to the discovery of her slain stepdaughter's body. The raw materials, it might be said, made the story a playwright's dream as well. But Maria's story seems never to have been admitted to the respectable stage. "No theatre with a reputation to lose," says a modern historian of melodrama, "would let him [Corder] be represented on its stage, while every theatre which did exhibit the murder in the Red Barn was packed."

Murder melodramas had even humbler homes in the thirties. One was the "penny gaff," a playhouse improvised from rundown business premises, the former shop serving as entryway, the warehouse behind as playhouse proper, and the upper story as gallery. The London slums had many of these squalid entertainments, conducted by actors, singers, and dancers in the last phases of drink and decrepitude who performed to unruly audiences, ranging in age from eight to twenty (seldom higher) and composed almost exclusively of costermongers, street boys, and their girls. The atmosphere of these resorts, which besides specializing in reputedly obscene songs * and dances were known to be meeting and recruiting places for apprentice criminals, attracted the condemnation of moralizing students of urban life and the constant attention of the police. Henry Mayhew, who was not easily shocked, was unsparing in his denunciation of the gaffs, where the stage "is turned into a

---

* Including one that might well be revived in our own day: the "Pineapple Rock."

platform to teach the cruelest debauchery." It was among their youthful clientele that the popular taste for murder dramatized assumed its crudest form. So did the dramatization itself, advertised typically by a handlettered placard when there was no money in the till to pay a printer: "FOR THE BENEFIT OF MR. TWIG, On Tuesday next will be performed the Grand National Dramar [*sic*] Of GREENACRE, or THE MURDER OF CARPENTER'S BUILDINGS." The gaffs, as James Grant, an observant journalist of the 1830s, commented, "evince a remarkably strong predilection for 'horrible murders'; and the moment that accounts of any such occurrence appear in the newspapers, a piece embodying the most shocking incidents in that occurrence is got up for representation at these establishments. The recent atrocity known by the name of the Edgeware murder, was quite a windfall to many of the Penny Theatres. Pieces founded on the most frightful of the circumstances connected with it were forthwith got up, and acted to crowded houses, amidst great applause. It will hardly be believed, yet such is the fact, that so late as November last—that is, full ten months after the occurrence took place—it was represented in these establishments to numerous audiences." Age cannot wither, nor custom stale, the vigorous representation of a real murder.

Murder melodramas turned up, too, at the fairs that remained as favorite an entertainment for early nineteenth-century Londoners as they had been for their Elizabethan ancestors. At Bartholomew and Greenwich fairs, for example, a familiar attraction for many years was John Richardson's dramatic theater, a spacious tent accommodating a thousand spectators on rows of planks. Such sensational dramas as *The Monk and the Murderer* (1807), compositions filled to the brim with Gothic terror, had in their starveling casts many future celebrities of the English stage, most notably Edmund Kean. In a festive locale where the competition included conjurers, freaks, menageries, acrobats, fire-eaters, learned pigs, and booths selling refreshments and a thousand kinds of gimcracks, it would have been unrealistic—and unprofitable—to expect people to sit patiently through the whole of an uncut drama. And so, as Dickens described Richardson's pitch at Greenwich Fair in *Sketches by Boz*, "illuminated

with variegated lamps, and pots of burning fire . . . you have a
melodrama (with three murders and a ghost), a pantomime, a
comic song, an overture, and some incidental music, all done
in five-and-twenty minutes." Although Richardson's show was
celebrated for its ample supply of costumes, logistics as well as
economics limited the innumerable smaller troupes which moved
from fair to fair in the country to a wardrobe as truncated as
their scripts. Mayhew heard of a company which played *Maria
Marten* in cavalier costume and *The Murder at Stanfield Hall*
(Rush) in garb of the time of Charles II.

At the fairs, in fact wherever in city or village there was
the prospect of a profitable audience, Punch and Judy showmen
put on what, from our special point of view, may fairly be called
a murder drama. From the beginning of his long career Punch,
imported to England by itinerant continental showmen at the
time of the Restoration, was of course primarily a murderer,
the number and nature of his victims differing as the routine
evolved through the years but always including his wife and
their infant child. At some point along the way, the figure of the
Hangman was introduced, the climactic episode in the play being Punch's expiation on the gallows. Still later—the most recent
historian of Punch and Judy suggests that it may have been
early in the nineteenth century—an inspired piece of business
was inserted in which Punch, pretending that he does not know
how to put his neck into the noose, tricks the Hangman into
showing him, whereupon Punch triumphantly hangs the Hangman. It is, as our authority says, "an enchanting and evergreen
bit of business. . . . The Hangman took his place very easily in
the show in a city where public hangings attracted vast crowds
all night before an execution, and where the last dying speeches
of executed criminals were hawked everywhere upon the pavements." In this period the Punch and Judy show in effect added
another dimension—a different slant, that of the folk tale—to the
subject of murder and execution.*

There were many touring marionette shows in nineteenth-

---

* Sample of a last dying speech, puppet-play version:
HANGMAN: I have been a very bad and wicked man.
PUNCH: I want a slice of bread and jam.

century England. In their repertories the traditional materials of puppetry, dating back to Elizabethan times, were replaced by simplified versions of the melodramas performed by the London companies and by Vincent Crummles's strolling troupe in *Nicholas Nickleby.* Thus once again, under the changed conditions of the age, the inherited folk materials gave way to contemporary journalistic and theatrical themes; even the marionettes tended to follow the news. But once successful, a play based on a topical occurrence or a best-selling novel held the booth—if that is the proper term—for many years. Evidently the only reasonably full records of plays performed on the marionette stage date from the last third of the century; prominent in these lists are *Jonathan Bradford* and (most popular of all, appearing in the repertories of at least ten companies) the deathless *Maria Marten.*

In the sixties, *East Lynne* and *Lady Audley's Secret,* immense successes in fiction and on the living stage, quickly made their way to the puppet theater as well. And mention of these plays requires us to return for a moment to the stage itself in that decade. Domestic melodrama, gradually ceasing to be the near-monopoly of the minor theaters and the penny gaffs, had become welcome in the West End playhouses patronized by the well-to-do, and re-named, by analogy with the parallel trend in fiction, the "sensation drama." The murders extensively reported in the *News of the World* and *The Times* furnished the story materials and the energizing spirit that went into these new productions. Sometimes they borrowed the plot line directly, but more often they simply took over useful incidents and characters. In 1883 the playwright Henry Arthur Jones, writing on "The Theatre and the Mob," described the commercial value of these materials: "In melodrama we find that those plays have been most successful that have contained the most prodigious excitement, the most appalling catastrophes, the most harrowing situations, and this without much reference to probability of story or consistency of character. The more a play has resembled a medley of those incidents and accidents which collect a crowd in the streets, the more successful it has been. On the whole, a melodrama has succeeded much in proportion as the general impression left by it is the same as the general impression left by the front page of the *Illustrated Police News*."

Significantly, it was in 1868, when the sensation drama on the London stage was matching the success of the sensation novel in the circulating libraries and the magazines, that Dickens added to his repertory of platform readings the scene of Bill Sikes's murder of Nancy. One of the most taxing solo dramatic performances ever devised, the act, which Dickens insisted upon including in his programs as many as ten times a week, sent his pulse from a normal 72 up to 124 and reduced him to utter prostration the moment he left the stage. A doctor was in attendance at every performance. Biographers have properly emphasized this repeated compulsive enactment of a terrible murder as a contributory cause of Dickens's fatal stroke in 1870; psychological interpreters have argued, perhaps less conclusively, that it reveals both an abnormal preoccupation with violent death and a subconscious death wish. Whatever the Bill Sikes performance may tell us about Dickens's state of mind at the end of his life, it says a good deal about the appetites and susceptibilities of his audiences. Part of the satisfaction Dickens derived from his demoniac portrayal of the murder was the hysteria it provoked in them. At one performance at Clifton, Dickens afterward reported to his daughter, there was "a contagion of fainting. And yet the place was not hot. I should think we had from a dozen to twenty ladies borne out, stiff and rigid, at various times. It became quite ridiculous." Ridiculous it may have been, but it was also the most impressive evidence possible of the receptivity—the morbid avidity, some might say—which the Victorian audience brought to the dramatic representation of murder.

ii

Murder was presented to the Victorians in still other forms, inert rather than living or with the show of life. Among these were waxen representations of celebrated criminals and tableaux of the dramatic high points in their careers, a field in which the renowned Madame Tussaud was the unchallenged monarch.

Hers was by no means the first waxwork exhibition in England.
A Mrs. Salmon had had one in Fleet Street as early as 1711,
when she was mentioned in the *Spectator;* Boswell found a
quarter-hour's amusement there in 1763; and still later it was one
of the sights of London to which David Copperfield took Peggotty on her visit from Great Yarmouth. Madame Tussaud's own
maternal uncle, the Swiss physician Christopher Curtius, from
whom she learned the art of wax modeling, toured his show
through England, under the management of her future husband,
in 1791. There were undoubtedly other such exhibitions then,
but I have seen no evidence that any contained what was to
prove Madame Tussaud's most popular specialty, the figures of
famous evildoers.

Her inspiration undoubtedly came from the Caverne des
Grands Voleurs which Dr. Curtius had added in 1783 to his
Parisian waxwork display in the Boulevard du Temple, an institution much favored by royalty. The accidents of the French
Revolution and the ensuing counterrevolution, furthermore, had
forced Madame Tussaud into intimate, if on their part posthumous, contact with men whose bloody deeds far eclipsed any
commemorated in the Caverne des Grands Voleurs; for in those
years her art was called into requisition to copy in wax the heads
of leading political casualties, brought to her studio fresh from
the guillotine. The figures of the most famous participants, on
one side or the other, in the turbulence of revolutionary and
Napoleonic France were the nucleus of the collection she
brought to England with her in 1802. With this assemblage of
surpassingly lifelike effigies—her valid boast was that they
wholly lacked the unpleasant yellow flesh tone of her competitors' figures, thanks to a secret formula for eliminating the waxen
cast from waxwork objects—Madame Tussaud toured the British
Isles for the next thirty years, exhibiting in assembly rooms,
theaters, and inns in every principal city and town.

About 1822 the revolutionists, Marat, Hébert, Fouquier-
Tinville, and the rest, were placed in a separate room, subject to
an extra 6*d.* admission charge. To these were added, as occasion
suggested, such native figures as those of Burke and Hare, described by a placard of 1833 as "(taken from their faces, to ob-

tain which the Proprietors went expressly to Scotland); which have excited intense interest from the peculiar nature of their crimes, and their approach to life." By the end of the forties these "wolves of the West Port" had been joined by Corder, John Holloway ("the atrocious wretch who murdered his wife in a manner too horrible to describe"—that is, by taking her body apart with a penknife and depositing the head, arms, and legs in a privy and her trunk and thighs in a Lover's Walk near Brighton), and "Eliza Davis, who was killed in Frederick Street, near Regent's Park." This last murder was committed not far from Baker Street, where the enlarged exhibition, after its many years on the road, had settled in 1835. The "Separate Room," also called "the Dead Room" and "the Black Room," received its permanent designation in 1845, thanks to a *Punch* contributor who had invented the term as a joke. Thus it was that when the Duke of Wellington, a frequent visitor to the exhibition, begged to be notified whenever a new figure was added, he specified: *"not forgetting the Chamber of Horrors."*

Conveniently overlooking the fact that the Chamber of Horrors had been in existence, under other names, long before the profitable outburst of homicidal activity in the late forties, the catalogue sold at the door in 1860 explained:

In consequence of the peculiarity of the following highly interesting Figures and Objects, they are placed in an adjoining room. The sensation created by the crimes of Rush, Mannings, &c., was so great that thousands were unable to satisfy their curiosity. It therefore induced the Messrs. Tussaud [the founder had died in 1850] to expend a large sum in building a suitable room for the purpose, and they assure the public that so far from the exhibition of the likenesses of criminals creating a desire to imitate them, Experience teaches them that it has a direct tendency to the contrary.

The mendacity here is less noteworthy than the moralism. The pious disclaimer, encountered wherever a representation of crime was on sale as a commercial commodity, was followed through in the body of the catalogue, where appropriate didactic remarks were appended to the listing of each figure.

The *pro forma* insistence upon the moral value of the exhibition probably neither uplifted nor depressed the countless

Victorians who visited it in the course of the years. They came
to enjoy themselves in an untroubled, uncomplicated way among
the grisly exhibits. A writer for *All the Year Round* well captured
the atmosphere:

"And every one of these here has been hung," said a powerfully-built
gentleman in top-boots, speaking to himself aloud with immense relish. "Every one of 'em hung," he said again, smacking his lips.

He was standing in the middle of the Chamber of Horrors, and looking dead at the new model of Dr. Smethurst, who, with his hand raised
in deprecation, and with a gentle smile upon his innocent countenance, appeared to be softly reasoning with the agriculturist, and saying, "No, dear sir, no—do not say so. *I* have not been hung—far from
it!"

To enter the Chamber of Horrors rather late in the afternoon, before
the gas is lighted, requires courage. To penetrate through a dark passage under the guillotine scaffold, to the mouth of a dimly-lighted
cell, through whose bars a figure in a black serge dress is faintly visible, requires courage. . . .

But, *what* a horrible place! There is horror in the dull cold light de-
scending from above upon those figures in the Old Bailey dock, all
with the same expression on their faces, upturned, inquisitive, be-
wildered. There is Horror in the unpicturesqueness of this aspect of
crime—crime in coats and trousers being more horrible (because
nearer to us) than crime in doublets and trunk-hose. There is Horror
in the inflated smiling heads, cast after death by hanging. . . .

Yet incongruities, or seeming incongruities, intervened. From
the main exhibition hall came strains of the house band, playing
"some of the stormier and more untidy passages of the overture
to the Bronze Horse, as well as . . . the last tune but one of the
Maritana Quadrilles." And, as the crowning touch:

What shall be said of the man who could stand at the door of the
Chamber of Horrors *eating a pork pie?* Yet such a man there was—
your Eye-witness saw him; a young man from the provinces; a young
man with light hair, a bright blue neckcloth, and a red and beefy
neck. His eye was on the model of Marat, assassinated in a bath, and
with this before him he could eat an underdone pork pie.

It is the last straw that breaks the laden camel's back; it was this last
horror that sent your Eye-witness out of Madame Tussaud's, as fast
as his legs would carry him.

Far from being truly incongruous, this spectacle of a youth eating a pork pie in the presence of murder was all too apposite, as

every Victorian aficionado of legendary crime in fiction and on the stage would have understood.

Whatever qualms the *All the Year Round* reporter felt did not affect the women who patronized Madame Tussaud's as unselfconsciously as they devoured newspaper accounts of a bloody murder. In the same year of 1860, a novelist named V. I. St. John deplored the phenomenon: "Young ladies who would blush or be indignant at your mentioning before them an ankle or a leg, will enter this loathesome den of horror, and gaze complacently at the faces of Rush, or Tawell,* or Greenacre, or at the expiring agonies of Marat in the bath, and they will ascend the steps of the guillotine, and feel the edge of the axe, and look at the pailful of sawdust which was placed ready to receive the head; and do all this with a face unmoved."

Madame Tussaud's prospered for exactly the same reasons that Catnach's flying and stationary hawkers did, and the latter profession was quick to recognize their common interest. One standing patterer told Mayhew, not long before the founder's death, that "he thought of calling upon that 'wenerable lady,' and asking her . . . 'to treat me to something to drink the immortal memory of Mr. Rush, my friend and her'n.'" She, and the sons who succeeded her in the business, assiduously kept up with the crime news, eliminating outdated figures if necessary in order to accommodate the newest sensation. On March 28, 1879, Kate Webster was arrested in Ireland; scarcely more than two weeks later, on Easter Monday of all days, her likeness was unveiled, to great fanfare, in Baker Street.

The purported lifelikeness of the wax figures was underscored by authentic relics which were also proudly exhibited in the Chamber of Horrors: the proprietors of minor theaters were not the only ones to snap up the *realia* of recent crime. An executed murderer's clothing, by long usage the perquisite of his hangman, no longer was disposed of, as had been customary, to the Jews; now the hangman had regular and far better paying customers in the representatives of Madame Tussaud. So well

---

* John Tawell, an excommunicated Quaker and former convict who had fallen into a prosperous way of business following his release in Australia, killed his former mistress, Sarah Hart, by a large dose of prussic acid in 1845.

known was her establishment's anxiety to buy up and display the clothing and accessories related to a murder that some survivors took special precautions against her agents. When the contents of Road House, scene of the Constance Kent murder, were auctioned off, the family withheld the little victim's cot lest it end up in the Chamber of Horrors. The old-time broadside salesmen, though generally sympathetic to the aims of the Tussaud institution, resented this aspect of its enterprise. "Daniel Good," one of Mayhew's informants said of the London coachman who killed his mistress, "was a first-rater; and would have been much better if it hadn't been for that there Madam Toosow. You see, she went down to Roehampton, and guv 2*l.* for the werry clogs as he used to wash his master's carriage in; so, in course, when the harristocracy could go and see the real things—the werry identical clogs—in the Chamber of 'Orrors, why the people wouldn't look at our authentic portraits of the fiend in human form."

People like Daniel Good, having been executed, were in no position to protest Tussauds' exploitation of their notoriety, but those who were more fortunate sometimes made trouble. Smethurst evidently was not one of them; he seems to have preferred to sue his second "wife's" estate rather than the waxwork establishment. But in 1894 the adventurer and shady financier Alfred John Monson, who had just been let off with the verdict of Not Proven in the sensational "Ardlamont Mystery" trial for the insurance-murder of a wealthy young man named Cecil Hambrough, entered two successive suits against Tussauds', one for a restraining injunction and the other for libel. His complaint was that, to the daily pain of himself and his family, his effigy was being displayed in the Chamber of Horrors, dressed in the clothes he was said to have been wearing the day of the "fatal accident" and holding the very gun with which he had been alleged to have killed Hambrough. The Tussauds, however, were able to show that Monson himself had been behind the negotiations which had resulted in their acquiring the clothes and the gun; he had accompanied his agent and accomplice to their door in a cab and then gone to a nearby hotel to await the proceeds of the deal. Monson won the suit, his damages being assessed at one farthing—a judgment calculated to convey to the plaintiff in a civil suit approximately the same message the Not Proven verdict conveys to the defendant in a Scottish criminal case. Since almost everyone believed that Monson had really killed Hambrough, the *Scotsman* doubtless was writing in a vein of heavy irony when it commented, "Thus are the rights vindicated of decent people to be protected against being publicly pilloried alongside of notorious murderers and thieves, and Monson himself recompensed handsomely for his own personal wrong." The Tussauds, in all probability, were also recompensed handsomely: what they laid out in legal fees must have been more than repaid in publicity.

If Madame Tussaud had no full-fledged rivals once she perfected her artistic, expository, and promotional techniques, she had persistent competition of a sort. There appear to have been hundreds of waxwork shows in England at the time, most of them small operations. It is said that the best of the exhibitions working the fairs was Ewing's, which was arranged in ten caravans. This may have been the one described at Bartholomew Fair in 1825, its personages reaching from Mother Shipton, Jane Shore, and Queen Elizabeth to diverse murderers such as Othello and Abraham Thornton.

Whether Dickens modeled Mrs. Jarley's waxwork display, in *The Old Curiosity Shop*, directly upon Madame Tussaud's in its touring years is not clear; if he did not, he must have had in mind some of her more ambitious competitors. Mrs. Jarley had her own chamber of horrors. Among the "historical characters and interesting but misguided individuals" available for inspection at the low all-inclusive rate of sixpence was "the woman who poisoned fourteen families with pickled walnuts"—Dickens's escalation, perhaps, of Madame Tussaud's "Phrenological Portraits of STEWART AND HIS WIFE, Who were executed in Edinburgh on the 13th of August, 1829, having confessed to the murder of Seven Persons by means of Poison, which they familiarly called doctoring." On view also, to quote Mrs. Jarley's spiel once the customers were inside, was "Jasper Packlemerton of atrocious memory, who courted and married fourteen wives, and destroyed them all, by tickling the soles of their feet when they were sleeping in the consciousness of innocence and virtue. On being brought to the scaffold and asked if he was sorry for what he had done, he replied yes, he was sorry for having let 'em off so easy, and hoped all Christian husbands would pardon him the offence. Let this be a warning to all young ladies to be particular in the character of the gentlemen of their choice. Observe that his fingers are curled as if in the act of tickling, and that his face is represented with a wink, as he appeared when committing his barbarous murders."

Mrs. Jarley's patter was stringently modified, along with the exhibits, when the patronage included parties of young ladies from nearby schools. No more arch chatter about a maiden's proper choice of a gentleman, but serious instruction; murderers were out, moralists were in. By deft alteration of costume, the waxen figure of Grimaldi, the famous clown, was converted into that of the grammarian Lindley Murray, and "a murderess of great renown" into—of all people—the eminent writer of moral and religious tracts, Hannah More. Miss Monflathers, head-mistress of the most elegant Boarding and Day Establishment in one town, considered the resultant figures to be "quite startling from their extreme correctness."

The humblest counterpart of the Jarley "delight of the Nobility and the Gentry," calling at villages too tiny to accommodate or reward the most necessitous strolling players or the most travel-worn wax figures, was the peep show, a booth containing painted pictures which were successively raised or lowered by the showman into the view of customers gazing through circular apertures fitted with magnifying glasses. In his autobiography, the self-styled "Lord" George Sanger, the Victorian circus impresario, recounted his debut in the entertainment business in the 1830s, when he and his father carried a peep show from place to place. The pictures, measuring four by two-and-a-half feet, were painted by a drunken Irishman named Jack Kelley, whose tumbledown atelier in Leather Lane, Holborn, was patronized by all itinerant showmen. An ordinary picture cost 3s. 6d., while a battle piece, with hundreds of figures painted in, ran to 7s. 6d. One of the Sangers' most successful productions was a series of scenes narrating the Red Barn murder. Sanger recalled his patter:

"Walk up!" I would pipe, "walk up and see the only correct views of the terrible murder of Maria Martin. They are historically accurate and true to life, depicting the death of Maria at the hands of the villain Corder in the famous Red Barn. You will see how the ghost of Maria appeared to her mother on three successive nights at the bedside, leading to the discovery of the body and the arrest of Corder at Eveley Grove House, Brentford, seven miles from London." When we had our row of spectators getting their pennyworths from the peep-holes I would describe the various pictures as they were pulled up into view. The arrest of Corder was always given special prominence, as follows: "The arrest of the murderer Corder as he was at breakfast with the two Miss Singletons. Lee, the officer, is seen entering the door and telling Corder of the serious charge against him. Observe the horrified faces of the ladies, and note, also, so true to life are these pictures, that even the saucepan is shown upon the fire and the minute glass upon the table timing the boiling of the eggs!"

A veteran one-handed peep showman estimated to Mayhew that there were about fifty of these caravan shows in the whole country. They worked the villages during the fair and feast season, returning to the London streets and markets for the autumn and winter. The subjects offered were of remarkable range—from the Queen of Sheba's visit to King Solomon to the murder of Weare, and from the building of the Tower of Babel and Wellington at Waterloo to the death of Maria Marten. The murders were the best draw in the "carawan shows," along with battles. "Anything in that way," Mayhew was told, "suits them. Theatrical plays [i.e., paintings of scenes in popular plays] ain't no good for country towns, 'cause they don't understand such things there. People is werry fond of the battles in the country, but a murder wot is well known is worth more than all the fights. There was more took in with Rush's murder than there has been even by the Battle of Waterloo itself."

Among the patrons of all these entertainments in city, town, and village were many children (who, said the peep showman, "is dreadful for cheapening things down"). The taste for murder usually begins at an early age, and the popular amusements of Victorian England did all they could to cultivate it among the young. When plays, puppet shows, waxworks, and peep shows were unavailable, children readily improvised their own representation of a horrid deed which was dominating their elders' talk at the moment. George Augustus Sala, the Victorian journalist and *bon vivant,* remembered how, when he and his London middle-class playmates tired of "playing at Dickens" (acting out scenes and characters from the newly published *Pickwick Papers*), they would "play at Greenacre." They made a cardboard model of Newgate, including a practicable drop; and a twopenny doll, suitably dressed, served very well as the condemned murderer.*

One favorite entertainment of nineteenth-century English children, however, was virtually untouched by the enthusiasm for murder. This was the toy theater, the pasteboard miniature stage for which, over the years, at least fifty firms provided sets of cut-out scenery and characters and simplified scripts for the performances to be offered before admiring home audiences. Although most of the juvenile plays were adapted from current hits in the real theater, they did not participate in the trend toward domestic realism; in this respect theirs was a case of arrested development. As late as 1850 they continued to limit themselves to pantomimes and romantic dramas that had been in fashion thirty years earlier, before the vogue for melodramas laid in contemporary settings had gotten under way. At least ten plays based on Scott's novels were available for juvenile production, and there were plenty of older nautical, Oriental, and Gothic melodramas: Isaac Pocock's *The Miller and His Men,* for example, since 1813 an old standby in the toy theater as it was

---

* Murders could be adapted to the purposes of practical instruction as well as of innocent merriment. The political journalist William Cobbett recorded in his *Rural Rides,* under date of November 20, 1825, that his son Richard "had learned from mere play to read, being first set to work of his own accord to find out what was said about Thurtell, when all the world was talking and reading about Thurtell." Success in this attractive venture encouraged his parents to provide him with *Robinson Crusoe,* and "that . . . made him a passable reader." Recalling Sloppy's proficiency with the police news, one may well believe that as many Victorian urchins learned to read with the assistance of sensational newspapers and broadsides as from the Bible and Catechism which were the officially adopted instruments of infant literacy in elementary schools.

in the London minors, was in the German romantic tradition. But virtually the only drama in the newer vein—and its setting was a century removed from the present—was *Jonathan Bradford,* which probably was put into the juvenile repertoire because its four-room set offered an unusual challenge to parlor producers.

One reason for this unexpected neglect of plays that proved so successful in the living theater of the day may have been the printers' and stationers' awareness that parents would not take kindly to the introduction of sordid tales of contemporary murder into their homes (though those tales obviously arrived there in other ways). Another reason was offered by William Archer later in the century: the picturesque melodrama, with its colorful, exotic settings and costumes, was well adapted to the interests of children at play, whereas the realistic genre that grew up alongside it, limited as it was to familiar settings and drab everyday costumes, simply lacked saleable theatrical glamor. This was a form of theater whose physical components could be bought, in Robert Louis Stevenson's famous phrase, "penny plain and twopence colored": but what, in pasteboard sets for a murder melodrama laid in gray Victorian London, was to be colored?

If, for whatever reasons, one did not find miniature representations of murderers and murder scenes set up in the parlor, ready for an appreciative audience after tea, their place might be occupied by three-dimensional objects of the same size and nature. In the period 1840–80, a profitable sideline of Staffordshire potters was the production of cheap portrait figures of royalty, politicians, nonconformist divines, writers, actors, sportsmen, Crimean war heroes, and other celebrities. The Victoria and Albert Museum's collection, for example, includes china figurines of Falstaff, Newton, Chaucer, Handel, Napoleon, James Thomson, Milton, Shakespeare, Wesley, and George Whitefield —a fair sampling of early- and mid-Victorian culture heroes. But in view of the climate of the times the Staffordshire line would have been seriously incomplete had it not included the likenesses of malefactors as well. And it did. In the most comprehensive collection, made by Thomas Balston and now the property of the National Trust, housed at Stapleford Park near Melton Mow-

bray, appear Dick Turpin (a reflection of the popularity of
Ainsworth's novel *Rookwood*), James Rush and Emily Sandford,
the Mannings, and Dr. Palmer. A portrait figure of Corder is also
known to exist, although neither the Victoria and Albert nor the
Balston collection includes an example.

A sub-genre of the ceramic *memento mori*, equally scarce, is
the series known in the antique trade as "murder houses." The
Balston collection includes a representation of Palmer's house in
High Street, Rugeley. Two versions are known of Corder's Red
Barn, one showing Maria Marten standing at the door, the other
with cows and chickens in the foreground. The James Rush
series, however, is regarded as the masterpiece of the murder
houses; it includes three sites connected with the murders, one
of which, Potash Farm, is portrayed, with signal disregard of the
facts, as "a sentimental farmhouse with roses round the door."
Of all the diverse witnesses to the place murder occupied in the
popular Victorian mentality, this placid domestication of villains, their victims, and the scenes of their villainy in the form
of china knick-knacks strikes us as the most incongruous—yet
typical.

iii

In one further symptom of the British populace's enthusiasm
for murder, the dramatic and the monstrous were not diluted by
any such sentimentality. For "symptom" one should perhaps read
"source," or, rather, two related sources: the one surviving un-
diminished today, the other belatedly cut off by law in 1868.
Once a murder had been committed, the public could look forward to additional dramas, scheduled in advance, open to the
public at no charge, and conducted under the most dignified and
unimpeachable of all secular auspices, those of the law. I refer,
of course, to trials and executions.

The queue outside the Central Criminal Court in Newgate
Street, familiarly if not affectionately known as the Old Bailey,
is a durable London institution; seekers after free unrehearsed
entertainment swelled it throughout the Victorian era as they do
today whenever something notorious is being aired. But the few
seats available to the public in both the Victorian building and

its successor, the present one, limited the number of people who could take advantage of the free spectacle. Often the audience was select in more than one sense. We have already noticed that Victorian ladies in modish attire were present at the trial of the Stauntons in 1877 and of Adelaide Bartlett in 1886. Several decades earlier, the trial of the valet Courvoisier for murdering his master was one of the outstanding fashionable events of the season.

Those whose occupations prevented them from attending the trials in person were amply cared for by the press. Not only did the newspapers, beginning with Thurtell, report in detail, often verbatim, the narrative of the crime as it was gradually developed from the witness box, the cut-and-thrust of cross-examination, the forensic oratory, and the judge's lengthy summing-up: in the case of the more celebrated trials, the same copious materials were gathered together and printed in hastily produced books for crime addicts to read at their leisure and preserve for future re-savoring and study.

The drama inherent in a trial was, indeed, an important factor in the Victorians' absorption in murder. Any good trial had its interest, from the comedy of *Bardell* v. *Pickwick* to that longest-running of all nineteenth-century courtroom sensations, the case of the Tichborne Claimant in 1871–74. But a good murder trial was the supreme treat in that line, and novelists and dramatists were as quick to capitalize upon the public appetite for courtroom scenes as they were to exploit the fondness for murder itself. In Charles Reade's *Griffith Gaunt*, for example—set nominally in the first half of the eighteenth century but so lacking in period color that it could just as credibly be a tale of mid-Victorian life—the wife of the eponymous hero defends herself against the charge of murdering him, in an extensive trial scene involving page after page of quoted testimony and rendered additionally dramatic by Mrs. Gaunt's desperate conducting of her own defense. Another woman is tried for poisoning her husband in Wilkie Collins's *Armadale,* and there are still other notable trials in Trollope's *Phineas Redux* and Charlotte Yonge's *The Trial.* Naturally, dramatists found fictional trial scenes ready-made for stage use. The Liverpool trial of Jem

Wilson for the murder of Harry Carson in Mrs. Gaskell's *Mary Barton,* for example, eventually reappeared as the climax of Dion Boucicault's *The Long Strike.*

But—to return to real life—it was the open-air execution that attracted the big crowds. One of the ugliest scenes of London life in the eighteenth century was the ritual progress of condemned men and women through the streets from Newgate Gaol to Tyburn, a few yards west of the present Marble Arch. The route, leading past St. Giles's, one of the most obscene of all the city's rookeries, was lined with the worst elements of the rabble, jeering or commiserating with the wretches bound hand and foot in the cart of the condemned. The gruesome scenes at Tyburn Tree itself have been described so many times as to relieve us of any necessity for recalling them here. The point is that, after Tyburn was abandoned in favor of Newgate as the place of execution (1783), the mobs grew larger and more turbulent. If they could not have bread and circuses, they had, and grossly relished, the recurrent spectacle of one or more murderers being turned off by the current Jack Ketch. (The most famous nineteenth-century hangman, and the busiest—he sometimes declined invitations to officiate at scheduled executions by saying he "had a little job" to do elsewhere—was William Calcraft, who presided at the rope on hundreds of occasions between 1828 and 1874.)

The same proceedings were duplicated on a smaller but still impressive scale in the assize towns throughout the kingdom. Gleeson Wilson, for example, was hanged at Liverpool in 1849 before an audience of one hundred thousand,* a large proportion of whom had come on cheap excursion trains the railways ran from "all available points." And as an epilogue, a kind of reward for faithful attendance, the authorities responded to popular demand by displaying the body of the hanged murderer, preliminary to its being dissected by surgeons. The latter operation was required in capital cases by a law of 1752, largely in-

---

* This and all succeeding attendance figures are drawn from contemporary sources, for whatever they may be worth. Some strike me as being considerably exaggerated.

spired by the novelist Henry Fielding, who as a Bow Street magistrate was prominent in the eighteenth-century movement for the reform of the criminal code and of the police. Thurtell's body, as we have seen, was diminishingly on view at Bart's during its leisurely dissection. Burke's was exhibited, fittingly enough in the anatomical theater of the College at Edinburgh, for one day, during which some thirty thousand sightseers viewed it; an equal number gathered the next morning, but the college officials decided that one such day was sufficient. At Brighton in 1831, twenty-three thousand of the curious pressed through the magistrates' room of the town hall in the space of six hours, to see the remains of John Holloway, who, as also noted above, had killed and dismembered his wife. This practice of exposing hanged men's bodies ended when the dissection requirement was repealed in 1832, probably as a result of the Brighton episode.

Nevertheless, during the first thirty years of the Queen's reign, public hangings themselves remained the best attended of all the "sports of the people." Although they drew disorderly crowds in Scotland and the provinces, they were at their worst in London. The rabble predominated, but the middle and upper classes were adequately represented at the execution of more than ordinarily notorious murderers. Schools were dismissed so that the young gentlemen could absorb a wholesome lesson from beholding the demise of a wrongdoer. Rooms commanding a good view of the scaffold, rented out at fancy prices, were the scene of all-night drinking parties on the eve of the execution and of jolly breakfasts after the merrymakers had watched their fill of the proceedings through opera glasses and the trap had been sprung.* Once the criminal had been turned off, to the

---

* In *Bentley's Miscellany* for June 1837 appeared a satiric poem bearing the quadruple title of "Family Stories.—No. V.— Hon. Mr. Sucklethumbkin's Story. The Execution. A Sporting Anecdote." When it was included in the first series of his popular *Ingoldsby Legends,* the author, the Rev. Richard Harris Barham, added a footnote saying it alluded to "the euthanasia of the late Mr. Greenacre." It is a mordant recital of the adventures of Lord Tomnoddy and his friends, gay blades all, when they attend an execution. They hold a party in the Magpie and Stump public house, the

accompaniment of the tolling bell of Saint Sepulchre's, the crowd, typically numbering tens of thousands, dissolved into a *mêlée* of brawling, drunken toughs and their women, many fighting to get to the scaffold and have a closer look at the dangling body. The drop of the trap likewise was the cue for the broadsheet vendors to start their strident merchandising.

Once in a while, the festivities were not confined to the execution site itself. One September evening in 1841 a man named Robert Blakesley, after spending most of the day in the company of various City policemen who should have had more than a suspicion that he planned something sinister, burst into the King's Head public house in Eastcheap, stabbed his estranged wife, who was acting as barmaid, and then with the same butcher knife killed the proprietor of the house, James Burdon. According to one of Mayhew's patterers, Burdon's widow kept the King's Head open on the morning Blakesley was hanged, "and the place was like a fair. I even went and sold papers outside the door myself. I thought if she war'n't ashamed, why should I be?"

Thackeray and Dickens were among the huge crowd that watched Courvoisier hanged in the summer of 1840. Thackeray's classic essay describing the event, "Going to See a Man Hanged," ended in an impassioned plea for the abolition of capital punishment. He was so shocked by the experience that he suffered from profound depression of the spirit for the next fortnight. Dickens did not immediately comment on the event except indirectly, in the Newgate scenes in *Barnaby Rudge,* but six years later he recalled the Courvoisier hanging in one of a series of letters on capital punishment he contributed to the *Daily News* during his brief editorship of that paper. In 1849 he attended the

whole upper floor of which they have rented for the occasion, but at daybreak they all pass out, thus missing the big moment. They awaken only after the body has been removed. "Here's a rum Go! . . . We've missed all the fun!"

In 1849, jaded with London sensations, the "Swell Mob," a coterie of wealthy rakes, chartered a special train to go to Norwich for the hanging of Rush. But the police spoiled the fun by intercepting the train at a way station and sending the delegation back to town. The police did not often treat honest enthusiasts so unsympathetically, but they had much on their hands that day.

monstrous festival of the Mannings' execution outside the Horsemonger Lane Gaol and at once wrote two blistering letters to
The Times, now not advocating the abolition of capital punishment but urging that executions be conducted decently and in
private.

Protests on both humane and security grounds—for these
grisly carnivals brought together, in a confined space, a dangerous concentration of known but unjailed criminals—mounted
year by year, until in 1856 a Select Committee of Commons unan-
imously recommended that public executions be ended. The
House of Lords promptly blocked the move. Then, in the middle
sixties, sentiment having been newly stirred by the riotous scenes
at the hanging of Müller in 1864, a Royal Commission took up
the subject afresh. (The public discussion of the matter in these
years, incidentally, may well have inspired Browning's graphic
description of the public beheading of the villain Guido Fran-
ceschini in the last book of *The Ring and the Book.*) In 1868
the Capital Punishment Amendment Act finally made private
executions mandatory.

As a minor consequence of this reform, the "gallows literature" trade, already hard pressed by superior newspaper coverage, suffered its coup de grâce. With criminals being put to
death in strictly regulated privacy, it would have occurred to
even the most languid intellects that shrilly hawked last dying
speeches had something bogus about them; if anyone could report the pious prose traditionally attributed to condemned criminals, it would have been the regular newspapermen, who until
1879 were allowed to witness executions within the prison walls.
But somehow, apart from statements uttered to attending clergy-
men in the condemned cell, convicted murderers were no longer
as communicative as they were purported to have been in the
heyday of the broadside and chapbook.

Necessarily, too, there was a change in the popular attitude
toward murder. No longer could the announcement of a new
homicide stir in the breasts of the multitude the pleasant ex-
pectation of a rowdy block party at the foot of the gallows. In
the ordinary course of events, the climax of the story was now
to be reached when the jury returned its verdict and the judge

delivered his sentence. The execution, described after the exclusion of the press simply by a curt official statement affixed to the prison gate, was anticlimactic. Then too, with the softening of manners in the mid-Victorian era and the diminution of the London mob, partly as a result of long-overdue slum clearance, the enthusiasm for public hangings probably had been fading in any case.

The last such event, on May 26, 1868, was the execution of Michael Barrett for his role in the dynamiting of Clerkenwell Prison, a sensational episode in the Irish patriots' long campaign of terrorism against their English oppressors. We are told that— only four years after Müller—"it took place . . . amid the most complete apathy on the part of the London populace." The overnight crowd numbered scarcely two thousand, and when the hour of the hanging neared, it swelled only moderately. There was no struggling for places; few if any ribald songs were sung; the solitary street-preacher who turned up was listened to with totally unwonted civility; and the tract distributors encountered no jeering or blasphemy. Barrett's appearance on the scaffold evoked a mixed response, some clapping their hands, some groaning and hooting, but even this expression of opinion was a matter only of minutes. And after the ceremony was over, the dispersing crowd failed to seriously inconvenience street traffic in the neighborhood. It was not like the old days at all.

The deletion of this single once-potent element in the popular response to murder did not, however, reduce its fascination. Could we say that henceforth—that is, in the century leading to our own day—the response would acquire a more intellectual, more specifically aesthetic, cast? At least it had lost, unlamented, the quality of sadistic brutality which complicated the public attitude so long as the last chapter of the current sensation was symbolized by the gallows erected in front of Newgate. Victorian murder continued to be a popular entertainment, but in somewhat purified circumstances.

5

Murder and the
Literary Life

PROBABLY the most curious by-product of the famous Palmer poisoning case was a book, published in London some four years after the doctor's execution, which translated the entire trial record, along with an account of Palmer's sporting activities, into classical Greek.* No further evidence is needed that if murder was popular among the Victorian masses, its hold upon the educated mind was just as compelling. I have not tried to discover how many statesmen, scientists, philosophers, peers, and other members of the class who read classical Greek as easily as English were students of the murderous art, but the incidence of enthusiasm among them may well have been as high as it was among men—and women—of letters. And there it was high indeed.

It is a little surprising to find so many Victorian intellectuals, otherwise the essence of sobriety, rectitude, and lofty ideals, joining the masses of tradesmen, artisans, and laborers in their passion for murder. And yet, given the atmosphere described in the preceding chapters, what else might we expect? The great

* Its author purported to be X. B. Καβουρ—a reflection of the current fame of the Italian statesman Camillo Benso Cavour. There is said also to have been a narrative of the Rush case, translated into *modern* Greek.

writers of the age grew up and lived their mature lives in a social climate flavored by Catnach broadsheets and Surrey melodramas and gore-filled Sunday papers; had they encountered current murder in no other way, which is most unlikely, they would have found it amply reported in *The Times*. The delight so many eminent Victorians expressed in murder assures us that, despite whatever "eminent" connotes, they were first and foremost simply Victorians.

I have remarked, in connection with the sensation novel, that mid-Victorian fiction tended to imply that murder occurred much more frequently in contemporary society, figured in the experience of many more people, than it actually did. And yet it is strange how many famous Victorian writers' lives were somehow brushed by murder. Between the two—the pervasive interest in murder as a perennial excitement to be followed day by day in the newspapers, and the accident of personal associa-tion with such a real-life event—it is more understandable than it otherwise would be why murder has as prominent a role as it does in Victorian literature.

The pattern of appreciation and participation was well set in the preceding era by Sir Walter Scott and Charles Lamb. When Scott was ten years old there had been a murder in his own family: his great-aunt Margaret Swithin, living in a house near St. George's Square, Edinburgh, was brutally killed with a coal-axe by her berserk maidservant, who after the deed ran into the street brandishing the bloody weapon and crying for witness to her guilt. The adult Scott attended criminal trials whenever he had the chance, and in his library at Abbotsford he prized a sizeable collection of criminal narratives and printed trials; the soporific effect which, he recorded, the perusal of the Thurtell "variorum edition" had on him must not be thought typical of his normal reaction toward such reading matter, which was, on the contrary, one of constant delight. Scott also took a certain pawky pride in telling Maria Edgeworth in 1823 that his son-in-law, John Gibson Lockhart, was defense counsel for one Robert Scott, "a clansman of mine, who, having sustained an af-front from two men on the road home from Earlstown fair, nobly waylaid and murdered them both single handed. He also cut off their noses, which was carrying the matter too far, and so the jury thought—so my namesake must strap for it, as many of *The Rough Clan* have done before him."

Charles Lamb, four years Scott's junior, had the unique distinction among English writers of living his whole life with a murderess—his sister Mary, who had knifed their mother to death in 1796 while in one of her recurrent fits of insanity.* The memory of that event, traumatic as it had been to Lamb, did not prevent his sharing the general murder fever of the 1820s. Thurtell, we know, was much on his mind, as he was on everybody else's, including Scott's and De Quincey's. In a charming stream-of-consciousness letter to his Quaker friend, the poet-banker Bernard Barton (January 9, 1824), Lamb complained of a "whoreson lethargy" which weighed upon his spirit at the moment. "I inhale suffocation—I can't distinguish veal from mutton—nothing interests me—tis 12 o'clock and Thurtell is just now coming out upon the New Drop—Jack Ketch alertly tucking up his greasy sleeves to do the last office of mortality, yet cannot I elicit a groan or a moral reflection." After some Elian free embroideries on this attack of the spleen, Lamb returned, as if by compulsion, to the overriding theme: "Who shall deliver me from the body of this death? It is just 15 minutes after 12. Thurtell is by this time a good way on his journey, baiting at Scorpion perhaps,† Ketch is bargaining for his cast coat and waistcoat, the Jew demurs at first at three half crowns, but on consideration that he may get somewhat by showing 'em in the Town, finally closes."

Five years later Burke and Hare were in Lamb's thoughts. "We may," he wrote another correspondent, "set off the Scotch murders against the Scotch novels—Hare, the Great Un-hanged" —as opposed, he meant to imply, to "the Great Unknown," the

* The story was recalled during the trial in 1872 of the elderly school-master and classical scholar John Selby Watson, who at the age of sixty-six had killed his wife. He seems to have been a long-suffering husband whose dismissal from his school post at Stockwell was the last straw. Reprieved on the ground that he was of unsound mind while committing the act, he died in a prison for the criminally insane in 1884. Watson is one of the few murderers to have earned a place in the *Dictionary of National Biography*.

† The zodiacal sign of the Scorpion was a way station on the route to Hades.

by-now superfluous sobriquet behind which the author of *Waverley* once had been concealed.

Lamb had no way of anticipating that not long thereafter, in December 1832, he would walk right into a murder-in-the-making. At Enfield, where he and Mary were then living, their friend Edward Moxon, the agreeable "printer of poets" who was later to marry their adopted daughter Emma Isola, unexpectedly dropped in. The maid being busy, Charles walked down to the Crown and Horseshoe inn to fetch an extra pint of porter for the guest. "Now," Lamb subsequently wrote in a letter dated the last day of the year, "I never go out quite disinterested upon such occasions. And I begged a half-pint of ale at the bar which our sweet-faced landlady good-humouredly complied with, asking me into the parlour, but a side door was just open that disclosed a more cheerful blaze, and I entered where four people were engaged over Dominoes." It was a typical pub scene, but, as events proved, a scene with a difference. One of the domino players invited Lamb, whom he did not know, to join in the game. "Not to balk a Christmas frolic," Lamb did, but he soon discovered he had forgotten how to play, and withdrew. Then another of the players, who he later learned was a young man named Benjamin Danby, surprised Lamb by telling him he had known him as a child in the Temple, where Danby's father had been a hairdresser. Lamb did not recognize him but "perfectly remembered his father." This amiable chat completed, Lamb returned to his cottage, somewhat overdue, with Moxon's pint of porter.

The men at the inn, besides Danby, were three local residents named Cooper, Sleath, and Johnson. The subsequent ballad identifies Danby accurately:

> This young man he was a sailor,
>   And just returned from sea,
> And down to Enfield Chase he went
>   His cousin for to see;
> Little thinking that ere night—
>   Would prove his destiny.

After Lamb went home, Danby played the traditional part of the drunken sailor, flashing the money he had just been paid at the end of his voyage, tossing for drinks, and steadily becoming more incapable. At the end of the evening, his chance companions, instead of seeing him safely to the home of his cousin, with whom he was staying, took him to a secluded spot in Holt White's Lane, leading from Enfield Town to Enfield Chase, cut his throat, and robbed him.

The next morning, after the body was found, Lamb was summoned to the coroner's inquest "to say what I knew of the transaction. My examination was conducted with all delicacy, and of course I was soon dismissed. I was afraid of getting into the papers, but I was pleased to find myself only noticed as a 'gentleman whose name we could not gather.'" (So much for Elia's celebrity!) In retrospect, Lamb felt that there had been something peculiar in the domino players' behavior; they had looked on him "a little suspiciously, as they do at alehouses when a rather better drest person than themselves attempts to join 'em." But perhaps not: "One often fancies things afterwards that did not perhaps strike one at the time. However, after all," Lamb concluded, "I have felt queer ever since. It has almost sickened me of the Crown and Horseshoe, and I sha'n't hastily go into the taproom again."

But his queasiness did not prevent him from trying to persuade his friends to come visit him at "murderous Enfield"; he could put them up, he said, at the Crown and Horseshoe, where "Johnson and Fare's sheets have been wash'd—unless you prefer Danby's *last* bed." It is not written that anyone took advantage of this proffered hospitality, which was a little suspect anyway, since neither the murderers nor their victim had been staying at the inn. The local sensation, however, continued to serve as grist for Lamb's epistolary mill. Six or seven weeks after the murder he was writing to the same Mrs. Badams to whom he had addressed his report of December 31: "By the way, Cooper, who turned King's evidence, is come back again Whitewash'd, has resumed his seat at chapel, and took his sister (a fact!) up to Holt White's lane to shew her the topography of the deed. I intend asking him to supper. They say he's pleasant in conversation. Will you come and meet him?" Evidently the projected party never took place.

Although Lamb never knew it, he had already had intimate contact with still another murderer. In the 1820s, as a member of the brilliant circle who made the *London Magazine* one of the best literary periodicals of the era, he had often been in the company of Thomas Griffiths Wainewright, a dandiacal but talented young man who contributed art criticism to the magazine under the pen name of "Janus Weathercock." Wainewright was a favorite of Lamb's and he returned the esteem. But while he was enjoying the company of such gifted men as Lamb, De Quincey, and Hazlitt, he had already begun to engage in serious crime. In 1822 and 1824 he forged signatures to power-of-attorney documents in order to collect from the Bank of England a legacy of £5,250 from his grandfather, the founder of the *Monthly Review*. It would have come to him eventually in any case, but Wainewright, whose style of living had thrust him deeply in debt, was a young man in a hurry. In February 1828, again impatient for a windfall, this time the estate of his still-healthy uncle, he shook the tree by giving George Edward Griffiths strychnine. To his disappointment, Wainewright discovered when the estate was turned over to him that it had shrunk considerably since Uncle George made out his will in his nephew's favor. Still, £5,000 was a respectable return for the small trouble the deed cost him.

Two years later, when his mother-in-law objected to his insuring her daughter—his wife's sister—for a large amount, he poisoned her, and not long afterwards, the policy being but two months old, he achieved his original purpose by successfully administering strychnine and antimony to the younger woman. When the Eagle Insurance Company refused to pay and his creditors pressed him, he fled to France and from that safe haven sued the company. By mistake, the suit was entered in the Court of Chancery, and no reader of *Bleak House* will be surprised to learn that four years were required to extricate it from that fathomless quagmire and transfer it to the Court of Exchequer. After one jury disagreed, a second found in favor of the insurers. Upon his return to England in 1837, Wainewright was arrested on the old forgery charge, convicted, and transported to Van Diemen's Land, where he died ten years later. But because his career as a poisoner was revealed only in the

course of the belated trial of his claim against the insurance company, his old friend Lamb never learned of it: he had died in 1834.

Thomas and Jane Carlyle were in physical proximity to
murder at least once during their long residence in Chelsea. In
May 1844, Jane wrote her cousin Jeannie Welsh: "You have
read in the newspaper *our* murder I hope—you cannot think
how much more interesting a murder becomes from being committed at one's door." Well, two or three blocks away; or, as her
husband measured the distance when he reported the sensation
to his brother in Canada, "a gun-shot from this." The case was
that of a middle-aged French chemist, Augustus Dalmas, who
had been courting Mrs. Sarah M'Farlane, a widow who had been
caring for his four children since his wife's death. Walking
across Battersea Bridge with her on the night of April 29,
Dalmas cut her throat from trachea to spine. No motive was
established. "He was *mad*, it does seem," Carlyle commented,
and the authorities agreed. After Dalmas was convicted and
sentenced to death, he was reprieved, confined for a time as a
criminal lunatic, and finally transported for life.

Jane's obvious delight in murder is a fair sample of the enjoyment, perhaps not always avowed, which many well-bred Victorian women found in the subject. We need not subscribe to
the stuffy opinion of one of the Carlyles' earlier editors, that her
allusions to murders and murderers then in the headlines point
to a decided "morbidity of mind." If Jane was morbid, so, on the
same kind of evidence, were plenty of other lively women in her
time.

Murders sometimes supplied her pen with topical analogies,
as when she described her husband's new portrait, by Gambar-
della, as *"Greenacre-Carlyle"* because of the "gallows-expression"
it attributed to the sitter. It is not certain that Carlyle appreciated the comparison. Nor is it probable that, had she known of
it, the Carlyles' noble friend and patroness, Lady Ashburton,
would have been much flattered by Jane's remark, in a letter to
a relative, that "Maria [Manning] has a strange likeness to
(never tell it)—Lady Ashburton!" Jane was jealous of the lady's
attentions to Carlyle, and the malice implied in her fancy is
unmistakable.

"What a bore that we cannot get done with the Mannings,"

she observed in another letter, in 1849. But the industry with which she clipped newspaper articles and pictures relating to that infamous pair and sent them to Jeannie Welsh makes it quite plain that she did not want to get done with them. Nor did the years witness any diminution of her interest. When her friend George Rennie called at Cheyne Row in 1856, after a long absence, their talk was of prayer, the possibility of war with America, and Palmer—"Nice topics for dear friends meeting after a dozen years!" she remarked. But first things first, and the achievements of the physician-poisoner were undeniably the supreme topic of the day. "Palmer," Jane wrote in her journal on May 29, "is convicted after a horridly interesting Trial lasting twelve days. From first to last he has preserved the most wonderful coolness, forcing a certain admiration from one, murderer tho' he be!"

Meanwhile, another talented literary lady, this time in the Midlands, was doubly involved with murder. In 1848 Mrs. Elizabeth Cleghorn Gaskell, wife of a Manchester clergyman, published *Mary Barton,* a novel of life among the factory hands in the age of Chartism. In one episode in the book, the son of a millowner whose hands are on strike is fatally shot by an unknown assailant who in the end is revealed to have been the heroine's father, a Chartist and one of the strikers. Local readers with long memories immediately recognized the incident as based on the murder in January 1831 of the son of Thomas Ashton, a Manchester cotton manufacturer. Rewards totaling £2,000, half of which was put up by the government, resulted in the arrest three years later of two men who, it was proved, had been hired for the job by the Spinners' Union, furious because the Ashtons had discharged one of their number for union activity. One of the defendants was quoted as saying that "he would shoot all the Ashtons if the unions would give him 10 *l.* apiece for doing so." Not surprisingly, both were executed.

Among *Mary Barton's* readers was the dead man's sister, now a married lady, who at the age of twelve had been the last person to speak to her brother. On coming to the account of the murder, she fainted, and her brother-in-law wrote Mrs. Gaskell to protest what the family deemed the deliberate revival of painful memories. In a letter of August 1852, Mrs. Gaskell apologized for whatever distress her adaptation of the Ashton case might have caused the survivors.

Her regret may have been all the keener because in the interval between the publication of *Mary Barton* and her receipt of the protest, murder had struck within her own circle of friends. ". . . such a tragedy here yesterday, which you will see in the papers," she wrote a correspondent in January 1850. "We know Mrs. Novelli! She was a Madonna-like person with a face (and character I believe) full of thought and gentle love. . . ." The Madonna-like person, a thirty-year-old widow, was the victim of her brother-in-law, Alexander Novelli, a Manchester merchant two years her junior, who after killing her had taken his own life. At the inquest his solicitor testified that while administering the affairs of his late brother, who had died sixteen months earlier, Novelli "complained that inspecting the accounts affected his head." Another witness revealed that the murderer's mother had been insane, two of his brothers also had died by their own hands, and a surviving sister was a lunatic. In the circumstances, the jury's verdict was hardly to be faulted: murder and suicide, the perpetrator "being at the time of insane mind."

At this very time, also, murder touched the life of Charles Kingsley, novelist, advocate of Christian Socialism, and rector of Eversley, Hampshire. In 1850 there was an outbreak of burglaries and other crimes in the neighborhood, and at Frimley, ten miles from Eversley, the fifty-four-year-old curate of the parish, the Rev. George Edward Hollest, was fatally shot by burglars who broke into his bedroom at three o'clock in the morning and with whom he—reputed to be "a very strong and active man"— imprudently chose to struggle. Kingsley consequently put bolts and bars on his rectory doors and slept with loaded pistols at his side. On one occasion he used them, when an intruder approached at night. "Unfortunately," wrote John Martineau, son of Harriet Martineau's cousin, who was a pupil at Eversley, "Mr. K. had one of the short little pistols loaded with three slugs and not a bullet, and at fifteen yards such a little pistol would hardly send them into a man far enough to hurt him much, especially through thick clothes." Supposedly nobody thought at the time of the equally futile "pop guns" Thurtell had used upon Weare. Thurtell and the pious Charles Kingsley: it is an odd thought.

Naturally, the privilege of being in the immediate neighborhood of a murder was not granted to many Victorian men of letters (or their wives). The cases just described were exceptional. The connection most writers had with contemporary homicide normally was more vicarious; but it took many forms, the most *outré* of which was Richard Monckton Milnes's collecting mania. Milnes, later Lord Houghton, was a wealthy patron of letters, always alert for new talent, and the friend of many of the greatest Victorian authors. He is possibly better remembered today for his extensive collection of pornography and other erotica, which may have confirmed his protégé Swinburne's masochistic bent, than for having written the influential first biography of Keats. He also, however, collected mementos of famous crime—autographs and woodcuts of Courvoisier and the hangman Calcraft, and relics such as a swatch of the dried skin of a notorious murderer, which he kept pressed inside an appropriate book.* Like Sir Walter Scott fifty years earlier, Milnes had a personal library of criminal trials that was among the best in existence, as was his extensive file of scrapbooks containing the letters of criminals and newspaper accounts of their deeds.

In 1831 Milnes had taken his B.A. at Trinity College, Cambridge, where he and several friends shared an emphatic taste for murder. One of them was William Makepeace Thackeray, whom Milnes accompanied in 1840 to see Courvoisier hanged. The expedition actually was Milnes's idea, for he was an early opponent of the death penalty and wished to study the temper of the crowd, numbering forty thousand as it turned out, at a public execution. He is the person designated as "X" in Thackeray's essay on the occasion. Although the sight appalled Thackeray, he nevertheless retained a lively interest in current crime, and

---

* Milnes's biographer, James Pope-Hennessy, does not identify the former tenant of this gruesome souvenir, but I wonder if it was not William Burke. By judicial order, Burke's skin was tanned, the end product being very thick and of a dark blue color, the texture of morocco leather; then (whether by judicial order or not) it was divided into vendible segments and sold. William Roughead's grandfather kept his inch-square sample in a snuffbox, and Scott is said to have cherished another piece in his library.

was in the habit, not universally appreciated by his hostesses, of having himself announced in their drawing rooms by the name of some murderer then enjoying notoriety.

A third Trinity College man in 1828–31 was Alfred Tennyson. The abundant anecdotal material in print has as little to say about his interest in crime as it does about his fondness for rude limericks, no doubt partly because his contemporaries, when they recorded their memories of him, felt that such enthusiasms were beneath the dignity of a Poet Laureate. There is, however, no question that Tennyson was, in this regard as so many others, a true Victorian. In 1859, visiting the Tennysons at their Isle of Wight home, the Oxford mathematics don, Charles Lutwidge Dodgson ("Lewis Carroll") wrote to a cousin, "Up in the smoking-room the conversation turned upon murders, and Tennyson told us several horrible stories from his own experience— he seems rather to revel in such descriptions—one would not guess it from his poetry." Nor would one guess that the author of *Alice in Wonderland* would relish such descriptions; and his rather prissy tone suggests that he didn't.

Later in the century Tennyson had a similar talk-fest with another don, this time Benjamin Jowett, translator of Plato and master of Balliol College. The story comes from H. B. Irving, son of the great actor and himself a well-regarded writer on true crime, who recalled his father telling him that "sitting up late one night talking with Tennyson, the latter remarked that he had not kept such late hours since a recent visit of Jowett. On that occasion the poet and the philosopher had talked together well into the small hours of the morning. My father asked Tennyson what was the subject of the conversation that had engrossed them. 'Murders,' replied Tennyson." One would give much to know which Victorian atrocities especially appealed to the Laureate.

Still another member of the Trinity College coterie in Tennyson's time was Edward FitzGerald, who liked to quote to his correspondents, as evidence of his delight in murder trials, the lines in *The Beggar's Opera,*

> The charge is prepared; the Lawyers are met—
> The Judges all ranged, a terrible show!

Once, remarking on his having ordered a copy of the *Newgate Calendar,* he wrote, "I don't ever wish to see and hear these things tried; but when they are in print I like to sit in Court then, and see the Judges, Counsel, Prisoners, Crowd: hear the Lawyers' Objections, the Murmur in the Court, etc." There is no more striking proof of the depth to which the Thurtell case impressed itself into the Victorian mind than a passage in a letter of FitzGerald's to Fanny Kemble in 1879, more than fifty years after the event: "I like, you know, a good Murder . . . only the other night I could not help reverting to that sublime—yes! of Thurtell—sending for his accomplice Hunt, who had saved himself by denouncing Thurtell—sending for him to pass the night before Execution with perfect Forgiveness—Handshaking—and 'God bless you—God bless you—you couldn't help it—I hope you'll live to be a good man.'"

FitzGerald's early biographer, Thomas Wright, describes his delicate discrimination: "Murders whose incidents were picturesque or suggestive of chiaroscuro, or which exposed the bed and secret recesses of the soul, whether of the assailer or the victim, excited his deep and perennial interest; whereas a brutal common murder, unaccompanied by startling psychological accessories, only disgusted him." Wright could have been speaking, with equal or greater applicability, of Robert Browning; for this was precisely Browning's attitude. The acuteness of his interest in the psychological springs and circumstances of murder are sufficiently attested by such short dramatic monologues as "Pippa Passes" (Part I), "Porphyria's Lover," and "The Laboratory," three studies in *crimes passionels,* two accomplished and the third prospective. From one point of view, *The Ring and the Book* may be called the most elaborate literary edifice ever built on the foundations of a true murder story. Browning and his father often discussed the murky details of contemporary murders. In one letter, sold with the Browning papers in 1913, the elder man discoursed on the Constance Kent affair and included, so great was his concern for detail, a plan of the Kent house. Near the end of his life, the poet impressed a fellow-diner with the breadth of his command of criminal lore. He was, wrote the publisher Kegan Paul, "acquainted with the minutest details of every *cause célèbre* . . . within living memory."

Of all Victorian writers, Charles Dickens was the most powerfully attracted by crime. His interest in crime and punishment was so many-sided and so revealing of his character that it has been the subject of a large scholarly study by Philip Collins, one chapter of which deals extensively but not exhaustively with the single topic of Dickens and murder. A number of recent critics, following Edmund Wilson's lead, have explored and speculated upon the fact that Dickens's concern with violent death, climaxed by his "reading" of Sikes's murder of Nancy, amounted to a virtual obsession. Fortunately there is no need here to go into the psychological implications of this compulsive concern or its reflections in Dickens's fiction. But it is pertinent to recall, for one thing, that Dickens was the best public relations man any police force was ever blessed with. He had a lifetime love affair with the Metropolitan Police, and in a number of journalistic articles, based on many excursions with his officer friends, in uniform or plain clothes, he describes their work, particularly in the slums and on the Thames. One of the very first fictional detectives is Inspector Bucket in *Bleak House,* modeled to some extent on Inspector Field of Scotland Yard.

Dickens followed murder in the newspapers as attentively as anyone, and in his letters he commented on the Müller and Pritchard cases in the mid-sixties. In his periodical, *Household Words,* he printed several of his own articles on contemporary murderers. One (June 14, 1856) is a vigorous psychological piece on Dr. Palmer, arguing that the defendant's much-remarked-upon calmness in the dock was "deportment . . . always to be looked for and counted on, in the case of a very wicked murderer. The blacker the guilt, the stronger the probability of its being carried off." To clinch his point, Dickens, who would have made a fine historian of crime, quoted from the newspaper coverage of Thurtell thirty-two years before to show how strikingly parallel to Palmer's had been Thurtell's conduct. Later in the same year, Dickens published in *Household Words* a piece on a favorite topic of his, prison philanthropy and prison hypocrisy, as illustrated by the currently notorious case of the pious Mr. Dove, who declared that his murder of his wife had been conducted under divine guidance. And in the issue for January 3, 1857, Dickens used a recent daylight murder in a shop in Parliament Street as a peg on which to hang the argument, loudly revived in our own day, that the lenience of the courts and the pedantry of the law are encouragements to crime. "Technicalities and forms of law, *in reason,* are essential to the preservation of the liberties and rights of all classes of men"; but. . . .

In 1849, as we shall soon see, Dickens inspected the scene of the Rush murders in Norfolk and wrote about them in the *Examiner,* and in 1867, on his second tour of America, he paid a special visit to the Harvard Medical School to examine the locale of one of America's classic crimes, Professor Webster's murder of his colleague, Professor Parkman. After he moved to Gad's Hill Place, Kent, in 1857, one of the favorite walks upon which he took visitors led to a stile in nearby Cobham Park, where in 1843 a London oil-paint manufacturer, Mr. Dadd, had been stabbed to death with a spring-blade knife wielded by his son, a promising young artist. "Dickens," recalled one such guest, the journalist Edmund Yates, "acted the whole scene with his usual dramatic force. . . . The murderer . . . escaped, but was afterwards secured: he had been travelling on a coach [in France], and his homicidal tendencies had been aroused by regarding the large neck, disclosed by a very low collar, of a fellow-passenger, who, waking from a sleep, found Dadd's fingers playing round his throat. On searching Dadd's studio, after his arrest, they found, painted on the wall behind a screen, portraits of Egg, Stone, and Frith, Dadd's intimate associates, *all with their throats cut*—a pleasant suggestion of their friend's intentions."

One finds it hard to believe that Dickens did not put that story to use somewhere in his fiction, it was so much to his taste. But his accumulated stock of such lore was so immense that he could not possibly have used it all in several lifetimes as productive as his. It is generally accepted that he drew Hortense in *Bleak House*—Lady Dedlock's maid who kills Mr. Tulkinghorn—from Maria Manning. Some Dickensians also find traces of Mrs. Manning in Mr. Jaggers's housekeeper, Molly, in *Great Expectations*. Slinkton in the short fiction "Hunted Down" is certainly based on Lamb's friend Wainewright, whom Dickens, on one of his frequent prison tours, happened to see before his transportation to Van Diemen's Land. Philip Collins suggests that in Slinkton, Dickens was also recalling Dr. Palmer, another killer of persons he had insured, including close relatives. Others have proposed Wainewright as a model, to some extent, of both Rigaud (in *Little Dorrit*) and Jonas Chuzzlewit; and still others have maintained that Chuzzlewit's murder of Montague Tigg has certain parallels with Thurtell's murder of Weare. Such identifications of Dickens's supposed "inspiration" for his murderous characters and episodes may or may not be persuasive, but they are all based on the solid premise that with his unflagging interest in the crime of the day it was only natural that he should have stored up the details of many cases for possible use in his fiction.

Availing himself of this premise, the present writer hazards another possible instance of Dickens's adaptation of a detail from a famous crime. At Courvoisier's trial, Lord William Russell's coachman and the butler from the house across the street testified that when Courvoisier was told of his master's death, he replied with agitation, "O my God, what shall I do? I have been with his lordship only five weeks, and what shall I do for my character?" In *Little Dorrit*, Mr. Merdle's physician announces that that eminent speculator, whose paper empire was about to crash, has just cut his throat in a Turkish bath:

"I should wish," said the Chief Butler, "to give a month's notice."
"Mr. Merdle has destroyed himself" [repeated the Physician].
"Sir," said the Chief Butler, "that is very unpleasant to the feelings of one in my position, as calculated to awaken prejudice; and I should wish to leave immediately."

Servants who devoted themselves to looking after number one were among Dickens's favorite butts, and it is conceivable that the Chief Butler's concerned reception of the news of his master's death owes something to Courvoisier's.

The two other Victorian novelists of permanent reputation who are traditionally categorized as sensation novelists, Wilkie Collins and Charles Reade, also maintained a keen interest in murder. As we have seen, certain elements of Collins's *The Moonstone* were suggested by the Constance Kent case of 1860, which, since it has been tantalizingly alluded to several times before, had better be briefly described now. This was the murder of a four-year-old boy, Francis Saville Kent, at Road, Wiltshire. It attracted intense national interest because it occurred in a substantial middle-class family—the father was H.M. Inspector of Factories for a district in southwest England—and because one of the chief suspects was the boy's sixteen-year-old stepsister, Constance. From the beginning, the Wiltshire constabulary proved to be totally out of their depth, and by the time, two weeks later, that expert help arrived from Scotland Yard in the person of Inspector Whicher, the scene had been overrun by bumbling police and sightseers, and any chance of discovering useful clues had vanished.* After shrewd investigation, Whicher decided that Constance, who today would be described as a badly mixed-up teenager, had killed the boy, and he forthwith arrested her. But the magistrates, accurately reflecting the strong local sentiment in her favor, set her free, whereupon Whicher, unyielding in his conviction that she was guilty, resigned from the police. Five years later Constance, then in an Anglican retreat at Brighton, confessed to the crime and was sentenced— the judge's sobs being echoed by everyone in the courtroom—to Millbank Penitentiary for life.

Her guilt is still disputed, notwithstanding her confession. An opposing school of thought has maintained from the outset that little Saville had his throat cut and was stuffed down the Kents' disused outside privy not because Constance hated his mother, her father's second wife—the most widely accepted theory—but because the boy, who slept on a cot in his nurse's

---

* One of the most farcical episodes in Victorian murder annals occurred the night after the murder, when a pair of rural policemen were assigned to stay in the house. Mr. Kent hospitably provided bread, cheese, and beer to solace their vigil, established them in the kitchen, and then, as usual, went the rounds of the house to lock up. He also, by inadvertence or design, locked the police in the kitchen. "They heard me," he later testified, "but I don't know if I told them I was going to bolt them in. I did not go to bed, but remained in my library. . . . About half-past two one of the police knocked at the door and asked to be let out." Relating the incident of the captive constables at one point in the judicial proceedings, the police superintendent said, "They were, I understood, to have the whole range of the house, but they only had the kitchen range." This witticism was rewarded with a laugh.

room, happened on the fatal night to be a witness to untoward events. As Dickens put it laconically in a letter to Collins, "Mr. Kent intriguing with the nursemaid, poor little child awakes in crib and sits up contemplating blissful proceedings. Nursemaid strangles him then and there. Mr. Kent gashes body to mystify discoverers and disposes of same." The nursemaid, Elizabeth Gough, had both preceded and followed Constance as the prime suspect in the case—she had in fact been arrested twice, but was released both times for lack of evidence.*

In the background of the murder lay a circumstance far more shocking than the comparatively unremarkable domestic situation resulting from a father's taking a second wife (in this case, the motherless children's governess). The first Mrs. Kent, mother of Constance and William, had gone insane after bearing her first three children, but her loss of mind did not deter her husband from begetting six more on her body. A modern historian of the period, W. L. Burn, cites the case as evidence that "if one seeks the closely-guarded, authoritarian, almost sealed community, the mid-Victorian family can provide it; in practice it did not always possess the enchantment which the distance of a century lends it." Which would seem to be a temperate interpretation indeed.

Charles Reade seems not to have directly used any contemporary murder in his fiction, but he was fully prepared to do so. In the huge scrapbooks of pamphlets and clippings he kept as documentary raw material for his novels and plays, the homicides of the era were amply represented, along with every other subject that agitated public interest. His principal association with the murders of the time was through the Penge case in 1877, so called because it took place at Penge, Kent. In this unpleasant affair the offenders were Louis Staunton, his brother Patrick, Patrick's wife, and Louis's mistress, Alice Rhodes, who bore a child to him while in jail. Louis had married Harriet

---

* In 1857 Constance, then thirteen, and her brother William ran away from home. They were picked up by the Bath police and taken back home. Dickens seems to have adopted the episode in *The Mystery of Edwin Drood* in which Helena and Neville [suggested by "Saville"?] Landless run away from home because of their cruel stepfather. Helena, like Constance, was dressed in an old suit of her brother's and had cut her hair boy-fashion.

Richardson, a young lady of weak mind but some property, and once the latter was safely his, he and his colleagues proceeded to maltreat and starve her. She died, as planned; but whether from the maltreatment or from tubercular meningitis was the question that dominated the trial.

The verdict of Guilty was welcomed by the public, because the Stauntons were clearly an undesirable lot. But the medical profession protested the judge's refusal to admit testimony by the defense doctors confirming the meningitis hypothesis, which would have made the allegation of murder untenable. The indignation spread to the London press. Reade's contribution to the furor was a series of six letters called "Hang in Haste, Repent at Leisure," printed in the *Daily Telegraph*. Reade wrote not as a novelist and playwright but as a barrister who had qualified at Lincoln's Inn in 1843. The verdict, he declared, was "the greatest judicial error of modern times," and in the course of showing why it was, he happened to reveal his attitude toward the profession that had brought him fame and money—an attitude probably concurred in by some other Victorian novelists, though they refrained from expressing it. "Though I write novels at one time," he said, "I can write logic at another, and when I write a novel I give the public my lowest gifts, but I give them my highest when I write in a great journal upon life and death and justice." It is a pregnant commentary on the dignity of the novelist's profession in the Victorian age, at least as seen by one of its long-time practitioners.

Whereas Reade based his allegation of a miscarriage of justice largely on legal and "rational" grounds, the great twentieth-century Home Office pathologist, Sir Bernard Spilsbury, came to the opposite conclusion by way of the medical testimony. Having read and pondered every word of testimony in the case, he declared to the Medico-Legal Society in 1921 that the doctors had been handicapped by the rudimentary state of knowledge of morbid anatomy that obtained in 1877. To a modern specialist, the findings of the post mortem were "overwhelmingly in favour of starvation being the cause of death, as against tubercular meningitis." So the jury's decision, notwithstanding Reade's elaborately reasoned rebuttal, seems to have been the right one after all.

It is a far cry from the irascible, crusading Reade to the aesthetes who were his younger contemporaries, but that is the way Victorian literature was.* One is not prepared, really, for the discovery that Walter Pater, the somewhat embarrassed guru of the aesthetic movement, mingled a taste for the macabre among his better-remembered qualities. When he was a schoolboy at Canterbury, he and his friends participated in the general excitement over what Dickens, in *The Uncommercial Traveller*, called "the Chopped-up Murdered Man." This was the affair of a carpet-bag two young boatmen discovered as they rowed under Waterloo Bridge early in the morning of October 9, 1857. The bag had been lowered over the parapet on a rope, probably to avoid a splash when it hit the water, but it had lodged on an abutment instead. It proved to contain, in addition to a complete suit of men's attire save for hat and shoes, twenty human pieces, which upon being reorganized were found to constitute the whole body, except for the head, of a dark-haired adult male. The only solid clue was provided by a toll-taker who reported that at about 11:30 on the preceding night an old sallow-faced woman had paid her halfpenny toll to cross the bridge; he remembered her because she had had much difficulty getting a heavy carpet-bag through the turnstile. But who she was remained as mysterious as the identity of her gruesome burden. The case was never solved.

One wonders if, in later years, Pater ever discussed the Waterloo Bridge mystery with the youth who was to become his most famous disciple, Oscar Wilde. So far as the printed evidence goes, Wilde's interest in murder took a rather different bent. His essay in *Intentions*, "Pen, Pencil, and Poison"—the title was borrowed from Swinburne—is a characteristically Wildeian appreciation of Thomas Griffiths Wainewright in his dual role

---

* En route, a glance should be spared for Robert Louis Stevenson, who was a keen student of murder, especially of the antiquarian variety. *Kidnapped* and its sequel *Catriona* are based on the Appin murder case of 1752, and, as we have seen, "The Body-Snatcher" recalls Edinburgh's pride, the Burke and Hare case. For several years Stevenson and his friend Edmund Gosse proposed to write a series of papers on old murders, but this promising enterprise seems to have come to nothing.

of aesthete and poisoner. Wilde admired him in both capacities.

But of all the major figures on the English literary scene as Victoria's reign drew to a close, the most sensitive connoisseur of murder was Henry James. We shall have occasion later on to note his adulation of Madeleine Smith. The most considerable evidence of James's enduring appreciation of murder is found in his correspondence during the last years of his life with William Roughead, a kindred spirit. The letters, extolling "the dear old human and sociable murders and adulteries and forgeries in which we are so agreeably at home," are preserved in the Harvard Library. They are, in my judgment, the crowning validation of the literary man's love of the murderous art. "The riddles of the past," James remarked to Roughead, "are such a refuge from those of the present!"

The riddles of James's and Roughead's "present" have long since taken their place with those of the past. Not all of the cases in the following chapters can fairly be called riddles, although hardly one is without some element of unsolved mystery. But their deepest interest lies in what they reveal, not what they conceal; and to us that interest is as strong, though sometimes for different reasons, as it was to the Victorians who welcomed the cases as they unfolded, one by one, in close-printed columns of newspaper type.

6

The Tragedy at
Stanfield Hall

JAMES BLOMFIELD RUSH, 1849

"CHAMBER OF HORRORS," the handbill began. "MADAME TUSSAUD & SONS, Anxious to gratify the Public, respectfully announce that they have added a POR-TRAIT MODEL of [in enormous letters] R U S H taken from life *AT NORWICH,* DURING THE TRIAL. It represents him as he appeared dressed in black, &c. and conveys a good idea of probably the Greatest Criminal that has been brought to justice for several years." The unwonted conservatism of the "probably" suggests the abundance of Great Criminals the past decade or so had produced. But James Blomfield Rush was something special. Even the Mannings, who claimed the spotlight less than six months after his trial, failed to eclipse him in the appreciative popular memory.

Part of Rush's fame probably was due to the expansion his prior record underwent at the hands of the broadsheet composers, assisted by, or assisting, the inventive tongue of rumor. I am not aware that Rush was guilty of any but the crimes alleged against him in the Norwich trial, but opinion assigned him a liberal variety of others. Witness the commentary a buyer of the current catalogue read at Madame Tussaud's, once he was attracted inside by her screaming placards:

The annals of crime must place the name of Rush at the lowest depth of infamy; he was accused in early life of having set fire to a haystack; of having rescued a man from custody; of having afterwards murdered his Wife, his Mother, his Father-in-law, and, lastly, Mr. Jermy and his Son, and dangerously wounded Mrs. Jermy and her maid; of having seduced many young women—and committed forgeries of the blackest dye. He was executed at Norwich, amidst the deepest execrations of the assembled multitude.*

Probably the locale also had something to do with the feverish public interest aroused by the murder of the Jermys, father and son. Reading the trial transcript, we have a sense of gloom and remoteness, even though Norfolk, where the murders took place, is nearer London than many another, better-known county; even today, tourists do not flock in any great numbers to that flat land protruding into the North Sea. We have the impression of roads often impassable from the depth and viscosity of their mud, of stupid rural constables, and tenant farmers caught up in the brooding ill-will and downright hatred that seem to thrive and endure in such an environment. It is the sort of atmosphere in which it is easy to believe the worst of one's neighbor, as Rush's neighbors obviously believed the worst of him.

Behind the murders was a tangle of lawsuits, disputes over ownership, and intricate financial dealings which it is luckily unnecessary for us to examine. Rush (who in earlier days happened to have been a tenant of Edward Bulwer) was tenant of three farms to which Isaac Jermy, an Oxford graduate, lawyer, and holder of important Norfolk offices, held title but of which Rush maintained he was true owner. By the autumn of 1848 Rush was financially *in extremis,* bankrupt and in imminent danger of being evicted from Potash Farm, where he lived with Emily Sandford, the housekeeper-mistress he had brought down from London. The enmity he had long entertained for the prosperous and, from his point of view, malign Isaac Jermy led him, on the evening of November 22, to trudge across the fields to

---

* One notes that this summary omits another crime attributed to Rush, the murder of his grandmother as alleged by the patterers (see above, page 53). This is one instance of many in which contemporary "authorities" failed to agree on the number and nature of a prominent criminal's previous misdeeds.

Stanfield Hall, Jermy's pseudo-Tudor residence. There he burst
into the house and shot and killed both male Jermys, also seriously wounding the young Mrs. Jermy, whose arm had to be am-
putated, and a maidservant. The police were duly summoned,
and the next morning Rush was arrested at Potash Farm.

Whereas there was something ingratiating and romantic,
however spuriously so, about Thurtell, nobody had a good word
to say for Rush, who seems to have been a thoroughly bad 'un,
saturnine, always a troublemaker and, one hazards, more than
a little paranoid. It did not help his case that the furor over him
came only eight months after the long-lowering Chartist menace
had finally been dissipated by events in London, when the much-
feared mass march on Parliament had been forestalled by an
armed and barricaded citizenry (commanded by the aged Duke
of Wellington) and by a most opportune rainstorm. In Rush
were concentrated those unlovely traits of character which Tory
farmers and small-town businessmen had long been in the habit
of attributing to political radicals. Just as nine years earlier it
had been said that Courvoisier was inspired by reading *Jack
Sheppard*, so now the instant biographies prepared for catchpenny circulation traced Rush's villainy to the inflammatory
printed matter he had consumed in his young manhood:

He formed an intimacy with Cobbett—read his books with avidity,
and adopted not only his political, but his anti-religious views. Paine's
"Age of Reason," which Cobbett recommended, next became his
study, and as he drank in the draughts of poison it contained their
pernicious influence became visible in his whole demeanour. He no
longer sought and delighted in the society of his friends and equals,
but almost wholly addicted himself to the companionship of persons
of low taste and depraved habits. Political discontent, which was rife
among the agricultural labourers, he delighted rather to foster than to
quench. . . . He was known among his companions as a libertine.
. . . He made a boast of seduction.

The indictment is a perfect epitome of the conditioned reflex of
the time—a reflex whose origins could be traced back more than
half a century, to the "Jacobin" scare bred by the French Revolution. Underlying it was a simple syllogism: Chartists and radicals
in general are villains; Rush is a villain; therefore Rush must be
a radical. In another pamphlet issued at the time, it was asserted

that "Cobbett and Carlyle were once his favorite teachers."
Thomas Carlyle, if he saw this startling allegation, would not
have liked it. But as a matter of fact the wrong man was named;
what the hurried author or typesetter meant was not Carlyle but
Carlile—Richard Carlile, one of the firebrand radicals of the
1820s and '30s.

Rush typically insisted on conducting his own defense, receiving extraordinary procedural leeway from the judge in order
to do so. He cross-examined many witnesses at length, sometimes
truculently and often irrelevantly, and frequently interrupted the
direct examination. His fourteen-hour closing speech was a ram-
bling, turgid harangue which prompted the prosecutor, winding
up the Crown case, to observe that "the present trial has exceeded in the annals of judicial long-suffering anything that was
ever before experienced." Torturous it may have been, but it was
certainly not without its moments. At one point in the trial, Rush
was allowed to examine one of the exhibits, a wallet of his. After
he handed it back, it was discovered that a check for forty
pounds was missing. A search failed to turn it up, and Rush
solemnly denied any knowledge of its whereabouts. Several
days later he casually produced it; he had palmed it and hidden
it in the lining of his hat.

While Rush was reposing in Norwich Castle awaiting trial,
there had come into the region three famous Londoners on a
light-hearted bachelors' jaunt: Charles Dickens and his friends,
two stalwarts of *Punch,* the editor Mark Lemon and the illus-
trator John Leech. They had chosen Norfolk for their January
holiday, rather than the more salubrious Salisbury Plain or the
Isle of Wight, because of its current notoriety. Of course they
visited Stanfield Hall, which, Dickens reported to John Forster
back in London, had "a murderous look that seemed to invite
such a crime." As a keen student of Metropolitan Police methods,
he was caustically critical of the way the Norfolk constables
were going about their work: "We arrived between the Hall and
Potash Farm, as the search was going on for the pistol in a
manner so consummately stupid, that there was nothing on earth
to prevent any of Rush's labourers from accepting five pounds
from Rush junior [the murderer's son] to find the weapon and

give it to him." The city of Norwich, Dickens concluded, was "a disappointment, all save its place of execution, which we found fit for a gigantic scoundrel's exit."

Dickens's derision of the local police was somewhat unfair, because at the time he was unaware of the handicaps under which they were working. It is true that only after Rush's execution, late in May, was the fatal double-barrelled blunderbuss (not a pistol) finally discovered in a reasonably obvious place, the muck of the Potash Farm bullock yard, and then not by the police but by farm hands. But, as is made clear in an article in the *Examiner* (June 2) which has recently been attributed to Dickens, the sixty men requisitioned to help the police in their search had been hampered by the ground rules laid down by Rush's son—whom Dickens, it is apparent from the letter quoted, did not trust—and affirmed by the local magistrates. The searchers were free to tidy up the Potash Farm fields, collect the manure from various locations and deposit it in neat piles, and otherwise beautify the premises, but the bullock yard itself was not to be disturbed. In addition, it was stipulated that the search party had to be withdrawn after a certain period had expired. The Chief Constable of Norfolk, one Colonel Oakes, applied to the magistrates for a modification of this order but it was not granted. Responsibility for the failure to unearth the weapon earlier, therefore, had to be laid upon the magistrates, who seem to have resided in the palm of young Rush's hand.

In the courtroom, too, one feels that the police were at a disadvantage; the judge was more impatient with them than they deserved. One of their number, attempting to prove that the clock at Rush's farm was a quarter-hour ahead of that at Stanfield Hall—the supposed difference of time was a crucial point in Rush's alibi—testified that he had established the fact by noting the time at the latter place (8:55 A.M.), walking across to Potash Farm, a distance of almost a mile through rough fields and along soggy footpaths, and finding upon his arrival that the time was now 9:10. "There was a quarter of an hour's difference." The judge understood him to mean that there was that much difference between the Potash Farm and Stanfield Hall clocks, which, considering that a quarter hour or more had

elapsed, was but natural. "There was exactly a quarter of an
hour's difference in the time?" The constable clarified his answer: "I remember what time it was by the Potash clock. It was
half-past nine." He had proved his point—the Potash clock was
actually fifteen or twenty minutes faster than that at Stanfield
Hall. But this was too much for the judge to follow. "It is evident," he told the unfortunate policeman, "that you are so con-
fused and so inaccurate that your statements cannot be relied
on—you may go down."

The next day the force fared no better, but this time it was
the fault of their own ineptness. Two of the policemen were
exhibiting guns they had found in Rush's room. Rush, conducting his own defense, demanded to see the shot which was said
to be inside them. The policemen fumbled and struggled but
were unable to draw it, "the screw of the ramrod being worn." A
gentleman in the courtroom offered his services and immediately
conquered the recalcitrant weapon. "The prisoner," it is reported,
"laughed heartily at the awkwardness of the police."

The laughter, to which we must admit he was entitled, gave
way in other circumstances to a less genial mood. Notwithstanding the free-thinking, anti-religious bias attributed to him by
his many detractors, Rush donned the mantle of religiosity during his imprisonment and trial. He was a canting hypocrite, making loud protestations of his saintliness and conducting himself
in a repellently pious manner which convinced no one. The governor and chaplain of Norwich Gaol said he "took every opportunity of denying his guilt, professing perfect tranquillity and
unhesitating confidence in his acquittal. His constant language
was, 'Thank God, I am quite comfortable in body and mind; I
eat well, drink well, and sleep well.'" Those who watched over
him, however, reported that neither his sleep nor his appetite
suggested the serenity of an easy conscience. The aged William
Wordsworth, following the trial in the newspapers he received
at far-off Rydal Mount, commented: "What a miserable Man
must he be, if he has a grain of human feeling in his composition." Whether or not he did was a matter of dispute.

It is tempting to think that Dickens, who not only was in
the neighborhood early in the case but must have read all the
later newspaper reports of Rush's behavior, drew from it certain

hints for his portrait of Uriah Heep. Immediately after his return from Norfolk he was hard at work on *David Copperfield,* in which he used a number of elements plainly derived from his late excursion—the Yarmouth locale of the Peggotty scenes, for example, and the accurate representation of the East Anglian dialect. From James Blomfield Rush canting in the condemned cell to Uriah Heep in Mr. Creakle's prison, unctuously protesting his remorse and reformation, does not seem a long step. Although, as has recently been pointed out, Dickens may have derived the suggestion for some of Uriah's fraudulent piety from a book by the chaplain of Pentonville, naïvely quoting several revoltingly hypocritical letters written by felons under his care, and although modern scholarship insists that there were fewer "Dickens originals"—literal prototypes of characters—than sentimental fancy once held, still it may well be that Rush's transparent sanctimony helped Dickens in some measure to color the umble Uriah's portrait.

The Rush trial is as replete as any other Victorian murder record with minutiae of sociological interest. How long, for example, did it commonly take a Victorian woman to read a given number of pages in a popular circulating-library novel? The point was crucial to Rush's alibi, which rested on the argument that on the evening of the murder he was absent from his house only half an hour, less time than it would have taken him—or a rural Norfolk constable—to walk to Stanfield Hall, shoot the Jermys, and return. Emily Sandford testified that while he was away she read half a volume of *Whitefriars, or The Days of Charles II,* a three-decker published some five years earlier.* Unless she was an exceptionally fast reader, it seemed likely that Rush was gone considerably longer than he wanted the jury to believe.

The presence of a circulating-library novel in the Potash farmhouse suggests that, whatever the moral shortcomings of the household, it was not without culture. Another book figures in the testimony—a "Scottish history" Rush had brought home

---

* The author, Emma Robinson, figured in the Rush trial quite by accident, but fifteen years later she deliberately associated herself with another sensational murder. Her three-volume *Madeleine Graham* (1864) is a thinly disguised fictionalization of the Madeleine Smith case.

from London the Monday before the murder. He and Emily had read and discussed parts of it; on the very day of the murder, she recollected, he had spoken of the familiar story of Robert Bruce and the tenacious spider. The implication, which she did not spell out, was that Rush too, though he had tried and failed half a dozen times or so to carry out his own mission, was confident of succeeding at the next attempt.

Nor was the cultural talk at Potash Farm exclusively literary. Emily was a talented pianist, and Rush, whether out of genuine enthusiasm for music or to lighten her life in the dismal countryside, had bought tickets for one Madame Dulcken's concert at Norwich the very night of the murder. His begging off at the last moment is among the many details he elicited from Emily Sandford during one of the most remarkable passages of the trial, which occupies a dozen pages in the printed record. With a determination again suggestive of Bruce's spider, Rush drew from her what amounts to a total-recall narrative of their movements and conversation during the hours embracing the murder. Seldom in historical sources do we find so circumstantial an account of the minute-by-minute actions of two people over a certain span of time. Under Rush's insistent questioning, the unhappy woman reconstructed every movement during those crucial hours:

> . . . I did sit on your knee, but I asked you first why you stared at me so strangely, and you said, "Come and kiss me," and I did go over to you.
>
> Q. Where was the easy chair standing at that time?
> A. At the corner of the table, in the corner.
> Q. How far off the tea table?
> A. Close to the table, for you to take your tea off the table.
> Q. You had not then got your outside dress on, had you?
> A. You know I had not.
> Q. Did not you put your outside dress on before you sat down to tea? Now, for God Almighty's sake, remember yourself?
> A. I put on my morning gown because I had to change my best dress. I had to go to Norwich to change; I heard you come in, and I slipped on my morning gown.
>
> . . . .
>
> Q. Where was your morning gown when I came into the parlour to tea?
> A. I had it on, or, if you wish to have it more explicitly, it was my

nightgown.
Q. But you put on some other dress before I sat down to tea?
A. I am sure I cannot tell, whether it was before tea or after tea I put
   the dress on. You told me to put on the dress, or we could not go
   to the concert. I cannot tell whether it was before tea or after tea.
Q. . . . I ask you now to recollect where I stood when I fastened
   your dress before tea, after you had been sitting on my knee?
A. By the fireplace, I think it was, but I do not recollect anything certain about the dress at all. . . . I believe I did run up and change
   my dress. I ran up stairs and put on my dress when I thought I
   was going to the concert, and then when I came down the kettle
   was boiling.

And so the narrative dialogue proceeded. The whole passage
could serve, almost without amendment, as a working script for
a dramatization.

As the numerous references to the Rush case in earlier chapters have shown, it was exploited by every branch of the popular press. None of the commercial uses to which it was put
better illustrates the convenience of a well-timed murder to
authors and publishers than the appearance, in the mass-circulation *London Journal* from May 1849 to November 1850 and in
fifty-nine penny numbers published by Edward Lloyd, of John
Frederick Smith's *The Chronicles of Stanfield Hall*. This sensational fiction had nothing at all to do with the Rush murders;
on the contrary, it was set in medieval times. But the mere occurrence of "Stanfield Hall" in the title was enough to guarantee
its popularity, which was responsible for many reprintings in
the next thirty or forty years. If any merchandising device in
the publishing world proved its effectiveness time after time in
these decades, it was the practice (later exemplified by Ainsworth in connection with the Bravo case) of somehow taking
advantage of the free advertising offered by the notoriety of a
good murder.*

* To readers better educated than the majority of those who bought the
London Journal or novels in penny parts, the title *Chronicles of Stanfield
Hall* had extra meaning. In Tudor times the manor of Stanfield was owned
by the mother of Amy Robsart, who as the wife of Robert Dudley, Earl of
Leicester, died mysteriously of a broken neck in 1560, at Cumnor Place,
Berkshire. Whether she was a suicide or the victim of an accident or of
murder was never decided, but rumor had it that her husband was re-
sponsible and that the Queen herself may have been implicated. Since the

In the printed accounts of the Rush drama occur the names of two supernumeraries, the Rev. W. W. Andrew and Sir John Boileau. Ordinarily the fame of such persons, glimpsed momentarily in the excitement of a notorious murder case, extends no further. But they were responsible as recently as 1960 for a small but welcome addition to the already voluminous literature of *l'affaire* Rush. In that year a Cambridge University specialist in Victorian church history, Owen Chadwick, published a volume called *Victorian Miniature*, based upon his discovery of a mass of unpublished personal papers which documented from real life that familiar theme of Victorian fiction, the relations between the parson in the village and the squire at the hall. Over a period of more than thirty years, a rigorous evangelical clergyman named William Andrew had served the Norfolk parish of Ketteringham, only a mile or two from both Stanfield Hall and Potash Farm. The squire of the manor was a blue-blooded baronet, Sir John Boileau. Both parties left diaries and other papers which provide a running account, seen from decidedly different angles, of the always uneasy relations which prevailed between parson and patron. "The diary of the parson . . . tells us what he thought of the squire. The diary of the squire . . . tells us what he thought of the parson. At various periods of their life they thought much about each other." They agreed upon only one subject, the unacceptability of Puseyite (high church) ritualism. Upon all other subjects circumstances required them to discuss, they were perpetually at odds. They were both strong-minded and energetic men, and in their repeated collisions the tension was occasionally aggravated by the Reverend Mr. Andrew's equally strong-minded and outspoken wife.

The whole story is a diverting one, and it offers an uncommonly close insight into the conflicts of interest and principle which agitated many a country clergyman and his patron. But its special interest for us lies in the fact that Rush was a parishioner of Andrew, who began by being much impressed by his piety but later—some time before the murder—had noted a falling off in both his church attendance and his spiritual health.

---

ill-fated Amy spent the early years of her marriage at Stanfield, the Victorians might have observed with some justice that the place was accursed.

After Rush's arrest, Andrew often visited him in his cell, occasions which he described in his diary, and he was nearby, though not actually looking on, when the trap was sprung.

A week after the execution, Andrew, faithful to a promise he had made to his flock, preached on the Rush case. Since everyone knew he had had intimate association with the murderer, most notably in the period traditionally covered by the broadside confessions and last dying speeches, he preached to a dense crowd crammed inside the church and into the adjacent yard. These upwards of two thousand sudden churchgoers listened raptly to Andrew's wholly improvised sermon, which lasted two hours and twenty minutes—an impressive accomplishment in itself, but a poor thing when measured against Rush's fourteen-hour attempt at self-exculpation. The sermon was reported *in extenso* by the local press and a month later was printed (revised by Andrew from the newspaper text) in a pamphlet which is reported to have "sold in great numbers." For a while the obscure parson's fame rivaled that of the most popular authors of evangelical literature, and, as his confidences to his diary reveal, he had dangerous dreams of moving into a wider sphere of influence. But, no doubt wisely, he renounced ambitions more suitable to the clergy of Barsetshire and stayed to continue his abrasive relations with Sir John Boileau.

Sir John himself, meanwhile, had played a role in the Rush case, for he had been one of the murderer's examining magistrates. It was to him that Emily Sandford retracted her initial story, that Rush had been absent from Potash Farm for only a few minutes, and replaced it with the statement, repeated at the trial, that he had been gone considerably longer; to him, also, she imparted her belief that Rush was guilty. Like many a Victorian squire, Sir John exerted himself in good works: he arranged for Emily to emigrate to Australia, paid her bills, gave her a letter to the Bishop of Melbourne, and bought her a piano so that she could teach music in her changed condition. But when her identity was discovered in Melbourne, she was nearly mobbed and could find no employment. Rush's notoriety had preceded her to the Antipodes.

7

"Trust Not the Physician"

WILLIAM PALMER, 1856
THOMAS SMETHURST, 1859
EDWARD PRITCHARD, 1865

THE SOLID FOUNDATIONS of present-day medicine
were laid, in great part, in the nineteenth century. In many respects—public sanitation, antisepsis, anesthesia, refined techniques of diagnosis and surgery, essential knowledge in a diver-
sity of fields from morbid anatomy to microbiology—the history
of Victorian medicine is one of vital progress. No roster of the
great Victorians would be complete without such names as
Southwood Smith and Sir John Simon in public health, Joseph
Lister in antisepsis, Sir James Simpson in anesthesia and ob-
stetrics, Richard Bright and Thomas Addison in the identification
and description of diseases. The repute which eminent medical
men enjoyed is suggested by the fact that between 1850 and
1883 thirty-six were knighted and sixteen received baronetcies;
Lister was made a baron.

And yet, paradoxically, during this same period the profession was also the object of sustained suspicion, derision, and outright distrust. One of the most authoritative historians of modern
medicine suggests several reasons: the higher level of education,
which equipped more people to be critical of their professional
advisers; the expansion of the newspaper and periodical press,
which increased the facilities by which such criticism could be

vented; and the failure of medicine, so far, to have provided society with any tangible benefit comparable to those afforded by technology in such forms as the steam engine and the electric telegraph (the sole exception perhaps was Jenner's invention of inoculation, but this was accomplished before 1800). The best doctors, typified by George Eliot's Tertius Lydgate, were busy clearing away the accumulated rubbish of centuries of earnest but largely unscientific medical theory and practice, but they had not as yet advanced to the place where they could offer a therapeutics which would give dramatic practical effect to their new knowledge by preventing or curing disease. Medicine, in a word, was lagging far behind the times; or so it seemed to many impatient Victorians who were captivated by the wholly visible achievements of natural scientists, inventors, and engineers.

To these principal reasons for the low popular esteem in which Victorian doctors were held may be added another: the prominence a few of them had in celebrated murder cases, either as protagonists or as conspicuously incompetent and/or discrepant "expert" witnesses in trials. Whereas most of the genuinely great Victorian medical men worked in relative obscurity, their achievements recognized in the main only by their colleagues (again there were exceptions, such as the doughty fighters for sanitary reform, who found publicity to be among their most valuable weapons), those who proved morally or scientifically fallible won a notoriety wholly disproportionate to their number.*

When Victoria came to the throne, the public still held in vivid memory Dr. Robert Knox, who may have been an excellent technician but whose incredible indifference to the provenance of the fresh cadavers Burke and Hare sold him gave the branch

* It is useful to remember that during the fifties and sixties, when medicine and murder were repeatedly being associated in sensational trials, especially in Scotland, Simpson and Lister were quietly making medical history of a more constructive sort in Edinburgh and Glasgow. Lister, for one, followed the trials in the papers. In the uproar following Jessie M'Lachlan's last-minute statement of what had really happened at 17 Sandyford Place, he composed a letter affirming that all the medical testimony adduced during the trial harmonized with her version—and sent it to the one Glasgow paper which stubbornly insisted on her guilt.

of anatomy a noisome reputation that would long endure. Now that sharpened medical intelligence had discredited so many of the techniques and remedies formerly favored by orthodox physicians, without substituting more effective new ones, quackery was prospering mightily. When an occasional charlatan got into serious trouble, public opinion, ready as ever to simplify and generalize, seldom bothered to distinguish between quackery and legitimate practice; both were "medicine" and so were tarred with the same brush.

The prominence of empirics of various persuasions in the thirties and forties led Carlyle to adopt the term "quackery" as an all-purpose word to signify humbuggery, glibness, hypocrisy, wherever found in the degenerate society of the time. He had two currently famous medicine men in mind. One was St. John Long, a fashionable fraud whose theory, plausible on the face of it, was that the way to cure a disease was to encourage it to escape from the body it afflicted. His panacea, therefore, was what he called—accurately enough—a "Corrosive Mixture," a poultice composed of oil of turpentine, mineral acid, and other ingredients of questionable benignity. This he liberally applied to an appropriate area of his patient's skin, where it promptly ate a wound that would afford the disease an outlet. The procedure may possibly have alleviated cases of consumption, rheumatism, gout, abscesses of the lungs and liver, and insanity, as it was advertised to do, but it also killed. In 1830 Long was tried twice for manslaughter. The first time, he was convicted but let off with a £250 fine; the second time, he was acquitted. Enough of his patients survived to erect a monument in grateful memory of him when he died a few years later. His notoriety in other quarters was such as to earn him the possibly unique distinction of coverage in both the *Lancet* (which was unsympathetic) and the latest versions of the *Newgate Calendar*. Not only Carlyle mentions him; he is recalled, as well, in the pages of Thackeray and George Eliot.

Even more famous, thanks to Carlyle's use of "Morrison's Pill" as a leading motif in *Past and Present*, was James Morison, the self-styled "Hygeist" and proprietor of a profit-making institution called the British College of Health. Morison, who was one of the first great advertisers, was also one of five men in London in the 1840s who were said to have made £200,000 each out of the patent medicine business; Morison's pill was reported to bring in £80,000 a year. Such extravagant prosperity may be thought to have entitled Morison to the unqualified adulation of his mammonistic contemporaries, and to a degree it did; but there was a darker side to the Morison success story.

In 1834 at York, a "respectable-looking, middle-aged man," an innkeeper who sold Morison's pills on the side, was indicted for manslaughter in consequence of his fatally prescribing his favorite remedy, which he declared had cured him of cholera when it was raging in the town, to a twenty-year-old apprentice known to be suffering from smallpox. "These produced very copious evacuations, but 'the pills' were still administered, and the prisoner said medical aid was unnecessary." Medical witnesses testified that the wondrous pills were compounded of gamboge, aloes, colocynth, and cream of tartar, and that the powerful cathartic effect for which they were noted was extremely unsuitable in cases of smallpox. The innkeeper was convicted and sentenced to six months in jail.

Two years later at the Old Bailey, another "respectable-looking, middle-aged man" was in the dock in connection with the death of a thirty-year-old man who had suffered from nothing more ominous than a pain in the knee. When a moderate dosage of Morison's pills did not have the desired analgesic effect, the vendor upped it to thirty or thirty-six at a time, and after a due course of violent purging the patient died. This, unlike the affair at York where the patient was already suffering from an often fatal disease, was a clear case of Morison's pills directly causing death. But counsel for the accused put in the box a stonemason who deposed that he once took a thousand pills in twenty days and "found great benefit from them." Another said he cured his scurvy and fistula with ninety to a hundred a day. In all, more than thirty witnesses, including a surgeon and a clergyman, swore that "after having vainly taken the prescriptions of medical men" they had had recourse to the pill for their gout, rheumatism, scurvy, fistula, or whatever—and here they were, in robust health. "One person said, he had taken a hundred in twenty-four hours, and another that he had taken 20,000 pills in two years; he had paid £22 for them. . . . The counsel for the prisoner said, they had upwards of forty other witnesses, but they thought it unnecessary to call them." The purveyor of these heroic doses was convicted but recommended to mercy, and was merely fined £200.*

Although, so far as I have noticed, no qualified medical man found himself in the dock, charged with premeditated homicide, in the first fifteen years of the reign, the possibility was by no means unthought of. In *Martin Chuzzlewit* (1844), Dr. John Jobling, medical officer of the Anglo-Bengalee Disinterested Loan and Life Assurance Company, recalls to Jonas Chuzzlewit " 'a case of murder, committed by a member of our profession; it was so artistically done' ":

"A certain gentleman was found, one morning, in an obscure street, lying in an angle of a doorway—I should rather say, leaning, in an upright position, in the angle of a doorway, and supported consequently *by* the doorway. Upon his waistcoat there was one solitary drop of blood. He was dead, and cold; and had been murdered, sir."

"Only one drop of blood!" said Jonas.

"Sir, that man," replied the doctor, "had been stabbed to the heart. Had been stabbed to the heart with such dexterity, sir, that he had died instantly, and had bled internally. It was supposed that a medical

* Within a few years after these criminal cases were revealing the (un-licensed) practice of medicine in an unfavorable light, the profession achieved undesired notoriety, for another reason, in the very highest social circles. Early in 1839 the Duchess of Kent's young lady-in-waiting, Lady Flora Hastings, consulted Sir James Clark (Keats's physician during his last months in Rome, and now the Queen's own doctor) for "derangement of the bowel, pain in the left side and a protuberance of the stomach." Sir James prescribed rhubarb and ipecacuanha pills and liniment of camphor, soap, and opium—and privately expressed his opinion that Lady Flora, who was unmarried, was pregnant. The Queen and her intimates clung to their suspicions even after a subsequent examination, in which Sir James was joined by a gynecologist, reversed the former's snap diagnosis. In July Lady Flora died of a tumor on the liver. Her family were justifiably embittered by the Queen's failure to quell the rumors that had filled the court in the intervening six months, and Clark did nothing to quiet the storm by defending himself in the press. It was, says the Queen's best biographer, Lady Longford, "the most disastrous episode of her early reign." Doctors making erroneous diagnoses in such conspicuous places as the royal household did as much to deface the "public image" of their profession as agents prescribing mammoth doses of Morison's pills.

friend of his (to whom suspicion attached) had engaged him in conversation on some pretence; had taken him, very likely, by the button in a conversational manner; had examined his ground at leisure with his other hand; had marked the exact spot; drawn out the instrument, whatever it was, when he was quite prepared; and——"

"And done the trick," suggested Jonas.

"Exactly so," replied the doctor. "It was quite an operation in its way, and very neat. The medical friend never turned up; and, as I tell you, he had the credit of it. Whether he did it or not, I can't say. But having had the honour to be called in with two or three of my professional brethren on the occasion, and having assisted to make a careful examination of the wound, I have no hesitation in saying that it would have reflected credit on any medical man; and that in an unprofessional person, it could not but be considered, either as an extraordinary work of art, or the result of a still more extraordinary, happy, and favourable conjunction of circumstances."

It sounds like a device in a twentieth-century detective novel. But (unless, as is not wholly unlikely, there were actual cases of this sort which were so consummately artistic that they went undetected) the Victorian medical man, when he turned to murder, regularly favored poison over pointed, edged, weighted, or ballistic tools.* To some connoisseurs of murder, echoing De Quincey as early as 1827, this was regrettable: "Fie on these dealers in poison, say I: can they not keep to the old honest way of cutting throats, without introducing such abominable inventions from Italy? I consider all these poisoning cases, compared with the legitimate style, as no better than wax-work by the side of sculpture, or a lithographic print by the side of a fine Volpato."

None of the three eminent practitioners to be memorialized here left any explanation of his preference for killing *per ora,* but it is not hard to infer. If they were not precisely credits to their profession, they were sufficiently wise in its ways; and they knew that, in the existing state of toxicological learning, the consequences of the administration of poison could readily be interpreted as stemming from natural causes. That their confidence was well grounded, the medical testimony offered in their

* The sole exception was Dr. William Smith, who was tried in 1854 for shooting a young Aberdeenshire farmer for the sake of his insurance. The jury's verdict was Not Proven.

defense at all three of their trials proves. Their misfortune lay mainly in the fact that their motives could not be dissembled as satisfactorily as, ideally at any rate, their methods could.

Not until the late 1880s, therefore, would a medical man be suspected of using his manual dexterity, rather than his acquaintance with lethal chemicals, for fell purposes, and even then the suspicion remained a mere hypothesis. The extravagant, intricate, and intimate nature of the mutilations sustained by Jack the Ripper's victims nourished the theory that the Ripper, if not actually a surgeon, had had surgical training. But no one knows.

i

The first of the great Victorian murder cases starring a physician in the dock was Palmer's in 1856, a trial which the presiding judge, Lord Chief Justice Campbell, described in his diary as "the most memorable judicial proceedings for the last fifty years, engaging the attention not only of this country but of all Europe." Since the heads of the English bench are not ordinarily given to exaggeration, we must believe that the Palmer trial was something decidedly out of the ordinary. It was; bar and public agreed on that. But, whatever the fine legal points the trial presented, we are concerned only with its fame and impact among the commonalty, and particularly with its effect upon the reputation of the medical profession.

The excitement over the Palmer case may adequately be measured by a single fact: it was the first trial in English history to be granted a change of venue. Palmer's lawyers argued that the climate of opinion in Staffordshire, where the crime occurred, was such as to deprive their client of a fair hearing. Acquiescing in this judgment, Parliament hastily passed a bill permitting such trials to be held at the Old Bailey rather than at the county assizes. (This new law came in handy to defense counsel a few years later, when they succeeded in having the trials of both Madeleine Smith and Dr. Pritchard, whose alleged felonies had been accomplished in Glasgow, transferred to Edinburgh.) But it was not only in Staffordshire that Palmer dominated people's thoughts; the fever was nationwide, and the journalistic coverage was accordingly exhaustive. One paper alone, the twopenny *Illustrated Times*, doubled its normal sale with a "Rugeley number" which found four hundred thousand buyers, a staggering circulation for the time. On another level, the *Annual Register*, the principal reference work which reviewed the events of each year, devoted no fewer than 142 pages in its volume for 1856 to a comprehensive report of the trial—far more space than it gave to any other Victorian crime.

William Palmer of Rugeley held the diploma of surgeon from St. Bartholomew's Hospital, London. Unlike those possessed by some of his colleagues who were to become similarly entangled with the law, therefore, his professional credentials were legitimate. One must add at once that two or three years before the ill-advised episode which brought him to the gallows he had ceased all practice, the lure of the turf having proved much stronger than the more humanitarian, if less stimulating, atmosphere of the consulting room. Palmer's ambitions were directed toward the sudden though undependable riches of the horseplayer rather than the modest rewards of the healer; and at the outset his preference was signally vindicated. The first horse he owned, Goldfinder (*not* Goldfinger), a thirty-to-one shot, won the Tradesmen's Plate at the Chester meeting in May 1853, earning Palmer a cool £2,770. With so auspicious a beginning in a non-medical field, it is no wonder that he decided to confine the application of his professional knowledge to such unprofessional ends as his personal fortunes might require. But it was also regrettable for the prestige of medicine that in the immeasurable flood of words printed about him in 1856 he was always referred to as "Dr. Palmer." The idea of a doctor out to make a killing, whether at the track or in the sickroom, was irresistible to the Victorian imagination, but it was a disservice to the profession.

As is true of many of the murders which absorbed the Victorian public, it is a little hard to determine from the trial record alone what caused the extraordinary excitement in Palmer's case. But then we remember that here, as in other cases, only part of the story, and in some ways only the less inflammatory part, is spread upon the court record; the public, devouring columns upon columns of additional details, inadmissible as evidence, which were uncovered by the tireless employees of a press little inhibited by law, knew a great deal more about—and in particular against—Palmer than the jury was permitted to hear. Neither his character nor his career could be directly described in court. It could not even be placed on record when he was tried for Cook's death that two other murder indictments were standing against him, ready in the event this one failed.

The larger bill of mortality charged against Palmer by widespread supposition, but for which he was not called to official account, is, by any reckoning, impressive. The magic figure which appeared in print, in places ranging from pretrial pamphlets to the *Annual Register,* was sixteen, the same number which, by a coincidence that may not be wholly accidental, Burke had acknowledged as the sum of his achievement. Palmer, in contrast, acknowledged nothing. To strike a judicious balance between his total, incredible denial and the possibly inflated rumor of sixteen, we may follow the most conservative modern authorities in fixing upon half a dozen or so murders as the minimum toll. In doing so, we leave out of account the death of several of his numerous creditors whom he was generally believed to have murdered (the supply of these was perpetually being renewed), as well as of a drunken no-good uncle whom he encouraged in a fatal brandy-drinking bout, and four of his—Palmer's—legitimate children. Since these last died of convulsions, however, there is a sporting chance that they were really the victims of childhood diseases. Putting these aside, then, we have in the years 1847–55: (1) A man named Abbey, poisoned with brandy laced with strychnine, motive unclear. (2) An illegitimate child of Palmer's, one of fourteen attributed to him during the five years he was apprenticed to a physician in a town in Cheshire. (3) His mother-in-law, who died a fortnight after she moved in with him and his wife, and from whom he inherited some property. (4) A racing man to whom he owed £800 in unpaid bets, and who died in circumstances curiously prophetic of those to prevail in Cook's case. (5) Palmer's wife, who died after a single premium had been paid on a £13,000 insurance policy taken out in his favor.* (6) His alcoholic brother, called to heaven less than a year after Mrs. Palmer and shortly after the issuance of a policy for the same amount.

It was for these last two casualties that Palmer was indicted, to heap Pelion upon the Ossa of the Cook affair. The insurance companies, becoming restive after certain rumors floating about Rugeley and the sporting world reached their offices, had temporized before paying on Mrs. Palmer's policy, and Palmer subsequently did nothing to restore their confidence in him when he shopped around for insurance to the amount of £82,000 on his brother Walter. It is surprising in retrospect that he could have persuaded any company to issue a policy for even £13,000. But the company that did so regained its wits in time to refuse payment after Walter died in August 1855.

This was the situation when the Shrewsbury races began in the following November. It was not conducive to Palmer's peace of mind. But, with the inveterate optimism of the racing man, he was convinced that his stable, though heavily mortgaged to moneylenders who specialized in the finances of sport, would see him through. He bet heavily on his favorite horse, The Chicken, and The Chicken lost. Two days earlier, however, Polestar, a mare owned by John Parsons Cook, had won the Shrewsbury Handicap at odds of seven to two. At the moment, therefore, Cook was in the money and Palmer was decidedly out of it.

Twenty-eight-year-old Cook had been articled to a solicitor, but after he inherited £12,000 he, like Palmer, had renounced his profession for the sporting life. He and Palmer had known each other for some time in the close but not necessarily ethical camaraderie of stable and betting room, and, in view of Palmer's

---

* It was unknown, at the time, that Palmer wrote in his diary on this sad occasion, "Sept. 29th (1854), Friday—My poor, dear Annie expired at 10 past 1." Nine days later he recorded that he attended church and took the Sacrament. What was known at the time of the trial, though of course it was not introduced as evidence, was that just nine months after his wife's death, Palmer's maidservant bore him a child. Contemporary gossip, accepted by some modern commentators on the case, had it that "he slept with his maidservant on the very night she [Mrs. Palmer] died," but this, I think, is cutting it rather close.

readiness to do murder and of their relative financial positions toward the end of the Shrewsbury meeting, the events that followed were predictable enough. A little earlier, Palmer had forged his mother's name on certain papers designed to placate the moneylenders who were pressing him for the £12,000 he owed them. In order to pay off a portion of this debt and thus avoid exposure, after Polestar's victory Palmer went to London and, representing himself as Cook's partner, collected £1,000 of Cook's winnings at Tattersall's. Immediately after this, he availed himself of more of Cook's money by forging his name to a check and another document. He found himself, therefore, deep in a bog of fraud and forgery, from which he could extricate himself, if at all, only by making sure that Cook would not survive to discover how he had been defrauded.

Nearly all the succeeding events took place in the Talbot Arms Inn, Rugeley, which, as usual in that season, was doing a roaring business with the race-course crowd. The picture developed during the testimony is, in a way, a darker version of Frith's celebrated *Derby Day* painting. It stresses a side of the Victorian racing scene not emphasized, though certainly implied, in Frith's panorama of mixed humanity at the races: the murky transactions among stable-owners, money-lenders, professional bettors, touts, and hangers-on; the anxieties, the soaring but illusive expectations, the calamities and desperate stratagems to recoup one's losses . . . If one wishes to know in great detail what happened in a provincial hotel during a Victorian racing season when a guest became violently ill and remained so for a number of days, the trial of Palmer is the place to find it.

For that is what it is all about. Cook took sick on November 14, and he died on the night of the twentieth. So much was undisputed. What *was* disputed was the cause of his agonizing final illness, which was attended by severe gastric disturbances and rigidifying of the muscles, with the result that at death his body was bent in the shape of a bow, resting on head and heels. Was it, as the pliant eighty-two-year-old local physician who had served Palmer in previous contingencies certified, a case of apoplexy? Nobody took this diagnosis seriously. Was it, then, as the prosecution maintained, strychnia poisoning? This was more likely, but since there had never been a court case involving the alleged administration of this substance, there were no precedents to give sorely-needed guidance. Or was it, as the defense claimed, a case of idiopathic (self-generating) or traumatic tetanus? The trouble here was that although strychnine was known to produce tetanic convulsions, such convulsions could be produced from causes other than poisons. Or, as other possibilities suggested in the course of allegedly expert testimony, might Cook have died of arachnitis (inflammation of the membrane covering the spinal cord), or epilepsy, or angina pectoris? The doctors wildly disagreed. The chance of consensus was made additionally remote by the fact that no traces of strychnia were found in Cook's organs. But some witnesses argued that the poison could do its work and then be cast off, leaving no traces. It all depended on whom you listened to. The Attorney-General in his closing address was severe: "To me," he said, "it seems that it is a scandal upon a learned, a distinguished, and a liberal profession, that men should come forward and put forward such speculations as these, perverting the facts, and drawing from them sophistical and unwarranted conclusions with the view of deceiving a jury."

He was referring, of course, to the defense witnesses. But some of the Attorney-General's own specialists had not distinguished themselves. His leading expert witness was Dr. Alfred Swaine Taylor, F.R.C.P., professor of medical jurisprudence at Guy's Hospital (he was to occupy the post for a total of forty-six years) and author of what he modestly described as "a well-known treatise" on poisons and medical forensics, a *Manual of Medical Jurisprudence,* first published in 1844, which had already gone through a number of editions. Ten years after his appearance in the Palmer trial Dr. Taylor would produce a companion treatise of equal importance, *The Principles and Practice of Medical Jurisprudence.* He was generally regarded as the top man in his field—a field which, admittedly, had not as yet been intensively cultivated. He discoursed learnedly on the effects of strychnia, yet on cross-examination he had to admit, "I have never had under my own observation the effects of strychnia on the human body; but I have written a book on the subject." It is impossible not to detect irony in the opening address of Mr. Serjeant Shee for the defense: "We must be just to Dr. Taylor. Dr. Taylor has had an extensive reading upon the subjects upon which he writes, and it is not to be supposed that Dr. Taylor would hastily set down in his book what he did not find established on high authority; therefore, though having it at second hand, Dr. Taylor knows something upon the subject."

Other occupants of the witness box could present evidence that was more empirical than Dr. Taylor's. They described experiments upon animals and a number of recent cases involving the fatal, though accidental, administration of strychnia to human beings. Not all the authorities, then, rested their confident judgments upon the received "literature on the subject." But these elementary applications of the scientific spirit to the problem did little to clear up the inconsistencies and uncertainties with which the whole body of medical testimony abounded.

Moreover, there was some irregular conduct at the Rugeley autopsy which virtually ensured that the London analysts to whom the vital organs were submitted did not receive them in pure form. Dr. Palmer, presumably as a professional courtesy but certainly in defiance of any etiquette that should prevail in such situations, was allowed to be in the room while the doctors were at work, and more than one testified that he was jostled as he extracted certain of Cook's organs and was putting them in jars. Failure to tie both ends of the stomach upon removal resulted in its contents being mixed with other matter; at one juncture Palmer, seeking to be of assistance, handled the jars himself; and two slits subsequently were found in the parchment covers that were intended to seal the jars against any interference with their contents. A post boy testified that Palmer offered him £10 if he would contrive to upset the fly in which Cook's stepfather was to take the jars to Stafford, where he could board a train for London. This climactic accident did not occur, but by that time there had been so many other blunders and possible interferences that it is no wonder the results of the tests in the London laboratory were open to grave question.

All these porosities and dubieties divided both the medical profession and the laity into vehemently opposing camps. As soon as the verdict of Guilty was delivered, there was acidulous comment on the ease with which a jury of ordinary men had sliced the Gordian knot the learned doctors had tied and decided that, notwithstanding the experts' being at loggerheads, Cook had died of strychnia administered by Palmer, as charged. The medical schools were in a tumult; Dr. Taylor was alternately praised and damned; a large public meeting was held in London to protest the verdict and the resultant death sentence; representations were made to the Home Secretary; and *The Times* printed, among much else relating to the case, letters from scientists suggesting that further tests be made on Cook. One would think, though, that by this time there was little left of Cook to test.

All the controversy came to nothing in the end. But Palmer's death did nothing to quiet it, because as he stood in the shadow of the noose before Stafford prison, he uttered the classically ambiguous statement, "I am innocent of poisoning Cook by strychnia." The question, however, was now a strictly intellectual one. The concomitant moral issue disturbed only the hairsplitters. If Palmer was, in fact, hanged for a crime he did not commit, rough justice had been done anyway, because had he been spared on the Cook charge he would have leaped from the frying pan into the fire of the other indictments pending against him and would have deserved hanging on the strength of those antecedent charges, as well as of the dozen others imputed to him at the bar of public opinion. Those whose consciences troubled them would thus have found solace of a kind in the law of compensation.

Not that Palmer's fate weighed heavily on the nation. On the contrary, his villainy was generally accepted, even if the law's rebuke happened to be misoccasioned, and no tears marked his passing. The public mood was accurately epitomized by two incidental circumstances. One was the popularity of the angle chosen by two of the *Illustrated Times'* staff who covered the case, Henry Mayhew's brother Augustus and Charles H. Bennett, an artist formerly on *Punch*. Both men, wrote George Augustus Sala long afterwards, "were essentially funny fellows, droll dogs, merry men, mad wags, or whatever you may please

to call them from a facetious point of view; and rarely, I should
say, has an altogether ghastly and repulsive history been narrated by pen and pencil in such a whimsically droll manner. . . .
They managed to get fun out of everything:—Palmer's betting
book, John Parsons Cook's medicine bottles, and the overturning
of the post-chaise in which the police officers were conveying the
entrails of the murdered man for chemical analysis." * The
other element of the public mood is symbolized by the story of
the way the hangman's rope was made. It was the handiwork
of a porter at the Stafford railway station who admitted other
railwaymen to the fun, with the result that when they were finished they had a thirty-foot length (enough, perhaps, to serve
Palmer on all of the murder counts). The enterprising porter cut
the surplus into pieces of two or three inches and sold them at
a shilling each through the Stafford streets.

Long before this, however, certain souvenirs of the great
Palmer case—living souvenirs—had been disposed of at prices
which would have greatly pleased the doctor; they might, in fact,
if the sums had been realized two months earlier and judiciously
apportioned to his creditors, have saved him to be delivered to
the gallows on an account other than Cook's. In January 1856, his
stud was auctioned off at Tattersall's. The purchaser of his brood
mare, Trickstress, was the Prince Consort himself, who paid 230
guineas for her. The Chicken, whose inconvenient failure at
Shrewsbury had marked the beginning of the end for Palmer,
realized eight hundred guineas. One may make what he wishes
out of the fact that this valuable but unreliable horse was subsequently renamed Vengeance.

ii

Dr. Palmer was executed on June 14, 1856. Three years later,
a second doctor was in Newgate awaiting trial on a like charge.

* Actually, Sala was wrong on at least three points: it was Cook's, not
Palmer's, betting book that was missing; the post-chaise was not overturned;
and it was not police officers who were riding in it. But these inaccuracies,
though committed many years later, harmonized with the general tone of
the case insofar as it was set by the medical witnesses.

The Thurtell Murder, 1824. *Above,* the pond in which the body of William Weare was found. *Below,* the execution of John Thurtell.

The Irish "resurrectionists," William Burke and William Hare, arrested in 1828.

THE FLYING STATIONER, OTHERWISE PATTERER.

" All you that have got feeling, I pray you now attend
 To these few lines so sad and true, a solemn silence lend ;
 It is of a cruel murder, to you I will unfold——
 The bare recital of the tale must make your blood run cold."

" Mercy on earth I'll not implore, to crave it would be vain,
 My hands are dyed with human gore, none can wash off the stain,
 But the merits of a Saviour, whose mercy alone I crave ;
 Good Christians pray, as thus I die, I may His pardon have."

The Red Barn, where the body of
Maria Marten was buried, 1828.

William Corder, the murderer.

"PARTIES" FOR THE GALLOWS.

Newsvender.—" Now, my man, what is it ?"

Boy.—" I vonts a nillustrated newspaper with a norrid murder and a
likeness in it."

Punch, 1845

A COPY OF VERSES ON

F. B. COURVOISIER,

Now *lying under* Sentence of Death for the Murder of his Master, Lord W. Russell

F. B. COURVOISIER.

Tune.—" Waggon Train."

THE day of trial now is over,
  And Courvoisier is doomed to die.
the prime of life to suffer,
InOn the fatal Gallows high ;
For the dreadful murder of his master,
  A wnruing take thea by his fall,
May he improve those precious moments,
  And to his God for mercy call.

A valet to Lord William Russell,
  He might have lived in honest fame,
Respected by his fellow servants,
  And bear an honest name,
Of Plate and Jewels he robbed his master,
  And in the house did them conceal,
So cunningly he did contrive it.
  That quite secure he then did feel.

It happened that Lord William Russell,
  Chanced for to go down the stairs,
He cought him in the act of plunder,
  Which did his master sore enrage ;
Revenge and fear then filled his bosom,
  His wicked heart was bad indeed,
His crimes to him they were laid open.
  Which made him plan the horrid deed.

In the dead of night when in his slumbers,
  To his bedside he then did creep,
With a knife the dreadful deed committed,
  Which caused many a heart to weep,
But when that they had found him guilty,
  The pangs of conscience he did feel ;
Unable to bear the torment,
  The horrid crime they did reveal.

The Lord Chief Justice then passed sentence,
  While tears fell from his Lordships eyes,
Prisoner you have been convicted,
  You must prepare yourself to die !
No mercy you had on your victim,
  His old grey hairs you did not spare,
Then in this world expect no mercy,
  But to your God put up your prayers.

Make your peace with your Creator,
  Call to him by night and day,
And may the Lord above in glory.
  Wash your dreadful sins away ;
Your time is short your doom is certain,
  Employ your time to God above,
And may you for this dreadful Murder,
  Find forgivenes through his love.

A warning take then by these verses,
  Think of the Valet's dreadful fate,
Let Honesty then guide your actions,
  And in your stations be content ;
Now with his father and sister,
  In foreign land his fate to hear,
The disgrace that he will bring upon them,
  Will cause them many a briny tear.

CHORUS.

Then while we act in an upright manner,
  With a conscience, clear we need not fear,
Let those that in bad paths are steering,
  Think on the fate of Courvoisier.

PAUL & Co., Printers, 2, 3, Monmouth Co
Seven Dials.

Stock woodcuts used in the street literature produced by James Catnach.

THE LITERARY GENTLEMAN.

Illustrious scribe! whose vivid genius strays
'Mid Drury's stews to incubate her lays,
And in St. Giles's slang conveys her tropes,
Wreathing the poet's lines with hangmen's ropes.
You who conceive 'tis poetry to teach
The sad bravado of a dying speech,
Or, when possess'd with a sublimer mood,
Show "Jack o' Dandies" dancing upon blood!
Crush bones—bruise flesh—recount each festering sore—
Rake up the plague pit—write—and write in gore!
Or, when inspired to humanize mankind,
Where doth your soaring soul its subjects find!
Not 'mid the scenes that simple Goldsmith sought,
And found a theme to elevate his thought;

But you, great scribe, more greedy of renown,
From Hounslow's gibbet drag a hero down.
Embue his mind with virtue; make him quote
Some moral truth, before he cuts a throat.
Then wash his hands, and—soaring o'er your craft,—
Refresh the hero with the bloody draught;
And, fearing lest the world should miss the act,
With noble zeal *italicize* the fact.
Or would you picture woman meek and pure,
By love and virtue tutor'd to endure,
With cunning skill you take a felon's trull,
Stuff her with sentiment, and scrunch her skull!
Oh! would your crashing, smashing, mashing pen were mine,
That I could "scorch your eye-balls" with my words,
                                        MY VALENTINE

USEFUL SUNDAY LITERATURE FOR THE MASSES;
OR, MURDER MADE FAMILIAR.

Father of a Family (reads). "The wretched Murderer is supposed to have cut the throats of his three eldest Children, and then to have killed the Baby by beating it repeatedly with a Poker. * * * * * In person he is of a rather bloated appearance, with a bull neck, small eyes, broad large nose, and coarse vulgar mouth. His dress was a light blue coat, with brass buttons, elegant yellow summer vest, and pepper-and-salt trowsers. When at the Station House he expressed himself as being rather 'peckish,' and said he should like a Black pudding, which, with a Cup of Coffee, was immediately procured for him."

Maria Manning.

G. P. Manning.

The Manning house.

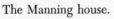

Discovery of the remains of Patrick O'Connor, murdered by the Mannings.

A cartoon in *Punch*, 1849, by Richard ("Dicky") Doyle, uncle of
the creator of Sherlock Holmes.

Staffordshire figurines commemorating the Rush murders.
Potash Farm, where James Rush lived with his mistress,
Emily Sandford, appears "with roses round the door."

Balston Collection

Mansell Collection

Dr. William Palmer in the dock.

Condemned cell in Newgate.

The jurors' retiring room.

Exterior of the court during the trial.

THE CASE OF MADELEINE SMITH, 1857

A courtroom sketch of Madeleine Smith. *Right*, Pierre Emile L'Angelier, the "inconvenient lover," from the photograph produced at the trial.

Scene outside Newgate Prison.

Mansell Collection

Headliners of the Sixties. *Left,* Dr. Edward William Pritchard, the
Glasgow poisoner. *Right,* Constance Kent—the case was never proved.

Mansell Collection

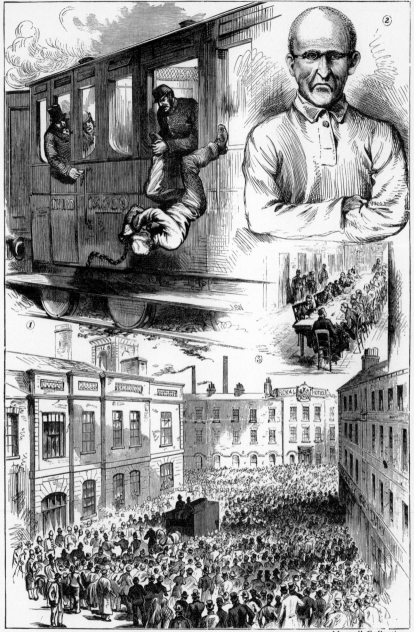

Incidents and scenes in connection with the convict Peace's attempted escape.
1. The attempt to escape from the train. 2. Charles Peace, alias John Ward.
3. The examination in the corridor of the police station. 4. The crowd
outside the town hall on the arrival of the van with the convict.

Three likenesses of criminals from the Chamber of Horrors at Madame Tussaud's. Madame Tussaud explained that a display of their likeness creates a contrary tendency to imitation. *Left to right*, Henry Wainwright and Kate Webster. *Below*, Thomas Neill Cream, the center figure.

Mrs. Bartlett.

Rev. G. Dyson
(Witness for the Prosecution).

The Pimlico Poisoning Case, 1886. Here Mr. Bartlett, father of the victim, is cross-examined by Edward Clarke, counsel for Adelaide Bartlett.

Mansell Collection

Florence Maybrick, the lady from Alabama, and James Maybrick.
He died under mysterious circumstances.

THE CASE OF FLORENCE MAYBRICK, 1889

Mrs. Maybrick making her statement to the court.

Dr. Thomas Smethurst, who had retired from the profession at least six years before he got into his great trouble, had been married since 1828 to a lady twenty or twenty-six years his senior (the evidence is conflicting). In 1858, while they were living in lodgings in Bayswater, he took up with a fellow-lodger, a spinster in her early forties named Isabella Bankes. Miss Bankes was evicted from the house because of her excessive familiarity with the doctor, but he followed her, bigamously married her, and settled down with her in Richmond. In his statement to the court after he was convicted of murdering Miss Bankes, Smethurst explained the second marriage in this somewhat cloudy language: "It is true that we united ourselves illegally, but it was for a permanency; and the marriage took place in this way:—At the request of the deceased—she was a person of property and good family connections, she knew that I was married—and, in order that she should be protected from reproach hereafter, this marriage was preliminary to one at a future period, in the event of my wife dying—she is now seventy-four years of age; therefore, it was fully intended that our union should be of a permanent nature."

But it was fated not to be of a permanent nature. Less than four months after her marriage, the new Mrs. Smethurst took sick with symptoms generally resembling those of acute dysentery, and only a little more than two months later, she died. The attending doctors had strong suspicions that something was amiss; furthermore, it transpired that Smethurst was the beneficiary of his late wife's newly made will. He was therefore charged with murder and brought to trial at the Old Bailey.

Things went badly from the outset. A juror was taken seriously ill on the first day and a mistrial was declared. During the second trial, the "painful details" incidental to the medical testimony required another juror to be removed to the open air. While he was taking deep breaths of the London smog outside the building, back in the courtroom the judge admonished the Crown counsel "that it was quite unnecessary to go into those matters with such minuteness, particularly as the jury probably would understand very little of such a subject"—advice which, if observed as a precedent, would have reduced the reports of many subsequent Victorian murder trials to mere pamphlet size.*

But the sensation of the trial was the fall from grace of the distinguished expert, Dr. Taylor. Testifying before the magistrates immediately after Smethurst was arrested, he had described how he had analyzed the contents of many bottles of supposed medicine found in Smethurst's possession. Only in Bottle 21 had he found incriminating evidence, namely arsenic. He repeated this statement before the coroner's jury. Before the trial itself began, therefore, Smethurst's guilt was widely assumed on the basis of the arsenic in Bottle 21. But when Taylor came to the witness box in the Old Bailey, he had to confess a crucial mistake. In his analysis he had used the standard Reinsch's test, which involved boiling the substance in question in hydrochloric acid and then dipping a piece of copper foil or gauze into the solution. But Bottle 21 happened to have contained chlorate of potassium, which had the effect of liberating arsenic already contained, as an impurity, in the copper. He had therefore been betrayed by his own analysis: the arsenic to whose damning presence he swore came not from the property of the accused but from his own laboratory supplies. And no arsenic was found in the new Mrs. Smethurst's organs.

This error provided one of the soundest bases for Smethurst's post-trial petition: the "universal prejudice created in the public mind" by Taylor's deposition before the magistrates and the coroner's jury prevented a fair trial. There seems to have been much substance to the claim. A barrister who watched the

* The bench's concern for the jury's limited powers of comprehension as well as its sensibilities was responsible for a number of moments of comedy in these trials. In the trial of Mrs. Maybrick the judge, admitting an exhibit in evidence, remarked, "I don't know, gentlemen, that you would be very much edified by looking at this arsenic." But medical ignorance was not confined to juries. In the same trial, his lordship "asked for the meaning of the term 'petechiae,' with which he confessed himself unfamiliar." Witness: "It is the Italian [*sic*] for fleabite, my lord." In the trial of Adelaide Bartlett a medical witness said, ". . . as far as I can remember, the lower part of the oesophagus was denuded of the epithelium." The Attorney-General, taking no chances, turned to the bench: "Your lordship does not need to have that explained to you, but perhaps it may be convenient to say that that long word means the gullet."

proceedings wrote that "Spectators, witnesses, prisoner's counsel, judge, jury, prosecuting counsel, one and all seemed weighed down, absolutely unable to escape from some mysterious weight hanging over their imaginations, which impelled them to a belief in the prisoner's guilt. Even the prisoner's counsel put his questions, as though this evil influence led him every time to expect an unfavourable answer, and he got it." The defense also failed to make adequate use of the considerable body of medical opinion it had on its side. This opinion held, in general, that Mrs. Smethurst, who was proved to have been from five to seven weeks pregnant, died of gastric complications attendant to that condition. An obstetrician appearing for the defense cited the case of "the celebrated Charlotte Brontë, who died of vomiting in pregnancy"—a convenient illustration he must have picked up in his non-professional reading, supposedly from Mrs. Gaskell's *Life of Charlotte Brontë,* which had appeared two years earlier.* Even the Crown prosecutor admitted in his opening statement that "he was not prepared to say positively that death was due either to arsenic or antimony, but it was due to some poison or other, when and where administered he was unable to say." The editor of the trial, himself a medical man, concludes that in his view "the evidence, both circumstantial and scientific, completely failed to prove the guilt of Smethurst."

But convicted he was, and at once both the medical and the legal professions raised an outcry. The *Dublin Medical Press* attacked Taylor in rhetorical periods customarily reserved for the nation's orators:

The man who, *par excellence,* was looked upon as the pillar of medical jurisprudence; the man who it was believed could clear up the most obscure case, involving medico-legal considerations, ever brought into a Court of Justice; the man without whose assistance no criminal

---

* A more remote link Smethurst had with literary history was occasioned by his having conducted, in 1847–52, a hydropathic establishment for "people of the first station and character" at Moor Park, Surrey, formerly the home of Sir William Temple. Here Jonathan Swift, Temple's secretary for several years, wrote *A Tale of a Tub* and *The Battle of the Books.* While at Moor Park, Smethurst, for his part, edited *The Water Cure Journal;* but his most extensive literary effort was *Hydrotherapia; or, The Water-Cure, Together with a Short Sketch of the History of the Water-Cure from the Remotest Antiquity, and Remarks on Sea-Bathing* (1843).

suspected of poisoning could be found guilty in England; the man whose opinion was quoted as the highest of all authorities at every trial where analysis is required, is the same who has now admitted the use of impure copper in an arsenic test where a life hung upon his evidence, the same who has brought an amount of disrepute upon his branch of the profession that years will not remove, the ultimate effects of which it is impossible to calculate, which none can regret with a deeper feeling of sorrow than ourselves, though, perhaps, in the end, a lesson may be taught which will not be lost upon the medical jurists, and which may tend to keep the fountain of justice clear and unpolluted.

When he regained his breath, the editorialist concluded: "We must now look upon Professor Taylor as having ended his career, and hope he will immediately withdraw into the obscurity of private life, not forgetting to carry with him his favourite arsenical copper." The valediction, though, was premature; notwithstanding this embarrassing episode, Taylor continued to be the high priest of British medical jurisprudence for eighteen more years.

Petitions, signed by many eminent lawyers and medical men, were handed in to the Home Secretary, Sir George Cornewall Lewis; three of the medical witnesses for the defense joined in a long, reasoned, particularized letter to the same official; the letter columns of *The Times* were filled with additional comment, most of it in Smethurst's favor. The Home Secretary compounded the furor by referring the case for adjudication to "the best-known surgeon in London," Sir Benjamin Collins Brodie. After studying the transcript, Sir Benjamin reported that "there is not absolute and complete evidence of Smethurst's guilt." Lord Chief Justice Baron Pollock, who had presided at the trial and had been severely criticized for his biased summing-up, justly complained that this was "a most unprecedented course"—Sir Benjamin, though competent to decide medical issues, had exceeded his authority by going into "matters & motives—probabilities—purchase of *poison* . . . in short . . . he overrules the conclusion of the jury." *

---

* Wilkie Collins used this and the following detail of the Smethurst case in his long and undeservedly neglected suspense story, *Armadale*, serialized in the *Cornhill Magazine* in 1864–66. In the novel, after the conviction of a woman for poisoning her husband there is a great outcry in the press: "Doctors who had *not* attended the sick man, and who had *not* been present at

Smethurst (who had an advantage Palmer did not enjoy, in that his record was clean) was therefore granted a pardon. The law, however, insisting on an ounce of flesh if it was to be deprived of its pound, had him rearrested and tried for bigamy. He was convicted and served a year at hard labor. At liberty once more, he had the effrontery to sue his late wife's next of kin, who were trying to prove her will void since, they maintained, it was signed under duress and the already-ailing testator was of unsound mind. Although this audacious move could not have been expected to create a favorable impression, nothing ventured, nothing gained. And Smethurst won his case!

If public confidence in expert testimony had been shaken by the doctors' disagreements in Palmer's case, it was shattered by the "absolutely and uncompromisingly contradictory" evidence in Smethurst's. "It is hardly to be wondered at," remarks the trial editor, "that a layman should have doubts as to the value of scientific testimony, if that were a sample." And apart from the all-too-palpable contradictions, there was the question of the various doctors' professional credentials. Smethurst himself had his M.D. from Erlangen University, and although the record does not specify, as it does in the later case of Dr. Pritchard, who was a fellow-alumnus of Erlangen, the likelihood is that he got it over the counter rather than earned it in the classroom and laboratory. Erlangen, like Giessen and Heidelberg, was noted for its sale of medical degrees on easy terms. Even so, an Erlangen M.D. was as impressive a credential as the "Archbishop of Canterbury's degree" held by one witness.

Q. What! Can he [the Archbishop] make a doctor of medicine?
A. [By the judge] Yes; and he can also make a master of arts.

---

the examination of the body, declared by dozens that he had died a natural death. Barristers without business, who had *not* heard the evidence, attacked the jury who had heard it, and judged the judge, who had sat on the bench before some of them were born." As a result, the Home Secretary consults the judge, who refuses to take any action but consents to "having the conflict of medical evidence submitted to one great doctor; and when the one great doctor took the merciful view, after expressly stating, in the first instance, that he knew nothing practically of the merits of the case, the Home Secretary was perfectly satisfied." The convicted woman is pardoned. But to satisfy public feeling that she should be punished a little, she is then tried and convicted on a charge of robbery.

Q. Did you take your degree as a matter of course?
A. [By witness] Oh, dear, no! It is a very uncommon thing. I had to
   get a certificate from two members of the College of Physicians,
   stating that they had known me for a length of time, and that I
   was a proper person to have the degree.

The Archbishop of Canterbury's fitness to pass upon the qualifications of a man proposing to undertake the cure of bodies may
have been marginal, but it was hallowed by long usage, for the
so-called Lambeth degrees had been given legal standing by an
act of 1533.

   In 1858, a year before Smethurst came to trial, nearly two
dozen corporate bodies and officials had the power to grant
licenses for medical practice. By an act of 1511, even before the
Archbishop of Canterbury received his diploma-granting privilege, men wishing to practice medicine in London, except for
Oxford and Cambridge graduates, had to be examined and approved by the Bishop of London or the Dean of St. Paul's, and
in the country by the bishop of the diocese—in every instance,
with at least nominal professional advice. By Smethurst's time,
medical education and licensing in Britain had become utter
chaos. Alongside the fellows and licentiates of the London College of Physicians and M.D.'s from British universities—the most
prestigious if not necessarily the most knowledgeable physicians
—all kinds of other so-called medical men assumed the title of
"doctor" or "surgeon": apothecaries, holders of diplomas from
continental medical schools, barbers, even chemists. No wonder,
then, that there was a strong movement to create one central
agency to standardize medical qualifications. This was accomplished by the Medical Act of 1858, which created the General
Medical Council. But the law was not retroactive, so that a pre-
1858 practitioner, however obscure his qualifications, could minister as before. Mid-Victorian murder trials therefore continued
to feature, as "expert" witnesses, medical men who conceivably
could not have passed the new standard examinations.

   The Smethurst case was not among the most "popular"
Victorian murders, in the sense that it did not enthrall the public
as Palmer's had done. The excitement it generated was chiefly in
educated circles; its sensationalism appealed to the intellect

rather than to the rude fancy. But even here, the student of Victorian social life does not go unrewarded. For this was the time —the middle and late 1850s—when the evangelical passion for strict Sabbatarian observance, which kept the Lord's Day unconscionably dull and joyless throughout the Queen's reign, reached its peak. In the early summer of 1855, Lord Robert Grosvenor introduced into the House of Commons a bill which, "to secure the better observance of the Lord's Day," sought to add to the existing Sabbatarian restrictions a ban upon the Sunday operation of trains and steamboats and upon the opening of public places of refreshment. For several Sundays thereafter, Hyde Park was the scene of riotous protests directed initially against the aristocrats who followed their custom of taking Sunday afternoon drives through the park. These high-born Sabbath breakers were greeted with groans, hisses, and cries of "Go to church!" On one such Sunday, 150,000 people were estimated to have gathered in the park, necessitating heavy police reinforcements (who were later charged, in respectable quarters, with over-reacting to the mob's unruliness) and sending over a hundred persons to the station house or the hospital. On another occasion crowds surged through nearby Belgravia, breaking the windows of mansions with paving blocks, Paris-style. The disaffection between classes was intensified by the knowledge that Lord Robert's bill specifically exempted Pall Mall clubs. In the end, the working-class protests, assisted by a substantial body of middle-class sympathizers, had their effect, and the provocative bill was withdrawn.

The most noteworthy literary documents reflecting the controversy are *Little Dorrit*, serialized in 1855–57, in which Dickens illustrates (and bitterly assails) the Sabbatarian obsession, and Trollope's *Barchester Towers* (1855), in which the Reverend Obadiah Slope's rabid Sabbatarianism wins him the influential partisanship of Mrs. Proudie and the detestation of her husband's broad-minded clergy. But alongside these novels stands, in a humble auxiliary role, the record of the Smethurst trial. It is no accident, but rather a faithful representation of the current spirit, that no fewer than three separate allusions to Sunday observance occur in the case. The Richmond solicitor whom Smethurst asked to come to Isabella's sickbed and execute her will testified, "I told him I did not like to do business on a Sunday, and that the law did not like wills being executed on a Sunday." Swallowing his scruples, however, he did it just the same, and collected his fee before he left the house. Dr. Taylor testified that he performed his analysis of specimens from Isabella, while she was still living, because "I was told that it was necessary to do something to save the life of this lady, and therefore, contrary to my custom of not making analyses on a Sunday, I proceeded with my experiment." It was as a result of this reluctant violation of the Sabbath that Smethurst was arrested the next day, but Isabella did not benefit by it; she died on the Tuesday. So pervasive were qualms about the desecration of the Day of Rest that, although Monday was traditionally the day appointed for executions in Surrey, where the alleged crime occurred, considerable opposition was expressed to the necessity of men working on the Sabbath to erect the scaffold atop Horsemonger Lane Gaol. The day therefore was altered to Tuesday, but thanks to Smethurst's reprieve, the gallows were not used.

And so the formidable presence of the English Sunday affected lawyers and doctors and all manner of men; it was sometimes a veritable matter of life and death, because it might have added a day to Smethurst's life had the crisis not been averted. Hangmen too must have a day reserved for their pious exercises And murderers? I have not tried to count the Victorian homicides that were enacted on the Lord's Day, but my impression is that murderers as a class were not Sabbatarians. At least, when a man or woman was set upon accomplishing the fatal deed, the Biblical admonition to keep the Lord's Day holy proved no deterrent. There may be some kind of significance in the fact that several of the goriest transactions in Victorian annals did occur on Sunday, and two of them involved maidservants doing away with their mistresses. Three of these murders are discussed in Chapter 12, though their conjunction there is not due to their happening to represent drastic violations of Sunday calm. It is worth noticing that one of these Sabbath breakers, William Sheward of Norwich, required a whole week to dispose of his victim's remains, so that it was not until late on the seventh day following that he could rest.

iii

As William Roughead suggests, Edward William Pritchard, M.D. (purchased), Erlangen, 1857, may well have "studied and improved upon the experience of Palmer" a decade before. In any event, he occupies a place of eminence in the gallery of Victorian physician-poisoners; the more so because he pursued his nefarious purpose while occupying a position of double trust, as son-in-law and husband of his victims as well as their medical attendant. Though he cultivated a plausibility which took in some people, there is no question that he was a nasty customer. It is good that the expressive Victorian word *scoundrel* has gone into semi-retirement, because it should be reserved for men like Pritchard, not degraded by application to inferior specimens.

He had been a naval surgeon for a time, and upon his retirement from the sea gave lectures on the exotic places he had visited. But some of his more attentive auditors noticed that he was not entirely consistent with himself, altering his version of places and experiences, along with his grandiloquent rhetoric, from recital to recital. At a time when Garibaldi was an English idol, Pritchard boasted of his friendship with the Italian patriot, even to exhibiting a cane inscribed to him—a cane which, unfortunately, some people recognized as having been in his possession for some time before the inscription was added. His vanity was impressive: one of his habits was to favor even casual acquaintances with visiting-card-size photographs of his magnificently bearded self. No professional advertising seems to have been involved; it was simply a matter of admitting a larger circle to the appreciation of his fine physical attributes.

In Glasgow, where he had settled in 1860, his insinuating manner enabled him to build up a fairly busy practice. But he was generally suspected and disliked by his professional colleagues, who rejected his repeated attempts to be admitted to the Faculty of Physicians and Surgeons and even to the various medical societies, which required only that the applicant possess a diploma and be of respectable character. Dr. Pritchard was noteworthy, too, for the untoward liberties he was reputed sometimes to claim with female patients in the privacy of his consulting room. And in 1863, two years before the events which brought him into national prominence, he had attracted the interest of the local police through a fire in his house involving the death of a servant girl. Although the blaze had begun in her room, she apparently had made no attempt to escape, the supposition being that she was already dead or unconscious. The insurance company, doubting along with the police that the episode was a mere accident, declined to pay Pritchard's claim.

Nevertheless, the doctor remained free to commit the deeds for which he was called to account—the slow, relentless disposition of his mother-in-law and wife, in that order, by antimony mixed in their food. He also favored aconite and opium, though perhaps not to the same lavish extent. He was proved to have bought extraordinary quantities of several poisons. One of the largest apothecary shops in the city sold to him alone as much antimony as it sold to the rest of the Glasgow profession in a single year. "In all my experience," said the proprietor, "I never furnished so much poison to any medical man." It was no wonder, then, that when the hapless ladies were analyzed they turned out to be saturated with lethal chemicals.

Pritchard's motives remain obscure. He stood to win a two-thirds life-interest in a sum of £2,500 if his wife predeceased him: an insufficient amount, one would think, to justify a murder. Or did he wish to free himself to marry a servant girl he had seduced some time ago? As for his mother-in-law, did he find it necessary to kill her because, having come to Glasgow to nurse her daughter and being a person capable of suspicion, she stood in the way of his perfecting his plan?

But it is futile to speculate about the motives of a man so out of the ordinary as to be able to write in his diary just after his mother-in-law's death: "About 1 A.M. this morning passing away calmly—peacefully—and the features retaining a life-like character—so finely drawn was the transition that it would be impossible to determine with decision the moment when life may be said to be departed." This was nothing compared to his performance, public and private, at his wife's death three weeks later. Just as she expired, he cried, "Come back to your dear Edward"; and when her coffin was opened at her father's home in Edinburgh he "exhibited a great deal of feeling" and kissed her cold lips. In his diary, meanwhile, he had written: "Died here at 1 A.M. Mary Jane, my own beloved wife, aged 38 years—no torment surrounded her bedside—but, like a calm, peaceful lamb of God—passed Minnie away. May God and Jesus, Holy Gh., one in three—welcome Minnie. Prayer on prayer till mine be o'er; everlasting love. Save us, Lord, for Thy dear Son."

Each of these famous cases of alleged poisoning by prescription (we must give Smethurst the benefit of the "alleged") brought to the witness box one medical man who took a particular beating. The luckless one here was a Dr. Paterson, whom Pritchard had called in to assist and advise him concerning the puzzling maladies that were afflicting his ladies. Paterson testified that while he was attending the mother-in-law, Mrs. Taylor, he suspected that both she and her daughter, whom he did not then examine or question but whose appearance disturbed him, were suffering from a visitation of something other than natural disease. He kept those suspicions to himself, however, and even when he revisited the house, at Pritchard's request, to see Mrs. Pritchard while her husband was in Edinburgh burying her mother, the obvious acceleration of her decline still did not prompt him to take any action. Only two days later, when her father, sent by Pritchard, came to collect a signed death certificate for Mrs. Taylor, did he move. Declining to provide the certificate (a refusal which led Pritchard to sign one himself, designating apoplexy as the cause of death), he instead wrote to the registrar that Mrs. Taylor's death was, in his opinion, "sudden, unexpected, and . . . mysterious." But when the second patient in Pritchard's household died shortly thereafter, Paterson resumed his silence. Even though he had seen her only four or five hours before the end and was convinced that she was dying of poison, he had done nothing except prescribe a sleeping draught.

This excessive punctiliousness, as it struck many people,

leads one to the belief that his private version of the Hippocratic Oath included the injunction that a doctor should mind his own business.

Q. As you thought Mrs. Pritchard was suffering in that way from antimony, did you ever go back to see her again?
A. I did not, and I believe that I never would have been called back again if I had not met Pritchard accidentally on the street.
Q. Why did you not go back?
A. Because she was not my patient. I had nothing to do with her.
Q. Then, though you saw a person suffering from what you believed to be poisoning by antimony, you did not think it worth your while to go near her again?
A. It was not my duty. I had no right to interfere in any family without being invited.
Q. Dr. Paterson, is it not your duty to look after a fellow-creature who, you believe, is being poisoned by antimony?
A. There was another doctor in the house. I did the best I could by apprising the registrar.
Q. Did you tell Dr. Pritchard?
A. I did not. Had I been called in consultation with another medical man, I should certainly have considered it my duty to have stated distinctly my medical opinion.
Q. But you stood upon your dignity, and did not go back to see what you believed to be a case of poisoning?
A. I had no right.
Q. No right?
A. I had no power to do it.
Q. No power?
A. I was under no obligation.
Q. You were under no obligation to go back to see a person whom you believed was being poisoned with antimony?
A. I took what steps I could to prevent any further administration of antimony.
Q. By never going back to see her?
A. No; by refusing to certify the death.

"I had discharged my duty," he said later, "so far as I thought incumbent upon me."

If there had been an appropriate charge to bring against Dr. Paterson, public opinion would have desired that he be convicted, as Pritchard was. His refusal to intervene when he saw two women dying of antimony poisoning was scandalous indeed. On the other hand, some commentators on the case have seen his role in a more sympathetic light; if he did not exert himself to save the lives of Mrs. Taylor and Mrs. Pritchard, he at least was primarily responsible for the detection of the crime. Better too late than never. Had he not communicated his suspicions to the registrar, his felonious brother in the profession might well have lived to kill another day.

Pritchard improved his last days in prison by transcribing texts of Scripture, which he dispensed to his visitors in lieu of the former photographs. This show of piety, however, failed to impress his ghostly counselor. "I shall see you in Heaven," the sanguine doctor told the clergyman. "Sir," said the clergyman coldly, "we shall meet at the Judgment Seat." Pritchard was hanged on July 28, 1865, before a crowd reported to have numbered one hundred thousand. Although they did not know it at the time, this was to be Scotland's last public hanging.

It must not be thought that by this trio of notorious cases within a single decade the British medical profession purged itself of its errors. To be scrupulously fair, we must remember that had it not been for the gradually developing expertise of toxicologists and pathologists, justice throughout the Victorian period would have faltered oftener than it did, and a number of callous murderers would have been spared the rope. Doctors —good doctors, learned doctors—were becoming ever more indispensable to the processes of the law. But, despite the professional reforms accomplished in the middle of the century, which after all had little to do with morality, a few doctors remained unvirtuous in the pursuit of selfish ends, as others remained incompetent as "experts." In 1881, for example, Dr. George Henry Lamson, a Bournemouth practitioner in financial distress, administered aconitine in a slice of fruit cake to his crippled eighteen-year-old brother-in-law, who stood to receive money from his parents' estate which Lamson thought he could make better use of, and right away. And, as we shall see in a later chapter, the most evil doctor of them all, Thomas Neill Cream, was waiting in the wings. The testimony in their cases, as well as in several others such as Chapman's, served only to confirm the popular impression conveyed by the trials of Palmer, Smethurst, and Pritchard: the Victorian medical profession was not consistently

one of the nation's first lines of defense against crime. Playgoers
who had attended Samuel Phelps's production at Sadler's Wells
(1851) of *Timon of Athens*—the first recorded staging of the
original drama—had special reason, in view of what they read
in the papers during the next two decades, to remember Timon's
advice to his hireling banditti:

> Trust not the physician;
> His antidotes are poison, and he slays
> More than you rob.

8

Henry James's Perfect Case

MADELEINE SMITH, 1857

CHRONOLOGY requires that Madeleine Smith's affair be placed here, where the Victorian period is but twenty years old; but she is the centerpiece of our little display. Who can sufficiently praise this determined and resourceful young lady? By disposing so efficiently of her inconvenient lover—a deed for which, it is true, she did not go unreprimanded—she earned herself a sure place among the immortals of British crime. Her story has everything: sex, a setting in well-to-do Scottish society, abundant echoes of contemporary conventions and prejudices, and, not least, more reverberations among high literary folk of the Victorian era than were called forth by any other immediately contemporary murder.

Madeleine was the daughter of a prosperous Glasgow architect. If Carlyle's favorite criterion of respectability applies (and it should, Scotsman to Scotsman), Mr. James Smith was unchallengeably respectable, for he kept not a mere gig but a carriage. Madeleine had finished off her education at a genteel boarding establishment in Clapton, a London suburb. A vivacious young woman of twenty-one, she had a healthy and assertive libido which ill comports with the received stereotype of the middle-class Victorian maiden as a shrinking, innocent, innocuous, slightly consumptive strummer of the pianoforte and limner of picturesque landscapes in sketchbooks. Beneath the conventional demureness lurked urgent passion, as is amply demonstrated in the letters she wrote to the thirty-year-old Jerseyman who was destined to be her victim.

Pierre Emile L'Angelier was a ten-shilling-a-week shipping clerk in a seedsman's warehouse. He was introduced to Madeleine in April 1855, and within a year she had become his mistress. The course of their love affair, which a modern pen can only characterize as torrid, may be traced in those incandescent, though regrettably iterative, missives. They are remarkable documents which no inquirer into the true state of Victorian sexuality can afford to overlook. Signed, typically, "thy ever-loving and ever-devoted Mimi, thine own wife," their candor was the subject of harsh comment from the judge in his summing-up at the end of the trial in which they were introduced as evidence. One passage in particular, he said, could not be read aloud, because the terms "perhaps . . . were never previously committed to paper as having passed between a man and a woman." This is doubtless an assumption incapable of proof, and it may reflect on the learned Lord Justice-Clerk's experience of the world, but he was certainly right in implying that Victorian women were not supposed to feel as Madeleine did, let alone articulate those feelings in flaming written words as she also did. Part of her guilt, in contemporary eyes, was that she was disloyal to her sex; part of her fascination to us is that she was uninhibited by the age in which she lived.

At any rate, Madeleine and Emile had a fine time for a while, and her reminiscent letters after their meetings were ecstatic and explicit. But her starchy Papa and Mama found out, to the extent of knowing that she was seeing an impecunious young man with a French name. Having other plans for her, they naturally forbade further interviews between the two. Madeleine and her lover therefore had to contrive surreptitious meetings in the house when her parents were absent or, in default of such opportunity, clandestine interviews at her bedroom window, which by happy chance was located in the basement, opening on an areaway.

This more restricted contact was satisfactory for a while, but in due course Madeleine became bored; and simultaneously, there appeared on the scene a more eligible suitor, of creditable nationality (Scots), appropriate social station, and reasonable financial expectations. Having had her fling, Madeleine was by now quite prepared to fulfil her proper destiny. But L'Angelier, alas, possessed her letters, and in addition he was not prepared to forgo the chance of an improving marriage which, despite his handicaps, he might still achieve if he played those letters right.

It was at this time, in February 1857, that Emile had two attacks of an undiagnosed gastric illness, from which, despite their severity, he in time recovered. At this same period Madeleine bought, on several occasions, sixpence' worth of arsenic from local chemists. On March 21 she wrote him, begging him to come to her window. The following night, returning to his lodging house, Emile was stricken again, with the worst attack yet; and within a few hours he was dead. A post mortem disclosed the presence in his organs of 82.7 grains of arsenic, the remnants of what one expert witness thought might have been as much as half an ounce—a truly formidable dose.

The pattern of events seemed to point to but one conclusion: Emile had died by Madeleine's hand. She freely admitted that on one occasion she had given him a cup of cocoa, in which arsenic was easily soluble, to fortify him on his long walk home. But there were difficulties in the hypothesis. It was true that the first time Emile was sick, he had been with her; but at the trial the prosecution was unable to show that she had as yet possessed herself of any arsenic. The second illness, on the other hand, could not be linked with any visit to Madeleine, though by that time she had bought the poison. In fact, it could not be established that he had even left his lodgings then. As for the fatal occasion, Madeleine declared that she had not seen him for the preceding three weeks, let alone that night. The one chocolaty tryst had taken place "a good time previously, on a date which she could not specify." *

Despite this inability to make a watertight case, the Scottish authorities charged her with murder, to the boundless interest of

* According to Emile's memorandum book, which was not admitted in evidence but was published soon after the trial, he saw Madeleine on several other evenings when it is known she had arsenic in her possession. In this respect the case against her was stronger than the prosecution was allowed to prove.

all Britain. Her nine-day trial was the sensation of the summer of 1857. Not within living memory, if ever, had the dock at Edinburgh, to which the trial was moved, been graced by so young, glamorous, *and* well-born a prisoner.

The papers of the time [one historian tells us] describe Madeleine as of middle height and fair complexion, an elegant figure, sharp and prominent features, restless and sparkling eyes; her brow was of the ordinary size and her face inclined to the oval; in spite of prison life her complexion was fair and fresh. She was dressed in rich brown silk, with a large brooch low set in the breast, a white straw bonnet simply trimmed with white ribbons, a white cambric handkerchief, and a bottle of smelling-salts in her kid-gloved hands. She is described as stepping into the dock with the air of a belle entering a ballroom. From the first to the last her demeanour was characterised by perfect repose mingled with an attitude of undaunted defiance. Only once did her composure give way: when her terrible letters were being read she covered her face with her hands.

It was also rumored—though supposedly not in print—that Madeleine, doubly blessed in that the judge was reputed to be not wholly unsusceptible to feminine charms and that the crinoline of the day facilitated the shy revealment thereof, took care that he should now and then be granted a glimpse of her neat foot and ankle. But so banal an embellishment, though probably inescapable under the circumstances, is unworthy of a place in a classic chronicle; even truth must be rejected if its vulgarity blemishes the artistic effect. More disturbing is the fact that such likenesses of Madeleine as survive do not reassure us of her comeliness. No photographs are known, and the courtroom sketches of her which appeared in the newspapers fail to substantiate the enthusiasm of the reporters and other spectators. So far as the dispassionate historian can tell, Madeleine was not necessarily a ravishing beauty, and perhaps not even a reasonably pretty adornment of a Glasgow drawing room. But involvement in the deed of which she was accused may have caused her to glow excessively in the eye of the beholder.

The jury's verdict, perhaps the only justifiable one considering the prosecution's inability to correlate Emile's visits to Madeleine with his illnesses, was Not Proven. It may well be that the jurors were affected to some extent by the defense's strategy of depicting L'Angelier's character in such a way as to touch off their xenophobic prejudices. The 1850s were a time when anti-Gallic sentiment, which had been present in Britain ever since the French Revolution, had become especially virulent. Between the French nation and the Romish church (whose establishment of an English hierarchy in 1850 had been greeted with a burst of hysterical anti-Papism) there was not much to choose; the British nation as a whole was never more confident of its own righteousness, and consequently never more convinced of the malign cunning of Roman Catholics and the sheer immorality of Frenchmen. The current Gallophobia aside, L'Angelier's prowess with women—which could not conveniently be denied, given the epistolary evidence produced in court—his reputed vanity, and the dramatic suicidal gestures in which he was said to have indulged when Madeleine was evincing a desire to jilt him: these fitted him with fatal neatness into the British, and even more the specifically Scottish, stereotype of the lubricious Frenchman on the loose in law-abiding, God-fearing society. The discovery of a cigarette case in his effects strengthened this impression, because in the 1850s cigarettes were still notoriously the preference of affected persons from Latin nations, in contrast to the honest cigars and pipes smoked by trueborn Britons. The verdict of this stolid jury therefore may have been intended to be as much a posthumous condemnation of L'Angelier as it was an expression of a certain measured doubt as to Madeleine's guilt.

The issue of the deceased's character as affected by his nationality was, of course, never made explicit, though it persistently hovered in the air. Much more specific was the concern with poison. Like the trials discussed in the last chapter, this one involved much toxicological evidence. And if anything is clear from the testimony in this and the other great trials for poisoning, it is that despite the legal requirement that purchasers designate what use they had in mind for the poisons they desired, and that they sign the chemist's book, it was quite easy to buy arsenic, prussic acid, antimony, or whatever else one fancied. Certainly Madeleine had no trouble; she merely claimed that she wanted to poison some rats. As the records of scores of arsenic murders reaching back to the seventeenth century attest, the rat-excuse was utterly conventional; by this time, one would think, chemists' assistants would have burst out laughing at a customer's invocation of the hoary fable. Furthermore, was it not odd that a young lady of Madeleine's social class would have gone shopping for such a commodity when menials were available to do the chore? But Madeleine, like uncounted numbers of men and women before her, got what she ordered. And when she came back for a fresh supply, she simply reported, with a smile, that encouraging progress was being made against the rats but another dose was needed to complete the job.

In the course of the testimony on the purchase and effectiveness of poison in mid-Victorian Britain—the trial transcript is a veritable textbook on the topic—there are some historically revealing, not to say macabre, touches. A physician recalled a case of a woman's taking arsenic by accident: "she was not a very strong-minded person; she was a hysterical and weak creature. She took it thinking it an effervescent powder, and she did not discover what she had taken till she saw a dog pulling about the room a paper on which 'Arsenic' was marked." And from another medical witness we obtain a sudden stark glimpse of life and death among the working class. "I have seen several cases of suicidal poisoning by arsenic," he said. "They were chiefly young females connected with mills and colour [dye] works. In many cases they had obtained the arsenic about the works; in others it was purchased. . . . The people about the works had great facility at that time in taking away arsenic." The matter-of-fact observation is pregnant with bitter sociological significance: dark, satanic mills, and desperate females . . .

To offset these reminders of what life was like outside the comfortable middle class there are occasional pleasant vignettes wholly void of any sinister meaning. As, for example, the recollection of a police constable who happened to meet L'Angelier as the young man was returning, serene in stomach, from one of his evenings with Madeleine: "He was standing near a lamp-post at the end of the back lane running from Mains Street. When I came along the point of the square, I turned along Mains Street, and he said, 'Cold night, policeman; do you smoke?' I said 'Yes, sir'; and he put his hand in his breast-pocket, and gave me two cigars and passed on."

Other women who figured in murder cases, such as Emily Sandford with her *Whitefriars* novel, were occasional readers, but Madeleine Smith, member of a class whose females had abundant leisure, read more than the rest. In her letters to Emile (one supposes, to add a certain requisite tone to chit-chat which was basically un-literary) she reported reading biographies of Sydney Smith, the late Whig clergyman and wit, and the Scottish judge Lord Cockburn. Cockburn in his day had been a celebrated pleader in criminal cases, but all she had to say about the book was that "the characters mentioned are too old for me to remember." The very image of the dutiful daughter who wishes to reassure Papa that he has not wasted his money on her education is seen in her comment on a recent life of Sir Robert Peel: "There is so much regarding politics in it, that I find it rather dry sort of reading; but papa asked me to read it, so I shall do it." Vasari's *Lives of the Painters* she liked more, because "the life of Andrea del Sarto quite makes me feel melancholy." Evidently Madeleine was unaware that only a year earlier, a man named Robert Browning, husband of the famous poetess Elizabeth Barrett, had re-told Andrea's story in verse. But such ignorance is easily forgiven, because few people read Browning then. Harriet Beecher Stowe's *Dred* "disgusted" our Glasgow maiden; Hume's *History* she read but did not evaluate; and of Macaulay's exceedingly popular history of England she merely said, "I like the 4th [volume] very much, but I don't mind the third much." Gibbon she "liked very much. . . . I found it interesting and instructive." She was less enthusiastic about Layard's recent book on Nineveh and Babylon: "I don't say I have read every word of it for many parts are dry and tiresome but you might not find it so."

It would appear that Madeleine did not have a large stock of critical ideas, let alone a sharply honed critical vocabulary. Superficially it might also seem that she credited Emile with a larger intellect than he really possessed; but, since she obviously knew her man better than we can, all this talk of books probably had the laudable aim of enhancing her value in his eyes. He must have made it plain to her that he liked women who read with serious intent. Apparently he also admired diligence, for she described a thirty-volume collection of the *British Essayists* as "a particular favourite of mine." "Next week," she told him, "I intend to begin a Book 8 large vols.—Francis Bacon's 'Works on Philosophy and History.'" Without necessarily impugning her sincerity of purpose, we may doubt that she ever got very far in this ambitious project.

But far from being merely a conscientious blue-stocking outside her amorous hours, Madeleine read for practical instruction. Like every educated Scot, she read *Blackwood's Edinburgh Magazine* and *Chambers's Edinburgh Journal*, the nation's two proudest achievements in the periodical line apart from the venerable *Edinburgh Review*. Here, ironies abound. From its inception, *Chambers's Journal* had been dedicated to the promotion of useful knowledge and morality among the people. In 1849, when Madeleine was thirteen, this favorite household paper had published an article deploring the current "Murder-Mania," blaming, among other causes, "the exciting and abhorrent details of slaughter offered by the public journals. . . . No doubt," the writer said, "the newspaper press only obeys a demand in presenting these minutiae of crime to its readers. The details we speak of, however, are not the less mischievous. Unquestionably, the *unsound predisposition* receives a direction and an impulse from the journals; and the atrocities, the horrors, and the sufferings that flaunt so wildly and pertinaciously in the eyes of the public, serve as so many sparks to ignite the latent mine."

Two years later *Chambers's* ran an article, subsequently identified as from the pen of one Charles Boner in Ratisbon, Bavaria, on "The Poison-Eaters." This was so sensational that, according to Boner in a follow-up article in February 1856, it had been copied or quoted in thirty-two journals on the continent as well as innumerable ones in Britain. Among the latter was the issue of *Blackwood's Magazine* for December 1853. The nub of the excitement was the assertion that arsenic taken in moderate doses has no deleterious effects on the human body but on the contrary may prove of benefit. The main instance cited was the habit peasants in lower Austria and Styria had of eating arsenic to improve their complexions. According to one authority, a "healthy but pale and thin milkmaid . . . had a lover whom she wished to attach to herself by a more agreeable exterior. She therefore had recourse to the well-known beautifier, and took arsenic several times a-week. The desired effect was not so long in showing itself, for in a few months she became stout, rosy-cheeked, and all that her lover could desire." It is true that she did not let well enough alone, and in the pursuit of still more pastoral glamor overdosed herself, with fatal results. But taken in moderation, the argument went, arsenic did have salutary effects. It was, said one Dr. Pearson, "as harmless as a glass of wine in the quantity of one-sixteenth part of a grain."

As usual when lay journals dabble in scientific topics, the experts protested the inaccuracy and potential mischief of these articles. The final word in *Chambers's Journal,* in an issue appearing just a year before Madeleine went on trial for murder by arsenic, was that the Styrian peasants may indeed acquire the appearance of blooming health from judicious intake of arsenic, but they know enough folk pharmacology to quit after ten days or a fortnight, by which time the desired results will have been achieved. "Lastly," a physician was quoted as saying, "let me urge upon all who adopt the Styrian system, to make some written memorandum that they have done so, lest, *in case of accident,* some of their friends may be hanged in mistake."

This was the time when Madeleine was enjoying the first fine raptures of having become Pierre Emile L'Angelier's mistress, and it is therefore possible that she had no leisure or inclination to peruse the superficially bland but potentially seductive pages of *Chambers's Journal.* But she could hardly have helped being aware of the controversy that had gone on for the past several years as a result of that first article in December 1851. The assumption works in either of two ways. On the one hand, it would suggest an obvious place where Madeleine could have learned of the fatal effects of arsenic taken in sufficient quantity: a useful fact to store away for possible later use. On the other— and this was, of course, the line of reasoning her own counsel seized upon—the widespread press discussion had revealed that arsenic was in common demand for non-lethal purposes, and that ladies like Madeleine might, with entire innocence of purpose, buy it at their neighborhood chemist's, though invoking the rat-extermination alibi rather than confessing to motives of personal vanity. In her sworn statement after her arrest, she said of her several purchases: "I used it all as a cosmetic, and applied it to my face, neck, and arms, diluted with water. . . . I had been advised in the use of the arsenic in the way I have mentioned by a young lady, the daughter of an actress, and I had also seen the use of it recommended in the newspapers." * Testifying at the trial, however, this young lady, a former schoolmate of Madeleine's at Clapton, denied recommending arsenic as a cosmetic and said merely that they had talked about Swiss mountaineers' using arsenic to improve their wind when they labored up steep slopes. This beneficial side-effect of arsenic-eating had been prominently mentioned in the magazine articles alluded to.

Representatives of the publishers were called to present sales figures for the issues of *Blackwood's* and *Chambers's* in question; they were seven thousand and fifty thousand respectively. A Falkirk surgeon testified that "I have frequently, since the publication of an article in *Chambers's Journal*, been asked by females as to the use of arsenic as a cosmetic," and a Glasgow chemist recalled a lady who "produced a number of *Blackwood's Magazine* containing an article on the use of arsenic for improving the complexion." Despite their occurrence in a sensational murder trial, these are proofs of "reader impact" which would warm the heart of any circulation manager or (in our time) any advertising space salesman. The tantalizing problem for us, however, is not whether Madeleine Smith, like other young ladies of the moment, was tempted to try this novel beautifier but whether she filed in memory the accompanying data on the fatal effects

---

* The newspapers and other contemporary authorities on beauty aids seem to have overlooked the fact that by law arsenic had to be mixed with soot and indigo, a precaution which would surely have diminished its efficacy in external applications. When taken internally, as in the case of L'Angelier, the coloring matter would remain in the system along with the arsenic; yet, oddly enough, none of the doctors noticed any such residue in his organs.

of arsenic when taken internally in liberal amounts. When Emile outlasted his welcome and the time came to dispose of him, did her mind revert to the blameless pages of *Chambers's Journal* . . . ? Either way, it was a question of saving her skin.

After the jury returned its ambiguous verdict, Madeleine went back to her family, but only briefly. Neither of her parents had attended the trial, and there is strong evidence that she was no longer welcome at the family fireside. At the time there was a story, accepted by Henry James and still preserved in some biographical accounts, that she almost immediately married a physician from Perth and emigrated with him to Australia, where he died. One such account adds that she herself died in Australia in 1893. But the truth, at least as regards her subsequent career, is quite different. On July 4, 1861, Madeleine, then living at 72 Sloane Street, Chelsea, married George Wardle, artist, at St. Paul's Church, Knightsbridge. How they met is not clear. One story has it that she had been living with a clergyman's family on the south coast of England and Wardle had been teaching drawing in a nearby school. Another, found in Violet Hunt's not always reliable book on the Rossetti-Morris circle, alleges that about this time she was "living in a London boarding-house very miserably" and working as a tapestry weaver for William Morris's newly founded firm of handicraftsmen and interior decorators.

If she was not associated with the Morris circle before her marriage, Madeleine joined it immediately thereafter, for her husband became a valued member of Morris's organization, rising eventually to the post of manager. It is said that he was a devoted student of medieval art as well as a talented draftsman and that he traveled throughout the country copying architectural designs and details for adaptation in Morris products. In their home in Bloomsbury the Wardles entertained freely. It appears that some of their guests knew of her dark past and some did not. The acute embarrassment which the latter's ignorance cost them gave rise to a number of stories, typified by that of the journalist George R. Sims, who was a dinner guest at the Wardles' when the talk turned to criminology and Madeleine

Smith's name was mentioned. Sims "remarked that if it was true, as was reported, that she was alive and married, her husband must be a brave man. He was continuing to air his views on the subject when one of his feet began to give him trouble; his neighbour was more discreet."

George Bernard Shaw, who saw Madeleine and her husband once or twice in connection with Morris's Socialist League, remembered her as "an ordinary good-humored capable woman with nothing sinister about her." After the death of her husband, who had left Morris's employment in 1889, she lived for a time in Staffordshire, then in London again, and finally in the United States, where she was married to one Sheehy. She died in 1928, in great poverty and at an advanced age, and was buried, as Lena Wardle Sheehy, in Mount Hope Cemetery, Hastings-on-Hudson, New York.

It is unlikely that Madeleine kept up the literary interests she had maintained in livelier if not happier days. Perhaps she would have been completely indifferent could she have known what an impact her case made on a number of leading literary figures. There was Nathaniel Hawthorne, for example, the American consul at Liverpool: he had come to Scotland on holiday while the trial was in progress, and in hotels in the Highlands he found the latest newspapers being read aloud to groups of ladies and gentlemen. Arriving in Edinburgh, he sought admission to another tourist attraction, the crown room in the Castle, but was told he had to present an order from the proper office in Parliament Square. By mistake he went first to the Justiciary Court, "where," he recorded in his diary, "there was a great throng endeavoring to get in; for the trial of Miss Smith for the murder of her lover is causing great excitement just now." How he was affected by this choice *crime passionel* he did not say; supposedly it had qualities which did not appeal to the author of *The Scarlet Letter.*

At this moment, too, the Edinburgh publisher John Blackwood was writing to his best-selling author, George Eliot:

The Madeleine Smith Trial keeps Edinburgh quite ahead of London at present. The girl will get off. She is a nice young woman but I really doubt whether she did poison the beast and at all events he deserved anything. I wish the dog had died and made no sign, as such exposures do much harm. I should like to hear Lewes [George Eliot's extralegal husband] on the subject as I think he has rather a turn for the analysis of remarkable trials.

George Eliot replied five days later:

I think Madeleine Smith one of the least fascinating of murderesses, and since she is acquitted it is a pity Palmer is not alive to marry her and be the victim of her second experiment in cosmetics—which is too likely to come one day or other.

Lewes, obedient to Blackwood's request, reported his opinion on the same day. It differed sharply from Blackwood's:

You want to know what I think of the Smith case. In one word I would say that it is very lucky for that miserable girl that her victim was a Frenchman and she a Scotchwoman. Under any other circumstances she must have been hanged. A more hideous case it would be difficult to find. I cannot feel the slightest approach to sympathy with her. I see absolutely *no* trace of goodness in her. From first to last she is utterly bad. As to Angelier's having corrupted her—in the ordinary sense of the word, he did—that is he gained her consent to what she seems far from reluctant in granting; but for all other "corruption" she seems to me more capable of corrupting him. Not that I have any sympathy with him. But he *had* good feelings. She has none.

While, however, the evidence against her is overwhelming and even the jury only returns a verdict of not proven—a moral condemnation though a legal acquittal—I must say the masterly defense of the Dean [John Inglis] was enough to shake a jury. It is one of the finest specimens of forensic argument I remember. Admirable in tone as well as masterly in legal acuteness. From the first I feared lest the *last* proof could be adduced; and the Dean takes up a strong position in showing the absence of such proof.

The sympathy felt for this girl is to me thoroughly incomprehensible. I understand the profound sympathy felt for her family. But it is clear the Dean believed her guilty—the judge summed up dead against her —the evidence in her favor was of itself a tacit avowal—yet the audience cheers her acquittal! Unless that cheer meant a condemnation of capital punishment altogether, it has a hideous sound in my ears.

So much for the combined opinion of Lewes and George Eliot, who obviously were not among Madeleine Smith's partisans. Neither was Jane Carlyle, a fellow Scotswoman, who later that month of July was writing her husband from her family home at Sunny Bank, where she was on a visit. First, she reported

(as "fact," naturally) one of the many stories then circulating
about the heroine of the hour:

. . . Miss Madeline [*sic*] Smith said to old Dr. Simpson, who attended her during a short illness in prison, and begged to use "the
privilege of an old man, and speak to her seriously at parting," "My
dear doctor, it is so good of you. But I won't let you trouble yourself
to give me advice, for I assure you I have quite made up my mind to
turn over a new leaf!"

Jane continued:

But about Miss Smith I have one thing to tell you which I think you
will be rather glad of, as giving the death-stroke to testimonials. The
Glasgow merchants are actually raising a subscription (it has reached
nine thousand pounds), "to testify their sympathy for her." One man,
a Mr. D———, has given a thousand himself—he had better marry
her, and get poisoned. [The probable fate of Madeleine's next suitor
seems to have worried most people; compare George Eliot's concern.]
Not that I believe the girl guilty of the poisoning; but she is such a
little incarnate devil that the murder don't go for much in my opinion
of her.

Haddington [Jane's home town] has half the honour of having produced this cockatrice. I knew her great-grandmother—a decent,
ancient woman, called "Mealy Janet," never to be seen but with a
bag of flour under each arm. She was mother to the "Mr. Hamilton,
architect of Edinburgh," and to one of the most curious figures in my
childhood, Mysie Hamilton, or "Meal Mysie" (she continuing her
mother's flour trade); she spoke with a loud *man's* voice, that used
to make us children take to our heels in terror when we heard it. I
remember the boys said Mysie was a ——— but what that was I
hadn't a notion, nor have I yet; my mother thought her a good
woman, and once by way of lark, invited her to tea. I bought a
pamphlet the other day containing the whole "trial," on the very spot
where Mysie Hamilton sold her flour, now a book-shop.

To George Eliot, Madeleine Smith was "one of the least
fascinating of murderesses," to Jane Carlyle a veritable "cockatrice"; it is fair to say that in their respective ways they were
prejudiced against her. Henry James, however, whose views
were uncomplicated by any loyalty to sex or nationality, was able
to look upon her with aesthetic detachment, and he found her
good indeed. His appreciation of "the prodigious Madeleine,"

as he called her—his friend Roughead's phrase was "our *prima donna assoluta*"—is unsurpassed in the connoisseurship of murder. It must be quoted in its enthusiastic entirety, from James's letter of June 16, 1914, to Roughead.

The case represents indeed the *type*, perfect case, with nothing to be taken from it or added, and with the beauty that she precisely *didn't* squalidly suffer, but lived on to admire with the rest of us, for so many years, the rare work of art with which she had been the means of enriching humanity. With what complacency must she not have regarded it, through the long backward vista, during the time (now twenty years ago) when I used to hear of her as, married and considered, after a long period in Australia, the near neighbour, in Onslow Gardens, of my old friends the Lyon Playfairs. They didn't know or see her (beyond the fact of her being there), but they tantalized me, because if it then made me very, very old it now piles Ossa upon Pelion for me that I remember perfectly her trial during its actuality; and how it used to come to us every day in the Times, at Boulogne, where I was then with my parents, and how they followed and discussed it in suspense and how I can still see the queer look of the "not proven," seen for the first time, on the printed page of the newspaper. I stand again with it, on the summer afternoon—a boy of 14—in the open window over the Rue Neuve Chaussée where I read it. Only I didn't know then of its—the case's—perfect beauty and distinction, as you say. . . . She was truly a portentous young person, with the *conditions* of the whole thing throwing it into such extraordinary relief, and yet I wonder all the same at the verdict in the face of the so vividly attested, and so fully and so horribly, sufferings of her victim. It's astonishing that the evidence of what he went through that last night didn't do for her. And what a pity she was almost of the pre-photographic age—I would give so much for a veracious portrait of her *then* face.

Here we have the unstinted tribute of one gifted artist to another, admiration mellowed by the golden haze of recollection.*

---

* Although James never ventured to use Madeleine's case as a *donnée*, others did. There have been several novels based on the affair, the first of which, an anonymous three-decker called *Such Things Are* (1862), ingeniously conflated it with the more recent Constance Kent sensation. Let an indignant commentator in the *Quarterly Review* tell how it was done: "These two crimes are taken out of their original associations, and, with some change of circumstances, are fastened upon two 'fast young ladies,' bosom friends to each other, and who, by a most marvellous coincidence, become the wives of two brothers. The one, some time after her marriage, is discovered by her horrified husband to be the person principally suspected

What pert young poisoner could wish a higher reward for her accomplishment?

---

of 'the famous Bogden murder;' the other, on the eve of her marriage, being threatened with an exposure of some passages in her earlier life, quietly gets rid of the obnoxious witness by a dose of strychnine, and, on the day but one following, figures as a bride in a 'quiet and unostentatious wedding at St. George's, Hanover Square.' " A motion picture, *Madeleine*, starring Ann Todd, revived the story in 1949.

9

A Deed of Dreadful Note

JESSIE M'LACHLAN, 1862

IN THE GREATEST of all Scottish murder stories there occurs an unexpectedly idyllic passage which, looked back upon, throws into grim relief the horrors that were soon to come. King Duncan, arriving at Macbeth's castle for what he has no reason to believe will be other than an enjoyable and relaxing visit, observes appreciatively,

> This castle hath a pleasant seat; the air
> Nimbly and sweetly recommends itself
> Unto our gentle senses.

And Banquo adds:

> This guest of summer,
> The temple-haunting martlet, does approve
> By his loved mansionry, that the heaven's breath
> Smells wooingly here; no jutty, frieze,
> Buttress, nor coign of vantage, but this bird
> Hath made his pendent bed and procreant cradle:
> Where they most breed and haunt, I have observed,
> The air is most delicate.

How wrong they both were! And how wrong, also, were three sisters—nothing to do with Macbeth's weird ones—who happened to be walking through the streets of Glasgow at four o'clock on the bonny, clear morning of Saturday, July 5, 1862, on their way home from their brother's all-night marriage party. The soft early-morning air, the rising sun, and the presence of many birds affected them as Duncan and Banquo were affected, with a sense of extraordinary peace. "When we were passing Sandyford Place," one of the sisters later deposed, "our attention was attracted by a great many small birds that had gathered in a tree which grew opposite the houses there; and it being a beautiful morning, still and calm, one of my sisters made the remark, how pleasant it was to hear the birds whistling on such a lovely morning, when everything else was quiet."

The girls also remarked on the presence of a light in two windows at 17 Sandyford Place. Illness? A late party? Sheer forgetfulness when the family retired? (Not very likely: this was Scotland.) They did not know, nor had they any reason to care. Returning from a happy marriage party, their thoughts understandably did not entertain the possibility that behind the Venetian blinds had recently occurred—or, perhaps, was occurring at that very moment—a deed unfit for the tender eye of pitiful day to look upon. And so the girls, two of whom were in domestic service and the third a cloakmaker, went their serene ways.

Number 17 Sandyford Place, by singular chance not far from the scenes of the Pritchard and Madeleine Smith murders, was the home of a prosperous accountant named John Fleming. With him and his family resided his father James, a spry senior citizen aged eighty-seven. There was also the usual complement of servants. On the weekend in question, the younger Flemings, like many comfortably fixed Glaswegians, had gone off to their summer place, leaving in their town house only "the old gentleman," as James would be deferentially called from the bench, and one servant, a young woman named Jess M'Pherson.

On Monday the son and *his* son returned to the city for business but did not go to Sandyford Place until late that afternoon. Jess, who normally would have been expected to welcome them, was nowhere in evidence. Upon being questioned, the grandfather claimed not to know where she was—"she's cut" (skipped) was all the light he could throw on the mystery. He had not seen her since Friday night. At no time, then or later, was he able to tell why her unexplained disappearance (she had been in the Flemings' service a fair length of time, and was a woman of steady habits) had not caused him any concern. But

inspection of the premises soon revealed what had happened to
her. She was found in her basement bedroom, nude from the
waist down, her head covered by a piece of carpet, weltering in
her own gore.* Forty wounds, the police surgeon counted; Macbeth's hireling assassin had done for Banquo with half the number.

Grandfather professed decent shock at the outrage. He was,
however, taken into custody. As the police investigation progressed, it was quickly learned that another servant-class person,
Mrs. Jessie M'Lachlan, who had formerly been with the Flemings and was now married to a sailor, had been present in the
house on the fatal Friday night, and that subsequently she had
both pawned some plate that was discovered to be missing and
shipped to herself at Ayr, under a false name, a quantity of
bloodstained clothing belonging to the unfortunate Jess M'Pherson. She was thereupon charged with murder and theft, and Mr.
Fleming, who by this time had spent eight days of his sunset
years in jail, was released with apologies for the inconvenience to
which he had been put.

Between the arrest of Mrs. M'Lachlan and the start of the
trial, feeling in Glasgow ran strongly against James Fleming.
Only one newspaper obstinately took his part. Notwithstanding
his great age (which some cynics maintained was only seventy-
eight, but he had a birth certificate dated 1775), he was not the
sort of patriarch to whom sympathy normally flows. "The old
gentleman" he may have been in the eyes of the judge, but to
those who knew him better he was a disreputable gaffer who had
worked most of his life as a handloom weaver, and now, in the
effulgence of his son's prosperity, spent most of his time in the
kitchen at Sandyford Place consorting with the servants and being obnoxious in one way or another. He and his tastes found

---

* Upon discovering the body, he later testified, John Fleming ran into
the street for help. He "met one gentleman at the entrance to the row. I
told him what had occurred, and asked him to come in; but he declined,
saying, 'No, no; you have said enough to frighten me from my dinner.' "
Bystanders' reluctance to get mixed up in a crime on grounds of queasiness
or detachment—one thinks of the notorious Kitty Genovese case in the New
York City borough of Queens a few years ago—evidently is not a phenomenon unique to our age.

their natural level in the servants' quarters. He had an insatiable inquisitiveness about everything that occurred in the household. It was well known that he got drunk when the means were available, and that ten years earlier he had been rebuked by the Kirk for fornication and bastardy—a feat which, at the age of seventy-seven, would more fittingly be recognized by a trophy. In view of all this, it was only natural that various servants in the Fleming household should have described him as "a nasty body," "a dirty body," and, more emphatically and conclusively, simply as "that auld deevil." He was not merely obnoxious; to those who had the misfortune to know him best, he was disgusting.

If, as is not unlikely, the educated younger members of the household had been reading Mr. Dickens's recent novel, *Great Expectations,* they might well have called him Aged P. Possibly they saw him in a different light than did the scandalized and exasperated servants below-stairs. However that may be, the old goat was the star of the trial. He may have been aged, but he was nowhere near his dotage. Alert and cagey, he delivered his testimony, sprinkled with many a confidential "ye ken," in Braid Scots. His account of the fatal weekend at 17 Sandyford Place did little to settle the blame one way or another, although his effort was to urge it in a direction away from him. He maintained, and no amount of cross-examination could shake him, that he had known nothing of the violent deed enacted in the basement which had deposited bloodstains on walls, door frames, and furniture, or of the time or agency of the partial clean-up operation which had left the stone floors still damp when the police arrived late Monday afternoon.

Why, then, had he answered the door on Saturday morning when the milkman's boy rang—something he had never done before, since this was the duty of one servant or another? The milkman and the boy, who became something of a national celebrity because of the crucial nature of his evidence, testified that Fleming, fully dressed in his black suit, had come to the door at about 7:40 that morning and said "he was for nae milk." Taken as a whole, Fleming's extensive reply to persistent questions of defense counsel on this point was a masterpiece of evasion and convenient failure of memory. It suited him to be senile when the pressure was on. Forced eventually, in the face of the milkmen's testimony, to admit that he had opened the door, he explained, "On Saturday morning, ye ken, Jessie was deed; she couldna open the door when she was deed." But how did he know she was dead? Recovering his wits, he said that of course he did not know it at the time, only later.

The judge, Lord Deas, did all he could to protect the aged gentleman from the imputation that he was telling neither the pure truth nor the whole truth. Indeed, whatever injudicious partiality the press and public had for Mrs. M'Lachlan was more than balanced by the judge's behavior throughout the trial; it could almost be said that the case for the prosecution was conducted from the bench. His summing-up was so transparently biased against her as to constitute a scandal. Before him, as he reviewed the evidence against Jessie, lay the dread black cap—the piece of cloth which, in English trials (where it was square), the judge placed on his wig when he pronounced the death sentence and which, in Scotland (where it was triangular), he simply held above his head. His openly bringing this ominous symbol with him before he even began his charge to the jury spoke louder than any words, and was a particular cause of offense to bar and laity alike.

As might have been expected, the black cap was needed. But only after the Guilty verdict was rendered—it was reached in fifteen minutes—did the climactic sensation of the trial occur. Jessie M'Lachlan's counsel read a long statement which the accused had dictated to them soon after she was arrested. They had withheld it from the case in the hope that the prosecution would fail to prove her presence at Sandyford Place and therefore would have made it unnecessary. The statement told how she and the deceased had sat companionably drinking with old Fleming in the kitchen on Friday evening; how Jess M'Pherson had incautiously uttered a remark or two about her "having a tongue that would frighten somebody if it were breaking loose on them," presumably an allusion to her privileged knowledge of one aspect or another of Fleming's unvirtuous behavior; how, while she, M'Lachlan, was absent on what proved to be a futile quest for replenishments for the convivial bowl, Fleming had

had an altercation with M'Pherson and had done her serious
bodily harm; how thereafter, through the summer night, M'Lachlan had cared for the sufferer; and how, finally, Grandpa, dis-
satisfied with his work, had resumed the cleaver, unmannerly
breeched with gore, and finished off the job in a peculiarly brutal manner. Because, as he sensibly informed her, Jessie M'Lachlan's bedside services had made her an accessory after the fact,
he had made her swear she would never divulge what had happened and then persuaded her to assist his design of making
the deed look like the accompaniment to a burglary by giving
her some of the household plate to pawn.

This narrative of the activities in the bloody basement,
which cleared up many points left unsettled during the trial,
made no impression upon the judge, however. How could it
have been expected to? He had already answered to his own
satisfaction the new questions it raised. He had let it be known
that he was privy to the secret that might have issued from
Jess M'Pherson's tongue had it been sufficiently loosened, for he
had gratuitously provided the key in connection with the testimony of a friend of the murdered woman who had met her in
the street a fortnight before she was killed. "She was looking
very ill; I never saw her looking so melancholy. I said, 'Jess,
what's wrong?' She said, 'I'm no' weel. You don't know how I
am situated; I live a miserable life. He [Fleming] is just an old
wretch and an old deevil.' I said, 'Tell me the right way of the
story; what has he done to you?' She said, 'I have something to
tell you, but I cannot tell you just now before your husband.'"
She promised to tell the witness, woman to woman, on the Sunday she did not live to see. Defense counsel properly, in view
of Fleming's reputation as an ancient but still aspiring lecher,
sought to establish that Jess's secret had to do with improper actions he had proposed or actually carried into effect. But the
judge sought to set the record straight: according to him, the
awful truth which Jess could not confide to her friend in the
presence of her husband was that she was thinking of emigrat-
ing.

Needless to say, no one believed Lord Deas, whose every
utterance from the bench was governed by his conviction that

Fleming was innocent as a naked newborn babe. In fact, had the judge been of a literary turn, he might have remarked that "that auld deevil's" largely unacknowledged virtues pleaded like angels, trumpet-tongued, against the suspicion of his guilt, and heaven's cherubim, in the form of circumstantial evidence, blew the truth of Jessie M'Lachlan's sole responsibility for the horrid deed in every eye. But he contented himself with merely re-affirming the jury's verdict and, under the frail canopy of the black triangle, sentenced her to death.

Public sentiment, which had been mounting day by day, now erupted. It was said that Glasgow doctors had their hands full treating patients afflicted with "extreme nervous irritability" as a result of their vicarious involvement in the case. The papers were crowded with special articles, enraged editorial comments, and letters to the editor. "Vindex," "Sigma," "One who Balances Probabilities," "Candidus," "Microscope," "A Lady who Admires Disinterested Truth Wherever It Is to be Found," and all their brothers and sisters—the sort of people whose pens were dipped in ink after every sensational trial—were heard from in unusually great numbers. Workers in factories and shops passed the hat to make up funds for the judicially maligned Jessie. Indignant meetings were held in every Scottish town, and in Glasgow alone, fifty thousand signatures were affixed to petitions demanding respite of sentence and a review of the case by the Crown. In shopwindows, in addition to crayon drawings of Jessie M'Lachlan and photographs of Jess M'Pherson, were displayed impudent and sometimes libelous caricatures: "The Sandyford Sweepstakes," in which, racing for the Crown Plate (the Gallows), the milkboy outran the judge and old Fleming; another in which "Lord Deas, as 'Lord Death,' attended by the Devil holding the rope, addressed a jury of 'Cuddies' [Scots: asses], while 'Old Gentleman,' with angel's wings and devil's tail, handed bags of gold to 'Black Fiscall' and 'Needy Sherriff' "; and a third in which the judge grasped Fleming by the hand as he cast aside Jessie's plea for mercy.

The campaign had its effect. After official inquiries into the case, Jessie's sentence was commuted to life imprisonment, a compromise that satisfied few, since if she was innocent she should have received a full pardon and if guilty she should have been hanged. Echoes of the case were heard in the House of Commons. But by this time the debate on the legal issues had ceased to affect Mrs. M'Lachlan's life. She had begun to serve what proved to be fifteen years in Perth General Prison. Upon her release she emigrated (in place of Jess M'Pherson, as Lord Deas certainly had not intended to enable her to do) to America. She is said to have died at Port Huron, Michigan, in 1899.

Who really killed Jess M'Pherson, and why? The authorities continue to differ. William Roughead, who edited the trial for the Notable Scottish Trials series, shared the generally held belief as it came down to him from the newspapers and other contemporary reports of the trial: Jessie M'Lachlan was innocent, and the evil old man had dispatched the maidservant even as Jessie maintained. But the latest student of the case, Christianna Brand, though sympathetic to Jessie throughout her book *Heaven Knows Who* (1960), ends with a metaphorical question mark.

10

The Murder that Thackeray Foretold

FRANZ MÜLLER, 1864

IN THE LITERATURE OF Victorian murder, the November 1862 issue of the *Cornhill Magazine* has a double significance, only half of which, so far as I know, has heretofore been recognized. In it was published an article on the legal problem of circumstantial evidence as posed by the M'Lachlan case, written by the already well-known literary barrister James Fitzjames Stephen, brother of the better-remembered Leslie Stephen and prospectively the uncle of Virginia Woolf. We shall meet him again when, as judge of the high court, he presides over the trial of Mrs. Maybrick. A few pages farther on in the same *Cornhill* appeared one of Thackeray's "Roundabout Papers" which contained a sentence or two of unintentional prophecy: "Have you ever entered a first-class railway carriage, where an old gentleman sat alone in a sweet sleep, daintily murdered him, taken his pocket-book, and got out at the next station? You know that this circumstance occurred in France a few months since."

Thackeray probably was referring to the second of two such murders which had been committed within a few months of each other in 1860. At 5 A.M. on December 5, a blood-splashed compartment on the train arriving in Paris from Troyes was

found to contain the body of M. Poinsot, the presiding judge
of the Imperial Court; he had been shot twice and brained, and
his watch and chain, wallet, traveling rug, and valise were missing. It was thought that the assailant had escaped when the train
slowed at Noisy-le-Sec, just outside the city, to pick up mail bags.
The *Sûreté* confidently identified him as a notorious adventurer,
army deserter, and suspected Prussian spy named Judd, who a
few months earlier had been arrested for a similar exploit, the
murder and robbery of a Russian army doctor on a train passing
through Alsace. Judd had slipped out of custody soon after his
arrest and thus had been free to strike again on the Troyes-Paris
run. There was some talk at the time that both homicides,
though accompanied by robbery from the person, in reality were
somehow connected with espionage. Judd was never re-captured.

In alluding to this French crime in a novel locale, Thackeray
seems to be suggesting that, though Britain had so far been
free of railway carriage murders, there was no reason why she
should be permanently immune. The compartmental arrangement of the carriages, with no communicating passageway, had,
from the very inception of enclosed passenger rolling stock,
added to the numerous hazards attached to railway travel. Between stations, unoffending passengers were wholly at the mercy
of drunks, madmen, and persons bent upon indecent assault. The
isolation of the compartment seemed an open invitation to murder. And so it proved, less than two years after Thackeray's mention of it. The man who introduced the railway carriage murder
to England was a foreigner, a German who had arrived in London at about the time the *Cornhill* piece appeared. It is improbable that he ever saw it, but he may well have read about
the French cases in the German papers.

A few minutes after ten on the evening of Saturday, July
9, 1864, two young City clerks boarded a train of the North
London Railway at Hackney station. The train had left Fenchurch
Street at 9:50 and had already stopped at Bow and Hackney
Wick (Victoria Park). The youths found an empty first-class
compartment, feebly lighted as was the practice so early in the
history of railways. After one had sat down, he told the other
that there was something sticky on his hand. The compartment

was just light enough for them to determine it was blood. The train fortunately had not started. They called the guard. He fetched a lamp from the brake van, and in its brighter light they discovered that the whole compartment, even the cushions and windowpanes, was spattered with blood. There were also a black bag and a stick—the property of the murdered man, as it turned out—and a hat which would prove one of the principal clues to the murderer. The guard locked the carriage and called the police. Later the carriage was detached from the train, returned to Bow station and shunted into a shed, where it would remain, locked, stationary, and silent, the fatal compartment untouched, while the murderer was found and brought to trial. Thackeray's offhand prophecy had been fulfilled.

The victim was soon found, lying unconscious on the right-of-way between Bow and Hackney Wick stations. Removed to a nearby tavern and then to his home in Clapton, he died the following night. He was Thomas Briggs, the seventy-year-old chief clerk for a firm of Lombard Street bankers, where, by coincidence, the young men who found the bloodstains also worked. Briggs had been returning home after having dined with his nephew in the suburb of Peckham. As events were reconstructed, his assailant had spotted him on the street or in the bus that carried him from the Lord Nelson public house up the Old Kent Road and across London Bridge to King William Street, near Fenchurch Street station. A man who knew him testified that he saw him in the train when it stopped at Bow station and said good night to him, Mr. Briggs replying in kind. Evidently, then, he was awake at this time; but for the greater glory of Thackeray's prescience it is tempting to think that he dozed off, or at least closed his eyes, after leaving Bow, thus seeming to enjoy the "sweet sleep" Thackeray specified for his hypothetical victim. The same man who bade him good night said that "he generally used to sleep going home in the railway carriage," and the presence of an extra amount of blood in one corner of the compartment led the police to believe that he was attacked when his head was resting against the brass rail. In any event, the murderer must have been with him in the compartment when the train left Bow. As the train prosaically puffed and clacked through the slum and factory district between Bow and Hackney Wick, he bludgeoned the elderly gentleman and took his watch and chain—overlooking £5 in his pocket—then dumped the body out the window.

The murderer was Franz Müller, a young and, until now, inoffensive German tailor who, as I have said, had been in England only about two years. By the time he was identified, he was on the high seas, heading for America, as he had told several acquaintances he had planned to do long before Briggs was murdered. He seems to have committed the murder to obtain funds for the voyage, because on the following Wednesday he booked passage on the sailing ship *Victoria*. The steerage fare, in those good old days, was £4.

The break in the case came through a Cheapside jeweler and a cab driver. When news of the murder appeared in the papers, the jeweler, whose name was John Death—a suitability only life, not the imagination of a novelist, could afford—came forward to say he had received Briggs's gold watchchain from a man to whom he gave some cheaper jewelry in part payment. Several days later, a cabman told the police that the box which had contained this jewelry had been given to his little girl by Franz Müller, who had happened to frequent his house. The cabby also identified as Müller's the hat which had been found in the railway compartment; in his understandable haste to leave the train at Hackney Wick, Müller had evidently exchanged hats with his victim. Briggs's was missing.

Although no one ever testified to having seen Müller and Briggs together, the fact that Müller had been in the vicinity of Peckham at the time Briggs was known to have taken the bus for Fenchurch Street,* the hat exchange, and the transaction

---

* In rebuttal, a Mr. and Mrs. Jones testified that he had been at their house, one-half or three-quarters of a mile from the place where Mr. Briggs's omnibus started, at the precise time when he was alleged to have been tailing his prospective victim. They also deposed that they had "two female lodgers, young women, who receive the visits of men," a statement which led prosecution counsel to characterize their house as a brothel. How many inmates constitute a brothel is a nice point of law which need not be examined here. This attempt at establishing an alibi for Müller was not very successful. As the editor of the trial says, "the character of Mr. and Mrs. Jones did not help their credibility, and the Solicitor-General dwelt with

with the jeweler converged to persuade the police that Müller was Briggs's murderer. And now, by a satisfying stroke of irony, the improved transportation which had supplied the setting for Müller's unprecedented crime also, as if by recompense, provided the means by which he was brought to justice. For when it was learned that he had embarked for America on a sailing ship, Inspector Tanner of Scotland Yard, who was in charge of the case, accompanied by a detective-sergeant, Mr. Death the jeweler, and Matthews the cab driver, took a fast steamer from Liverpool, arriving in New York twenty days ahead of the *Victoria.* The detail is certainly not relevant to the case, but one cannot help wondering how this heterogeneous quartet spent those twenty days in New York, presumably at Crown expense, waiting for Müller's ship to come in. At which hotel did they stay—the Astor House, or the St. Nicholas, whose luxury is said to have amazed visiting Englishmen? Did they favor Delmonico's with their patronage? And whither did their appetite for entertainment lead them of an evening, to Niblo's Garden or Barnum's Museum? . . .

Müller was arrested as soon as a boat could put out to the arriving ship, and after an extradition hearing he was returned to England under guard, reading *The Pickwick Papers* and *David Copperfield.* The news of this triumph of law and technology—foreshadowing, incidentally, the famous use of maritime wireless to capture Dr. Crippen in 1910—crowded the American Civil War from the columns of the London papers.

Probably the most impressive evidence of the case's hold on the public imagination is found in Matthew Arnold's preface to his *Essays in Criticism,* published the following year. Incongruously, this is the same preface which contains the ever-redolent poetic praise of Oxford "spreading her gardens to the moonlight, and whispering from her towers the last enchantments of the Middle Age." Before the passage in question Arnold had, in his customary fashion, been more or less suavely reproaching the philistines for the excessive value they placed on life. Also

---

almost undue vehemence on the little reliance that was to be placed on the clock of a brothel; it is difficult to see why the veracity of a clock should vary according to the character of the house in which it stands."

by custom, he used a topical instance as the text for his lay ser-
mon. "His avocations," by which he meant his duties as one of
Her Majesty's school inspectors, had lately required him to travel
almost daily on a branch of the Great Eastern Railway from
Woodford, Essex, where he and his family were living, to the
City.

Every one knows that the murderer, Müller, perpetrated his despica-
able act on the North London Railway, close by. The English middle
class, of which I am myself a feeble unit, travel on the Woodford
Branch in large numbers. Well, the demoralisation of our class,—the
class which (the newspapers are constantly saying it, so I may repeat
it without vanity) has done all the great things which have ever been
done in England,—the demoralisation, I say, of our class, caused by
the Bow tragedy, was something bewildering. Myself a transcendent-
alist (as the *Saturday Review* knows), I escaped the infection; and,
day after day, I used to ply my agitated fellow-travellers with all the
consolations which my transcendentalism would naturally suggest to
me. I reminded them how Caesar refused to take precautions against
assassination, because life was not worth having at the price of an
ignoble solicitude for it. I reminded them what insignificant atoms we
all are in the life of the world. "Suppose the worst to happen," I said,
addressing a portly jeweller from Cheapside [John Death?]; "suppose
even yourself to be the victim; *il n'y a pas d'homme nécessaire.* We
should miss you for a day or two upon the Woodford Branch; but
the great mundane movement would still go on, the gravel walks of
your villa would still be rolled, dividends would still be paid at the
Bank, omnibuses would still run, there would still be the old crush
at the corner of Fenchurch Street." All was of no avail. Nothing could
moderate, in the bosom of the great English middle class, their pas-
sionate, absorbing, almost bloodthirsty clinging to life.

There is something irresistibly comic in the picture of Matthew
Arnold, a modest-salaried civil servant, attempting to administer
the consolation of philosophy to worried businessmen in a com-
muter train. But, more than a century later, one still could do
worse than bring the Arnoldian "criticism of life" to his reading
of the daily headlines.

The case against Müller was so strong that the enduring
interest of the trial lies not in any suspense or forensic brilliance
(for it has little of either) but, rather, in its rich evocation of a
social locale: particularly, in this case, the tradesmen and other
occupation-types whom the accident of murder brought together

in the Old Bailey courtroom. For the first but by no means the last time in the history of British murder, attention centered upon the testimony of railwaymen—ticket takers, guards, stationmasters, engine drivers—which helped speed Müller to the gallows. From it we derive authentic details, some perhaps unavailable from any other source, of the routine working of Victorian railways.

The testimony provides technical data from other occupations as well. The hat found in the train was surely Müller's; Matthews the cabman testified that he had bought it for him. But was the hat found in Müller's possession when he arrived in New York the one Briggs had been wearing? The crown was considerably lower. The custom hatter at 18 Royal Exchange who had made it testified (as summed up in the words of prosecuting counsel) that it had been "cut down an inch or an inch and a half, and . . . not . . . by a hatter. . . . A hatter would have used varnish and a hot iron, and . . . this has merely been pasted on and sewed—and sewed very neatly and regularly. It has therefore been cut down, not by a hatter, but by one who understood sewing. In fact, it has been cut down by a tailor, and not a hatter." The operation had been made necessary, not to adapt the hat to Müller's head but to excise the portion of the crown containing Briggs's name. But under the lining remained fragments of the silver paper which the hatter had inserted to improve the fit on Briggs's head. The evidence of the hat was one of the sturdiest nails to be driven into poor Müller's coffin. It also enhanced his contemporary fame, because by drastically revising the shape of the purloined hat he inadvertently introduced and gave a name to a new style in mid-Victorian men's attire, a hat resembling a topper but reduced to half an ordinary top hat's height—the "Muller-cut-down." (The umlaut was sacrificed in the general abbreviation.) "Such an origin," note Willett and Phillis Cunnington, the modern authorities on nineteenth-century English costume, "is perhaps unique in the history of fashion." It is a distinction one is not prepared to challenge.

Apart from whatever unhappiness the gentlemen's hatter from the Royal Exchange may have felt over this faddish vulgarization of his art, his sojourn in the witness box was a sore tribulation. A tradesman of his quality did not like to get mixed up in sensational affairs like murder trials—especially when defense counsel sought to suggest that Müller might have come into possession of the cut-down hat through the regular channels of the second-hand trade. "My trade," he declared frostily, "is of a first-class, not second-hand. I know nothing of the second-hand trade in hats. My hats," he conceded, "may get into the second-hand trade. Servants sell their masters' hats very frequently." But it is clear that he could not countenance such debasement.

Mr. Briggs, it appears, bought but one hat (of excellent quality, of course) in a year. Perhaps one measure of Victorian difference in rank was the number of hats one bought annually: another witness, the cab driver, declared that he bought nine or ten—mostly second-hand, one would imagine—because his work kept him out of doors, in all kinds of weather. The more hats, the lower the social class? At any rate, this cabman was the most diverting witness in the trial. He was a remarkably dimwitted but sometimes cunning cove, whose answers to questions had something of the quality we associate with the comic routine of Shakespearean clowns:

Q. [Referring to Müller's alleged commissioning of his friend the cab driver to buy him a hat] In consequence of that you got one?
A. Yes.
Q. At what shop?
A. At the same.
Q. What same, what shop?
A. At the hatter's.
Q. Of course, but where?
A. Mr. Walker's, Crawford Street, Marylebone.

Defense counsel accused him of perjuring himself in hope of collecting the reward that had been offered for Müller's arrest and conviction. The lawyer professed himself unable to believe that, what with all the talk about the railway murder in pubs and cab ranks, and all the columns of newsprint and the blaring newsvendors' placards, Matthews had not heard of it for nine days. So Matthews maintained: that was why he had not come forward earlier with his vital evidence of the jeweler's box and the hat. But he was forced to admit that when police bills announced a substantial reward, he suddenly noticed them.

Q. Do you mean to say that you did not see the bills offering the £300 reward?
A. Yes; but if it had been a "plain" bill I should have done my duty.
Q. Do you expect a portion of the reward?
A. If I am entitled to it I should expect it.
Q. Then you do expect it. Why did you not answer me before? Have you ever said this, that if you had kept your mouth closed a little while longer there would have been £500 instead of £300 reward?
A. I never said so.
Q. Never anything like it?
A. No; I said that I was given to understand when I was before the coroner that there were bills offering £500. But if it had been a shilling I should have done my duty the same.
Q. I do not ask you to compliment yourself.

The record does not reveal whether the avariciously virtuous cabman collected the £300.

The scenes outside Newgate on the alternately showery and moonlit night before Müller's execution were shocking. The crowd, composed, as *The Times* reported, of "well dressed and ill dressed, old men and lads, women and girls," packed the streets, drinking beer, smoking, laughing, and yelling. After the workmen began to erect the scaffold at 3 A.M. the mob grew steadily in size and riotousness. Before sunrise there were intermittent noises of laughter and scuffling which puzzled the reporter until, with the coming of daylight, he could see that gangs of toughs were making their way from place to place, "bonneting" well-dressed members of the crowd (that is, pulling their hats down over their faces), garroting, and robbing them. "Sometimes their victims made a desperate resistance, and for a few minutes kept the crowd around them violently swaying to and fro amid the dreadful uproar. In no instance, however, could we ascertain that 'police' was ever called." The assaults and robberies continued unchecked until the hour of the hanging. "Latterly nearly 50,000 people were crammed between the walls of this wide thoroughfare. Wherever the eye could rest it found the same dim monotony of pale but dirty faces, which seemed

to waver as the steam of the hot crowd rose high." Once more
the London mob had had its holiday, courtesy of a cold-blooded
murderer. But this was almost the last such entertainment;
largely as a result of the wholesale garroting and robbing episodes, Parliament finally got around to forbidding public executions.

What were the effects of Müller's deed on railway travel?
None at all. The British public, resigned to the fact that the risk
on their lines was already much greater than on the Continent—
"fatal accidents," says a leading modern historian, "were more
than fifteen times as frequent as in Germany"—decided that the
additional possibility of misadventure at the hands of a fellow
passenger was an acceptable hazard, and so they kept on riding.
This confidence proved to be well founded. It was not until June
1881 that British rolling stock was again the scene of a murder.
This time the setting was the Brighton line, later to acquire fame
of a more genial sort in *The Importance of Being Earnest*. When
a train from London stopped at Preston Park, just outside Brighton, it discharged a man who was disheveled and covered with
blood, and, strangest touch of all, had a watchchain hanging
from his shoe. He explained his appearance and obvious mental
distress to the station officials by saying he had been set upon
in his compartment by would-be robbers; the dangling watch-
chain was witness to his quick thinking in concealing his valuables inside his shoe. The railwaymen, congratulating him on his
fast thinking and his avoidance of additional bodily harm, sent
him on his way. Not long afterward, however, the body of a gentleman of sixty-four, a Mr. Gold, was found reposing, bullet
wound in neck, at the entrance to a tunnel up the line. Hastily
revising their opinion of what had happened, the railway people
contributed to the police their joint impression of what the man
with the valuables in his shoe looked like, and the resulting
artist's profile sketch (receding chin, extraordinarily vain, vacu-
ous expression) was printed in the newspapers. An alert landlady saw it, and the murderer, a journalist named Percy Lefroy
Mapleton, was soon in custody.

Meanwhile, however, the famous ride of Charley Peace on
the Sheffield line had dramatized another serious deficiency of

existing railway carriage design, namely, the lack of lavatory accommodations. But it was not until about 1892 that the British passenger began to enjoy the luxury of corridor carriages with lavatories and henceforth could ride with enhanced convenience—and security.

11

A Spin Across London Bridge

HENRY WAINWRIGHT, 1875

You cannot carry with any degree of safety, either in a cab or by any other mode, a dead body along the streets of London.
—The Lord Chief Justice, Sir Alexander James Cockburn

SATURDAY, SEPTEMBER 11, 1875, was a warm, butter-turning day in London, and the mortgagee had taken possession of Henry Wainwright's brushmaking warehouse in the Whitechapel Road. Wainwright had lately been unscathed by prosperity; some ten months earlier, his salesroom across the road had burned down, and the insurance company, exercising the option it reserved in cases of reasonable doubt, had delayed paying his claim. Now, in taking leave of the warehouse, he was about to remove such chattels as remained on the premises to a new location, a building called the Hen and Chickens, just south of the Thames near the junction of Southwark Street and the Borough High Street. Here his brother Thomas had briefly been in the ironmonger's trade, but Thomas too had recently failed and his stock had been sold at auction. However, he still had the key to the building, whose deep and solid foundations, forming a cellar with remote and inaccessible corners, were well adapted for Henry's purposes. Henry had therefore borrowed the key.

The property he proposed to transfer this day consisted of two large and unwieldy bundles wrapped in black "American cloth" (oilcloth). He was then at a grain warehouse in the New Road, where, by the generous permission of the proprietor, he was carrying on his brush business until he could get back on his financial feet. Wainwright asked Alfred Stokes, who had been with him as a brushmaker for seventeen or eighteen years, "Will you carry a parcel for me, Stokes?"

"Yes, sir, with the greatest of pleasure." They went to the Whitechapel Road warehouse, and Stokes shouldered the two large bundles Wainwright drew from underneath some straw, not without complaint over their weight and strong odor. Outside the warehouse Wainwright relieved Stokes of the lighter one and, so encumbered, they trudged a quarter-mile down the road, at which point Wainwright went in search of a cab, leaving Stokes to guard the awkward freight. Yielding to normal curiosity, he began to open one parcel and quickly learned that he was in charge of, at the very least, one severed human hand. He did not venture to probe further

While Stokes was pondering the possible significance of this disquieting discovery, Wainwright arrived with a cab he had found at a nearby rank. He was then smoking a large cigar. Stokes helped him load the bundles onto the cab. He thanked Stokes for his trouble and said he would see him later. Then, as he was about to drive off with his bulky packages, Wainwright happened to see a young ballet dancer of his acquaintance emerging from a tavern and, to complete his enjoyment, asked her to go along for a ride on this nice Saturday afternoon. "I don't mind if I do," we can hear her answering as he gallantly handed her up. Off went the cab, laden with Wainwright, theatrical person, and bundles. It probably struck her as odd that, as soon as they were under way, he gave her a newspaper and invited her to read it while they rode. He said he wanted to think.

Stokes, left behind on the sidewalk, now sensed that something was decidedly wrong. He therefore took off in pursuit of the cab as it headed westward through Commercial Road, Ald-

gate High Street, and Leadenhall Street en route to London
Bridge. On seeing two policemen in Leadenhall Street, he
stopped, caught his breath, and urged them to join in the chase.
"Man, you must be mad," said they, laughing. So, panting and
perspiring, he resumed his run. Across London Bridge, the refuse-
swollen river gleaming dully in the sun. (The route, curiously,
was just the reverse of the one the elderly Mr. Briggs traversed
the night of his death.) Past old St. Saviour's, later to become
Southwark Cathedral, its tower grazed by a looming railway
viaduct. Into the Borough High Street, the brisk clop-clop of
the horse's hoofs, the ever more labored puffing of Stokes in pursuit. "I was so exhausted that I felt I should drop," he later told
the court. Before he did so, however, the cab stopped at the Hen
and Chickens. Not far away stood another policeman, whom
Stokes desperately accosted. This cooperative guardian of the
peace agreed to have a look into the matter. He went up to
where Wainwright was unloading the parcels with the cabby's
assistance, and, like Stokes earlier, began to open one. A horrified
glimpse, and he summoned a fellow constable, who joined him in
declining the £200 bribe Wainwright promised to have ready
for them in twenty minutes. Wainwright was arrested on the
spot.

Since Stokes, the lonely long-distance runner, does not appear again in the case, it may be noted here that after he testified to the strenuous part he played in Wainwright's apprehension, the judge awarded him £30 from the public funds for his
"perseverance." He had earned every shilling of it.

The prisoner Wainwright, custodian of those grisly bundles,
was a man of some consequence in the East End. The son of a
churchwarden who left an estate of £11,000, he had been a
member of Christ Church Institute of St. George's-in-the-East,
where he had been active in musical and elocutionary classes.
He also had participated in private theatricals and in 1867 was
lecturing, as far away as Leeds, on "The Wit and Eccentricity
of Sydney Smith." In earlier years he had promoted temperance
from the platform, but he seems subsequently to have lost his
convictions in this regard. His sociable inclinations as well as
his enthusiasm for the stage had brought him into the intimate

company of the management and artistes at the Pavilion Theatre, next door to his brush shop, and at their suppers a favorite recitation of his—an ominous choice—was Thomas Hood's famous poem, "The Dream of Eugene Aram."

Well-filled and satisfying though his leisure had been, his personal and business fortunes had declined. In 1872, being already in possession of a wife and several children, he had acquired a mistress, Harriet Lane, whom he set up in lodgings under the name of "Mrs. Percy King," and by whom he had two more children. By September 1874, however, his interest in this arrangement had faded, along with his ability to support it in the style to which it was accustomed. It was at this time that Harriet vanished from her place of residence, from which she was due soon to be evicted anyway, for drunk and disorderly conduct on the pavement outside.

The following month, whatever misgivings Harriet's friends and relatives may have entertained over her sudden disappearance were allayed by Henry's announcement that she had eloped to the continent for "a spree" with one Edward Frieake. Telegrams and letters were received to the same effect, signed by Frieake. This happened to be the name of a respectable Whitechapel auctioneer and longtime friend of Wainwright, who, upon learning of the unauthorized misappropriation, protested to Wainwright. In light of Frieake's current engagement to a young lady, who could be expected to take an intolerant view of his being romantically linked with another, we may well believe that those representations were fairly heated. Wainwright, amused, told his friend that he wasn't the fellow at all—the Teddy Frieake involved with the former Harriet Lane, more recently the *soi-disante* Mrs. King, was a younger man, a hanger-on in billiard saloons and similar places of entertainment. He was also a figment of Wainwright's imagination, except insofar as Henry had prevailed upon his brother Thomas to impersonate the said Teddy in his strategy of inducing Harriet to disappear.

The truth was that Harriet, in the flesh, had never left Whitechapel. Since approximately the day she was last seen at her lodgings, she had been reposing, with three bullets in her head and her throat cut, under the flagstone paving of the paint

room in the brush warehouse. Wainwright had thought to erase
her totally from the local scene by interring her with fifty pounds
of chloride of lime, purchased, it was proved at the trial, the day
before she left her lodgings.* He was one more victim of the vulgar error which assumes that when liberally applied to a dead
body put in earth, lime—any kind of lime—will quickly decom-
pose it. The Mannings had been on the right track when they
covered O'Connor with quicklime, although the quantity used
was insufficient for their purposes, and when the kitchen floor
was dug up, enough identifiable evidence of O'Connor survived
to hang them. Wainwright, despite what one must assume was a
superior education, chose chloride of lime, which, far from destroying flesh, has the quite opposite, and certainly undesirable,
effect of preserving it. It must have been a dark moment in his
life when, after all the trouble to which he had gone to dispose
of Harriet, he finally had to face the necessity of moving her
stubbornly existing remains from Whitechapel to Southwark.
That his well-laid plan had failed through a mere ignorance of
elementary chemistry must have rendered additionally disagreeable the chore of separating her into ten pieces for convenience
of packaging and shipping.

Even his misguided reliance upon chloride of lime, however,
might not have betrayed Wainwright, because if all had gone
well otherwise he might have transferred his bundles to the
former ironmongery and buried them there without anyone the
wiser. His crucial miscalculation amounted to no more than
failure to light his cigar soon enough. Had he done so the moment he extracted the bundles from beneath the straw, it is possible that Stokes would not have become inquisitive enough to
examine one of the bundles while awaiting the cab; especially
if (as the editor of the trial, H. B. Irving, sensibly observes) he
had given Stokes a cigar to smoke himself.

---

* This purchase, and the inquiries leading thereto among wholesalers,
acquired the sweet smell of legitimacy because in his line of work—"brushmaking" seems to have embraced the sort of merchandise now classed as
janitors' supplies—Wainwright was interested in providing "small stores"
to various purchasers, including, of all people, the police. In the last months
of his independent existence as a brushmaker, just after he killed Harriet,
he actually won a contract to provide the police with chloride of lime.

The record of Wainwright's trial, which led to his execution, is of substantial and variegated interest. Among the most curious of its aspects is the appearance of William Schwenck Gilbert's name as one of the barristers instructed for the defense in the police court hearing. Actually, it was Gilbert's way of getting out of jury duty. At this date he was no longer at the bar but instead was hard at work on *Broken Hearts,* a sentimental drama in blank verse. Having been called to jury service, he persuaded a friend to get him a nominal two-day brief in the Wainwright case so that, as a "practicing" lawyer, he could be excused. *Broken Hearts,* produced in December, was such a disaster that modern Gilbertians agree he could have spent his time better doing his duty as a citizen.

There could be no more vivid and authentic record than the trial provides of the physical and social ambience of an East London neighborhood at a moment in history. It is Charles Booth in miniature, without the sociology. The whole drama, as reconstructed from the witness box, occurs in perfectly ordinary houses, shops, and pubs, indistinguishable from a hundred thousand other ones in the Victorian metropolis except for the accident that they were somehow associated with a particularly macabre crime. The warehouse where Harriet was buried, a typical small-time business establishment, is portrayed with a detail impossible even to contemporary photography; for no photography could do justice to the Cockney complaints about the faulty drains and unremoved refuse piles which were the putative source of the disagreeable odor that had hung about the premises since Wainwright had deposited Harriet under the floor, nor could it explain the sudden disappearance of a dog which persisted too often in nosing in the vicinity of the paint room. Curiosity has been known to kill more than cats.

As in the Müller case, there is much information about occupational routines of the time. From several post office clerks, for example, we hear of the exact manner in which the G.P.O. at that date filed its daily accumulation of telegrams handed in at each office, numbering and docketing them. After being kept for a month, they were sent to be pulped. From a pawnbroker we learn that it was the custom to write only the last name of the customer on the ticket, then prefixing it with the generic "John" if it was a man, "Ann" if it was a woman. Tickets of goods that were redeemed were filed day by day and kept for two years.

We are enabled, also, to follow a perfectly unexceptional person, living in London in 1875, on a daily itinerary, just as Pepys enables us to do for the rounds of a quite exceptional person living in London in the 1660s. At 12:30 P.M. on September 10, Thomas Wainwright, the erstwhile "Mr. Frieake" who a year earlier had taken Harriet Lane on a fictitious spree to the continent, lunched with friends at the Black Lion, Bishopsgate Street. He was, as we have noted, out of employment, his ironmongery at the Hen and Chickens having been sold up. After lunch he went round to call on Henry, at work in the grain warehouse. Henry asked him to go and buy a garden spade and cleaver ("for chopping wood") at Mr. Pettigrew's nearby shop. The transaction at this (solvent) ironmongery was extended to a half-hour or forty-five minutes by his going out for a drink with Mr. Pettigrew. Mr. Pettigrew paid. Thomas then went by the warehouse to deliver the implements, charging his brother 5s. for what he had bought, at trade discount, for 3s. It was now 2:30 P.M., time for a spot of sherry at another public house. After this, to another place for dinner (a meal eaten in the middle of the afternoon at this date in some social circles), following which, back to the Black Lion; then to 1 Racquet Court, Fleet Street, at 4:30, and finally to the Surrey Gardens, a popular amusement spot, where he was with at least a dozen friends until 10:45 P.M. And so, Pepys-like, to bed. So minute a rendering of his movements that day supplied Thomas with an impervious alibi, for it was during those later hours that brother Henry was performing his butchery on Harriet's remains with the brand-new tool he had received, at a fraternal markup of sixty-six per cent, from Mr. Pettigrew's.

To the archaeologist, shards from a midden—prehistoric rubbish—are precious evidence of man's way of life before he learned to write. To the social historian, similarly, the contents of a man's pockets may illustrate the life of the time in a way no formal records do. What did a Whitechapel man in a small and

unsuccessful way of business carry with him on the day he took
a theatrical lady on a ride across the Thames? This is the inven-
tory made at the police station: £3 10s. in gold, 12s. 8d. in silver, some coppers, foreign coin, pawnbrokers' checks, twenty-
seven keys, a silver watch and metal chain, a tape measure, spectacles and case knife, rule, pencil case, two cigars (another had
been consumed during the cab ride), a memorandum book, and
a handkerchief. By contrast, Mr. Briggs, in a higher and more
prosperous way of life, carried with him four sovereigns, a florin,
10s. 6d. in silver and copper, keys, a silver snuffbox, a silk handkerchief—and half of a first-class railway ticket. He also had a
diamond ring on his finger and a gold fastening (for his watch
chain) attached to his waistcoat.

Details of mid-Victorian female costume: Harriet wore her
hair "done up in the back, with a large pad. . . . Her hair was
frizzed over the pad." The surgeon who inspected her remains
marveled—perhaps he was not a family man—at the formidable
contrivance the unfortunate lady bore, under the dictates of
fashion, on her head. In addition to a bullet embedded in it,
"There were also in the pad an immense quantity of hairpins.
. . . The hairpins in the pad were bent, broken, and rusty. They
were innumerable all over the pad, and sufficient to have arrested the progress of a bullet." History does not record what
effect, if any, this testimony had on the vogue for chignons.

Graphic vignettes of scene, habit, and character:

The testimony of an oilman neighbor in Whitechapel Road
who kept a pistol with him to practice marksmanship in odd moments: "I fired at anything I took it into my head to fire at." The
Lord Chief Justice: "Was it with the view of practising to make
yourself a shot, or at little birds hopping about, or had you any
particular mark to fire at?" Witness: "I had no particular mark."
(This in the midst of a crowded city!)

The sudden grim scene of shirtsleeved policemen digging
for evidential odds and ends at Harriet's late grave: "On the first
day," testified one of them, "we had candles and lanterns. In the
daytime it was perfectly light there from the skylight. Sometimes
children came round the door and looked through the keyhole

and watched us. There were fissures in the shutters, through which they looked when we were there." Slum children's free entertainment, a peep show with live actors.

And, by way of contrast, the delightful business of the third champagne glass: When Harriet was visited, shortly before her disappearance, by a gentleman (Thomas Wainwright, posing as Mr. Frieake), they sent her landlady, Mrs. Foster, across the street to a pub to buy champagne and borrow glasses.

Defense counsel, recalling the episode in his closing speech: "Mrs. Foster went and borrowed three glasses, and only two were used. There were only two persons for whom the wine came, and why did she get three? Possibly she thought they would ask her to take a glass."

Lord Chief Justice: "The same thought occurred to me."

Counsel: "I am happy to be confirmed by the Lord Chief Justice. Mrs. Foster was not asked to drink, and whether or not she thought the rising generation less polite than in her younger days, the disappointment was one likely to impress the matter upon her memory, and she said the bottles came upon two separate occasions, thereby flatly contradicting Mrs. Humphries' evidence." A landlady who has been pointedly not asked to share a bottle of champagne, even when she has brought her own glass, is not likely to have forgotten the incident or the surrounding circumstances.

From the human-interest point of view, then, Wainwright's is a most instructive case. Aesthetically, however, it is less satisfactory. Edward FitzGerald complained to Fanny Kemble that it was "a nasty thing, not at all to my liking." Like other spectators, he regretted that the Whitechapel brushmaker bore the same family name, less the medial *e*, that had been made famous many years earlier by the cunning activities of Thomas Griffiths Wainewright. There was a world of difference between an accomplished forger-poisoner and a hacker-up of a woman's body. So also thought Swinburne, who wrote in indignation to William Michael Rossetti: "I must express to you the deep grief with which I see the honoured name of Wainwright associated with a vulgar and clumsy murder, utterly inartistic and discreditable to the merest amateur. It is as though William Shakespeare were charged with the authorship (*pace Laureati*) of [Tennyson's] 'Queen Mary.'" This was a most unkind double-edged cut on Swinburne's part, but who can say that, strictly on the technical level, Henry the bungling brushmaker did not deserve it?

12

The Trouble
with Servants

KATE WEBSTER, 1879

A DURABLE Victorian assumption, energetically
promoted by *Punch,* was that policemen spent most of their time
in the kitchens on their beats, eating rabbit pie and flirting with
the cooks and parlormaids. Householders resented this open-
house policy, partly as taxpayers who felt they were not getting
enough municipal service for their money, partly as economists
who disapproved of feeding free-loading constables, and partly
as moralists who feared that under the sturdy guise of helmet
and tunic lurked the wiles of the seducer. They may have been
right. And yet one feels that, notwithstanding their annoyance,
they should have been grateful to have official protection on the
premises so much of the time. Given the all-too-notorious presence of murderers among the Victorian servant class, they
needed all the reassurance they could get. A policeman in the
house could reasonably mean added safety in parlor and bedroom, unless, like the hapless rural constables at Road House, he
was locked inside the kitchen.

The Victorian servant-neurosis originated in May of 1840,
when Courvoisier killed Lord William Russell. The event, wrote
the diarist Charles Greville, "frightened all London out of its
wits. Visionary servants and air-drawn razors or carving-knives

dance before everybody's imagination and half the world go to sleep expecting to have their throats cut before morning." A large concourse of menservants attended their colleague's execution. Nine years later, with Maria Manning, it was the ladies' turn. Maria had been in the service of the Duchess of Sutherland. It is not recorded whether there was a noticeable preponderance of maidservants among the tumultuous crowd that came to see her hanged—probably not, because it was harder for maids than for butlers, footmen, and valets to get time off, especially for frivolous purposes—but it is certain, at least, that the Manning case signally failed to strengthen employers' confidence in the reliability of their household staff. Particularly when it was revealed that in Maria's box, when she was arrested in Edinburgh, were found two letters of recommendation in which persons of the very highest rank attested to her kindness, affection, and pious inclination.

The social structure of the servant class mirrored that of Victorian society in general. There was the same hierarchical order, the same firm distinctions of rank and privilege. These depended upon the individual's position in the household, ranging in the case of men from the butler down to the groom and in the case of women from the housekeeper to the miserable kitchen maid and the "tweeny." They also depended, of course, upon the social class to which the household itself belonged. For these reasons, Courvoisier, a valet to a peer, and Maria Manning, a personal maid to a duchess, could be said to have belonged to the aristocracy of servant society.

They were therefore near the tip of the pyramid whose broad base comprised the bulk of the servant population. In 1861 they numbered well over a million all told—a few thousands more than the total employed in the textile industry. These hordes of domestic help worked in the households not of the rich or comfortable, but in the countless petty-bourgeois domiciles of people who could not afford more than one or two servants but had sufficient money—and it did not take much—to escape the ignominy of having none at all. For these lower middle-class householders there was a plentiful supply of cheap labor, girls from the workhouse such as Mrs. Snagsby's epileptic drudge in *Bleak House,* refugees from the oppressive life of the factory towns, peasant stock from the English and Scottish villages, and poor Irish, driven from their country by the terrible famine of the 1840s and the poverty and despair that knew no term. Of this last class in particular it may be said that their employment records probably could not have borne close inspection, and in some cases they also possessed unedifying police histories. One wonders if in many households equipped with this dubious sort of help there was not constantly an unhealthy tension, a vague sense of insecurity, bred not by any conscious memories of Courvoisier and Manning, who belonged to a quite distant, elevated sphere of servanthood, but by the all-too-obvious antecedents and dispositions of the pittance-waged menials currently on the premises.

Such certainly, in 1879, was the situation in the modest Richmond cottage of a widow in her middle fifties named Mrs. Julia Thomas. But before we look into her most sanguinary fate, our horizons will be broadened if we briefly review several antecedent cases whose worst features were combined in hers. Of these earlier cases, one anticipated the extraordinary procedure adopted by Mrs. Thomas's murderer, and the others the domestic situation which led to the bloodshed.

Between the Greenacre affair of 1836, in which the victim's remains were deposited in three locales, and the Waterloo Bridge mystery twenty-one years later, in which the body—though all (save the head) found in one place—was cut into twenty pieces, there had intervened a case which in this gruesome respect outdid them both. In 1851 the town of Norwich, not yet recovered from the Rush hysteria only two years earlier, was excited afresh by the recurrent discovery, here and there, of fragments of human flesh. The murderer, whoever he was, had done an astonishingly conscientious job on his victim, whoever she was; he had virtually diced her and strewn the results all over town. He had, in fact, realized Othello's expressed but unfulfilled desire to chop his own prospective female victim into messes. The case remained unsolved until 1869, when a Norwich publican and pawnbroker named William Sheward dropped into a London police station and confessed that it had been his first wife who had been so profusely distributed—by himself, an occupation requiring a week of full-time work. A prominent feature of the ensuing trial was the discomfiture of the two Norwich doctors who had reassembled the parts and confidently informed the coroner's jury that the victim had been a young woman of between sixteen and twenty-six years. They were now forced to eat their affidavits: the murdered woman was fifty-four at the time of her disintegration. Evidently Norfolk in the middle of the century was as backward in its medical forensics as, *teste* Dickens on the Rush case, it was in its police work.

Other murders which foreshadowed the Webster affair of 1879 had their roots in unsatisfactory labor-management relationships in a variety of homes. One, for instance, came to light on January 29, 1855, when a pair of boys looking for employment shoveling the newly fallen snow rang the bell at a house in Ordnance Terrace, Chatham. It was answered by a maidservant bleeding copiously from a cut throat; unable to speak, she pointed upstairs. When a doctor arrived at the house, he found the bludgeoned body of its occupant, a frail old lady named Catherine Bacon. When the maid Elizabeth Laws's injuries were attended to and she could again speak, she related a horrifying tale of how her late employer had been set upon in the cellar by two dustmen, who had used a cleaver so viciously as to leave bloodstains everywhere in the cellar and in the bedroom to which they dragged their victim's body. Then they had sliced Elizabeth's throat and departed.

This was, on the whole, a persuasive account, but one consideration thrust serious doubt upon its veracity, namely, the testimony of local pawnbrokers that Elizabeth had lately brought them certain portable belongings of Mrs. Bacon's. The girl was therefore charged with murder and tried. Great was the astonishment in court when, after lengthy deliberation, the jury delivered a verdict of acquittal. Rumor had it that the fly in the ointment had been one of the jurors, who belonged to a society agitating for the abolition of capital punishment. Anyway, Elizabeth was re-arrested on a charge of robbery, and upon conviction drew a six-month sentence. Now exempt from a revival of the murder charge, she told the true story of what had happened that snowy morning in Chatham. She had been in the habit of attending disreputable places of refreshment in the neighborhood and returning to Ordnance Terrace late at night, deep in her cups. At an interview in the cellar, her mistress took her to task for this unamiable dereliction, and Elizabeth, fed to the gills with Mrs. Bacon's nagging, seized a hatchet and struck her several blows on the head. The servant—not the apocryphal dustmen—then dragged the blood-bespattered old woman upstairs to her room, where, perceiving signs of life, she hit her liberally and conclusively with a piece of iron. Afterwards, when the snow shovelers rang the bell, Elizabeth, with admirable celerity of thought, contrived the story of the dustmen, cut her own throat, and opened the door.

In succeeding years there were other fatal encounters between mistress and maidservant, but the most sensational murder of this kind, because like Lord William Russell's it occurred in fashionable Mayfair, was that of Madame Riel in 1872. This lady lived in a house in Park Lane, her expenses being paid by General Lord Lucan, whose principal distinction in history is that it was his order to his brother-in-law, Lord Cardigan, which set in motion the disastrous charge of the Light Brigade. Madame Riel, like most of the employers who were done to death by a member of their household staff, was said to be a difficult person to satisfy. The latest servant who failed to do so, a Belgian named Marguerite Diblanc, received a month's notice; but notice was accompanied not by a month's wages, as was customary, but by a mere week's. Marguerite took issue with Madame Riel; Madame Riel was unable to appreciate her point of view; Marguerite throttled Madame Riel with a rope. Then, regaining her self-control, she helped herself to travel funds from what had suddenly become her late mistress' estate (in addition to the disputed severance pay and a few pieces of jewelry) and made for France. She was pursued, arrested, returned, tried, convicted, and sentenced to death, but her punishment later was reduced to penal servitude.

In the 1879 case of Kate Webster and Mrs. Thomas, the two themes of the painstaking dissector and the irritable maidservant neatly merge. Kate was an unfavorable specimen of a type which at best had little to recommend it. Thirty years old, Irish by birth, she had an imposing criminal record. Upon her arrival in England she had specialized for a while in lodging-house robberies, her technique being to apply for a room or even occupy one for a day or two and, while there, to lift any property of the landlady or the lodgers which appealed to her. As a result, she had been in and out of jail, one term of confinement having been the result of conviction on thirty-six charges of larceny committed in the vicinity of Kingston-on-Thames. When she was not incarcerated she was constantly on the move; during her years in London and the suburbs, she changed her habitation as often as her name. She had also had a murky love life resulting in a child to whom—anomalously, considering her inhumanity in other respects—she was attached by ties of genuine maternal solicitude.

No policeman with eyes sufficiently acute to qualify him for his job was ever likely to have looked upon Kate with sentimental longing, although he might well have been moved to appraise her from a professional standpoint. It is said that she had a "peculiarly sinister face, with . . . dark, gleaming and slightly oblique eyes"; she was "dark, morose"; she was "a compound of primitiveness, sharpness, greed, mother love, histrionic genius, extravagance, economy, sexual love, love of finery, sullenness, revenge, mendacity, coolness, cunning, self-possession, ungovernable fury, demoniacal savageness, and, over and above all, perhaps, superstition." She was, in fact, one of the most complicated and contradictory characters, servant-class or not, ever to come to the attention of Scotland Yard.

As might have been expected, things did not work out in Richmond. Mrs. Thomas was not an ideal employer—she was easily excited and vexed, and had a reputation among the neighborhood servants as something of a tartar—and Kate for her part was no paragon as a maid of all work. In her occupational role she was sloppy, surly, and irresponsible. After only a month, therefore, Mrs. Thomas gave her notice, and in the interval remaining before Kate's anticipated departure, for the sake of protection as well as of the added income which would help her sustain her pose of being a more genteel lady than she really was, Mrs. Thomas took in temporary lodgers. These, however, had left when, at the time stipulated for Kate's own leave-taking, she asked to be allowed to stay on for a few more days. Mrs. Thomas agreed, much, we may well believe, against her better judgment. No one need envy her state of mind thereafter; her situation was worthy of a Hitchcock film. Instead of writing her brother or her solicitor to ask their assistance in evicting this sinister creature, Mrs. Thomas temporized and, on Sunday evening, March 2, went to church and took the Sacrament. Her fellow communicants noticed that she was much upset. She had, as a matter of fact, come from an especially awful scene with Kate, who had returned from her Sunday afternoon outing late and noticeably the worse for drink. Despite all this, however, Mrs. Thomas went back to her house alone.

Kate was waiting for her. After bludgeoning her employer into submission, but not necessarily into total unconsciousness, she proceeded to mutilate, disembowel, and dismember her; a lengthy, laborious, and awkward procedure, especially since Kate, though muscular and possessed of great determination, was not practiced in this kind of operation. As the editor of the record of her trial remarks, "One cannot help thinking that once having begun it, she could never have carried it through to the bitter end had not her enjoyment of it more than equalled her anticipations." Having reduced Mrs. Thomas to manageable portions, she put them on the stove and boiled them, a procedure which accounted for the strong odor the neighbors noticed the next morning. More than once in her labors, pausing for refreshment, she repaired to the Hole in the Wall Inn nearby; the proprietress, a lady with the gladsome name of Mrs. Hayhoe, is reputed to have observed when the nature of Kate's exhausting activities became known, "I little thought when Kate came in and I chatted with her that she had left her mistress boiling in the copper." It was also said that a day or two later, when the product had cooled, "Kate went around amongst the neighbors, offering for sale two jars of fat, which she declared to be the best dripping." The record does not show that she made a sale, which was just as well for the comfort of Richmond suburbanites when they later read the newspapers.

It was quite a job to clean the utensils and set the house to rights after the rendering was complete; probably Kate, now liberated from the dictatorial presence of her employer, did a more thorough job than she had ever accomplished when Mrs. Thomas was still in health. Once these necessary chores were completed, however—by now it was Tuesday—she sallied forth in Mrs. Thomas's best clothes and paid a social call on acquaintances in Hammersmith, the family of a house painter named Porter, whom she had not seen for some time.* To them she announced that she had inherited a cottage in Richmond from an aunt and was now in process of selling it and its furnishings with a view to retiring to Ireland. She brought with her a black bag which she placed under the table as the group enjoyed tea. The bag, it later transpired, contained Mrs. Thomas' head, wrapped in brown paper.

After tea, Kate and the Porters' teen-age son returned to the Thomas house; on the way she disappeared for a little while, and on her return no longer possessed the heavy bag. At the cottage, she got him to help her carry an even heavier box to Richmond Bridge. It was a dark night. Kate made some excuse for the boy to leave her for a few minutes; he heard a splash; and the box was gone. It would turn up the next morning—the Wednesday following the fatal Sunday—downstream at Barnes. The discovery of the box, with its assortment of anatomical odds and ends, unfit for boiling, constituted the first intimation that

---

* It was the Porters' testimony especially which left a residue of information for the curious social historian. In accounting for their movements during their perilous involvement with Kate, they provided valuable details of the everyday routine an honest working-class family followed. We also are impressed by the way public houses were almost the sole fixed points in the physical and social topography of such people. Mentioned in the trial, either as places actually visited or as landmarks on a journey being retraced before the court, were, in addition to Mrs. Hayhoe's Hole in the Wall, the Rising Sun, the Oxford and Cambridge Arms (overlooking the Hammersmith racing reach, naturally), the Angel, the Bell and Anchor, the Anglesey, the Railway, the Thatched House, the Grapes, the Swakeley, and the Three Tuns. Daily life to these people seemingly consisted of movement from one pub to the next, even if they did not stop in—or, if they did stop, only to visit the water closet, as the Porter boy did.

There is also a modicum of instruction to be had from the revelation that in 1879 a jeweler was willing to pay 6s. for a second-hand gold dental bridge with two teeth on either side—the late Mrs. Thomas's, of course.

something was amiss in the Thames suburbs upstream from London.

Nobody in the neighborhood missed Mrs. Thomas, who had been something of a recluse, and outside the neighborhood, where she had not been known, Kate successfully passed herself off *as* Mrs. Thomas. Under this pretense she arranged for the sale of the widow's furniture and other effects to John Church, landlord of the Rising Sun tavern, Hammersmith, on whom she later tried to pin the murder and who, in the witness box, evinced a defiant inability to recall the circumstances of his earlier life, even in respect to the occupation he had followed or who had employed him. The sale proved to be Kate's undoing, partly because the arrival of a moving van aroused the suspicions of the next door neighbor, who owned the cottage, and partly because in a dress Church acquired he found a letter to Mrs. Thomas from a friend in another part of London. This friend, upon being visited by Church, who had himself become suspicious by now, readily confirmed that the "Mrs. Thomas" who had sold the cottage furnishings to him was an impostor. Furthermore, a dress which Kate had withheld from the sale—a black silk one, evil memories of Maria Manning—and which she left behind when she fled to Ireland, contained a letter from her uncle which helped the police, when they were finally called in, to trace her.

The belated discovery, more than two weeks after the murder, that Mrs. Thomas was missing, shed useful light on the origin of the box that had been brought ashore at Barnes. At the cottage the police found charred bones, a chopper, bloodstains which Kate had overlooked, and other evidence which explained all too adequately what had happened to Mrs. Thomas. The "Barnes mystery" which had occupied the papers for a fortnight was a mystery no longer.* Kate, brought back from Ireland, was tried at the Old Bailey in July. Despite her attempts to shift the guilt first to Church and then to Porter, both of whom luckily

---

* Just as it had begun to be a mystery, Kate and Mrs. Porter were inside Mrs. Thomas's cottage when a newsboy came along, yelling, "Supposed murder; shocking discovery of human remains in a box found in the Thames." Kate, not turning a hair, exclaimed, "I expect that's only a catchpenny, but we might as well have a paper," and went out and bought one. This coolness was entirely typical of her.

had stout alibis, she was condemned and hanged, leaving behind distasteful memories in Newgate, whose officials, though long inured to the language of desperate criminals, were appalled by the quality of Kate's.

The locale of executions having by this time been shifted to inside the prison walls, no immense delegation of Irish maid-servants gathered to witness her turning off. The newspapers, however, had another public event to cover: the sale by auction, undertaken by Mrs. Thomas's executors, of the effects Kate had illicitly appropriated. The reticent publican Church was a heavy purchaser, acquiring, among other mementos, the carving knife she had used. The cottage itself, however, was not in demand. Richmond was then a desirable neighborhood, as it remains to-day, but there were psychological disadvantages to occupying that particular property. When, finally, some intrepid people did take it, their worst trouble was in keeping servants, who were understandably uneasy over the memories of what their callous predecessor had achieved within those walls.

But elsewhere, as before, the shoe was on the other foot: it was the employers who worried, not the employees. Kate Webster's butchery simply intensified the effect already produced by Britain's succession of murderers from the servants' quarters. It was with good reason that many a nervous Victorian householder worried less about his staff's professional expertise than about their good will. The effect of Webster *et al.* undoubtedly was to make such householders scrutinize their prospective employees' credentials with extra care. (These, however, could not be expected to include any police record.) It also had the effect of making them more tolerant of their servants' shortcomings, forbearing to chide them for a summons unanswered, the brasswork unpolished, a roast of beef underdone. Anything for a sense, however ill-founded, that all was well below-stairs, and that the occasional queer look one detected on the face of a maidservant or even a footman was the result of dyspepsia from too rich food rather than anything personal. And yet, when we look at those quaint pictures of Victorian familial contentment in the parlor after dinner, Papa reading aloud from a religious novel, Mama busy with her needlework, the children disposed about the room in attitudes of innocent play—we cannot help wondering what apprehensions persisted somewhere deep in their minds: disquieting questions, that is, of what evil intentions were being weighed in the mind of that starchily capped maidservant we see lurking in the background.

13

Charley's Music Hall Turn

CHARLES PEACE, 1879

MURDER has many faces, most of them grotesque in one way or another. If—begging Aristotle's pardon, for he would have been revolted by the gratuitous amount of blood she shed—Kate Webster may be said to represent the mask of tragedy, her contemporary Charley Peace personifies the spirit of comedy. Alone among the celebrated malefactors of the Victorian era, he inspired the half-affectionate epithet of rogue. He captured the imagination of millions, and it is too bad that the broadside and chapbook had almost disappeared from the scene by the time his career reached its climax, for he was the material of which old-fashioned ballads were made. As it was, he did become a legendary figure about whom a whole body of romantic or amusing anecdotes grew up, to be propagated and amplified chiefly in boys' pulp papers.

In these papers, as in the marionette entertainments that continued to draw upon his career well into our own century, Peace was celebrated for his larcenous rather than his murderous achievements; he was a modern Jack Sheppard, committing his crimes with honest gusto, not a ruthless letter of blood. But, as is usually true of such figures, the romantic trappings of myth are belied by the prosaic facts. Charles Peace was, in truth, a conscienceless, mendacious villain, a lecher, a moral monstrosity. The fame he enjoyed for many years after his execution for murder was the result of his manner. He practiced his criminality with such an air, and he reminded one so often of star comedy turns in the music hall, that one tended to forget that he also killed people.

Apart from his claim—and none of his claims can be accepted without severe reservation—that his father was an animal trainer with Mr. Wombell's celebrated menagerie, Peace's antecedents are unknown. He began as a pickpocket specializing in fairs. Once, in pursuit of this vocation, when he was himself being pursued, he was forced to conceal himself for several hours in the ladies' lavatory tent. No captivity he later endured, and he endured many, brought back happier memories than this. Between 1854 and 1872 he was constantly in and out of prison, the usual charge being breaking and entering followed by larceny of greater or lesser degree. Penal servitude, indeed, was for him a way of life; he was a dedicated recidivist.

During the intervals when this old lag was engaged in more or less licit occupations, he made a living as a carver, gilder, picture-frame maker, hawker of small wares, and miscellaneous entertainer. In this last capacity he became known, in limited circles to be sure, as "the modern Paganini" and when in blackface as "the Great Ethiopian Musician." He was much in demand to support festivities at public houses, often with a single-stringed fiddle of his own construction, and he possessed, in addition to a wooden canary which could warble a tune, a number of conventional violins, some of considerable value though he had paid for none. One story has it that his musical talent extended also to playing difficult operatic selections on his teeth. He even turned up at schools, offering dramatic readings such as the Gravediggers' scene.

Peace seems to have had extraordinary equipment, both physical and temperamental, for acting. I have said that murder has many faces: so did Peace. He could manipulate his face, it is reported, so that he became completely unrecognizable even by his closest associates. He boasted that when his name was writ large on the WANTED posters, he often went to Scotland

Yard to read his physical description; nobody spotted him. In view of these accomplishments, it is a little anticlimactic to find that one of the chaplains who attempted to bring spiritual comfort to him in prison said that "in appearance he resembled a half-caste crossing-sweeper." This is not very kind, and yet it seems to do Charley Peace justice. However blind Scotland Yard may have been to his presence, his was not a figure easily overlooked. He was lame, or so it seemed: perhaps it was the assumption some people made on beholding his legs-apart walk, which suggests that he was bandy-legged. He was small, no taller than five feet four inches, and he had a maimed hand, a disadvantage he overcame to some extent by holding in it a false lower arm to which a stout iron hook was attached in the manner of Dickens's Captain Cuttle. Notwithstanding these manifold handicaps, he was agile and powerful, a monkey-like man to be feared. When, after sitting for his own wax portrait at Tussaud's, George Bernard Shaw inspected the Chamber of Horrors, he is reported to have lingered thoughtfully for several minutes before the figure of Charley Peace.

In 1875, after the fairly diversified career I have mentioned, Peace settled in a town near Sheffield, where he became acquainted with, and then a serious nuisance to, a couple named Dyson. He had originally framed some pictures for them, but in time he became an unwanted intimate in their home as well as a leering peeper through their windows. In the proceedings necessitated by the violent demise of Mr. Dyson, his widow was subjected to extended and strenuous cross-examination, the aim of which was to suggest that she had not, in fact, been married to her late "husband" and that she had had engagements with Peace in the attic of the empty house next door. However that may be, in 1876, in another suburb of Sheffield to which the couple had moved, allegedly to escape Peace's insistent attentions, Dyson was shot to death. Witnesses agreed that Peace had done it; there was no attempt at concealment. Nevertheless, Peace not only escaped but disappeared wholly from view. The view of the police, that is.

As they discovered when they eventually caught up with him, Charley made good use of the following months. His first necessity was to replenish his capital, and this he did by making a good haul of plate and jewelry from a gentleman's house at Hull and an equally satisfactory one of negotiable silk goods from a Nottingham warehouse. Some four or five months after Dyson's murder, Peace arrived in London and settled in Lambeth, where a wave of nocturnal burglaries immediately caused great consternation and puzzlement to the police, who had to admit to the press each day that "the gang," as they took it to be, had pulled yet another coup, but no suspects were in custody. When the Lambeth burglaries tapered off, a fresh series began downriver at Greenwich, where—though the connection was apparent to no one—a self-styled "gentleman of independent means" had just occupied a beautiful house, which he proceeded to furnish with no regard for expense. Night after night, the homes of leading Greenwich citizens were ransacked by a "gang" who not only operated with remarkable efficiency but showed great discernment in their choice of loot. The police were baffled, the public indignant, and the local papers full of letters to the editor.

Again a lull, and then, once more, a crime wave: this time in Peckham, where the gentleman of independent means, late of Greenwich, had moved to even more sumptuous quarters, accompanied this time not only by his wife, as she was called, but by a companion-housekeeper. He was now "Mr. Thompson," a resident well thought of by his new neighbors, who observed with approval that he went to church regularly and had musical tastes. His only peculiarity was that he liked to go to bed early. Nobody was then aware that he did not lie snug abed through the night, as is the habit of law-abiding people.

Hindsight is always wiser than perception attempted in the midst of events, and that is probably why nobody put two and two together: the larcenous persons operating in Peckham villas at night seemed to be unable to resist a good-looking violin whenever it happened to be stored near the family plate and jewelry—and simultaneously, Mr. Thompson's collection of violins was growing. At length he had so many that he could no longer accommodate them in his home, and he asked a neighbor if she would be so good as to let him store some in hers. Since

Mr. Thompson never played anything but sacred music, she was pleased to oblige him.

On the evening of Wednesday, October 9, 1878, the virtuous family at Peckham enjoyed, as was their pleasant habit, a little musicale, Mr. Thompson playing one of his treasured violins (one which later was traced to a pillaged home in Blackheath), one of his female associates singing and the other officiating at the piano. Mr. Thompson then went out on business. Early the next morning, at a villa in St. James's Park, Blackheath, a prowling constable intruded into the activities of a portico-burglar or, as we should say, second-story man, who in retaliation shot at him four or five times. The policeman, though wounded in the arm, grappled with the burglar and succeeded in detaining him until the arrival of reinforcements. Great were the joy of the police and the amazement of Peckham when the expertly elusive gang of housebreakers was revealed to be Charles Peace.

Peace, alias Thompson, also alias John Ward, was charged with burglary and feloniously shooting a constable, and was duly convicted and sentenced to penal servitude for life. But the Sheffield authorities were interested in him too, on a graver count, and arrangements were made to try him there. In January 1879, he was escorted onto a train, and in the course of the trip he was more than usually obstreperous. With apologies for the "disgusting" nature of the details, the editor of his trial record was forced to say plainly that Peace made "an excuse of necessity to leave the train at each stopping place"—there being as yet no lavatory accommodations on British trains—"and also behav[ed] in the carriage in a beastly and beastlike manner. . . . To put a stop to this behaviour, the warders provided a number of paper bags, and whenever Peace required one it was given to him and then thrown out of the window." Thus the right-of-way on the London-Sheffield line was littered with curious souvenirs of the progress of British justice.

After passing Worksop, Peace once again requested a bag, which he proceeded to use, or affected to use, his back being turned toward his guards in decent respect for their sensibilities. But he then varied the routine by following the bag out the window. Since the train was running at forty-five miles an hour and there was delay in communicating with the driver, it was halted only with some difficulty. The guards and trainmen, hastening back, found Peace somewhat battered but very much alive, and the hectic trip to Sheffield was resumed. He was deposited in the police station, where he made a big to-do of groaning, moaning, wishing he were dead, and otherwise salvaging as much as he could from the failure of whatever plan he had had in mind when he ejected himself from the train. No murderer ever came to human judgment in a touchier mood. The adjourned inquiry was held, in deference to the state of his health, in the candle-lit corridor outside his cell. As usual, Peace interrupted, complained of his ailments, and in general proved a most uncooperative prisoner. More or less recovered in body, though untamed in spirit, he was tried at the Leeds assizes and duly condemned for Dyson's murder.

Ordinarily, this would be the end of the story. But this is Charley Peace's story, which makes a difference. We revert to 1876, when Dyson was still living. In August of that year, there had been a sensational murder at Whalley Range, near Manchester, when a policeman named Cock was done to death. All suspicion pointed to one William Habron and his brother John, workingmen, who were known to have uttered threats against Cock. They were arrested and tried, and one brother, William, was convicted on what one must admit was impressive circumstantial evidence. His brother was acquitted. But two weeks after Peace's conviction, in February 1879, he stirred himself to write one of his magnificently illiterate letters. It began:

On the 27 & 28 of nov 1876 at Manchester assizes thare was tow brothers triad for the morder of Police man cox in Seymour Grove at Whalley range near Manchester ther was from seven to ten witnesses appeared against them & all of them but one perjered themselves against them to the uttermost. for I saw this trial myself & the only Person that spoke the truth was a civilian not the Lawyer's son for he did not speak the truth. The circumstances of the case are as folows.

Peace's narrative of the murder, for which he claimed responsibility, followed. According to him, the policeman had surprised him in the pursuit of his burglarious intentions. He concluded:

The two brothers who were charged with this Murder were named Frank [John] & Aaron [William] Harman. Frank was acquitted & Aaron was sentenced to death but recommended to mercy on account of his youth. & after wards repreved by the Secteary off State down to Life.

as a prooff of his in inosence, you will find that the ball that was taken out of coxs brest is one of Heleys No. 9 pinfire cartridge & was fired out of my revolver now at the leeds town Hall & if you take the ball out of one of Heleys No. 9 pinfire cartridge it & the one taken out of coxs body both will weight alike & allso bouth of them to fit into the one cartridge case. what I have said is nothing but the truth & this man is inosenc. I have done my duty & leve the rest to you.

Although considerable skepticism was expressed by the authorities, this document sufficed to win William Habron a pardon and an indemnity of £800.

Having done his good deed, Peace awaited his execution with equanimity. On the fatal morning he spent so much time in the lavatory as to arouse the concern of the warden, who had heard about the train trip. He then ate a hearty breakfast, complained about the quality of the bacon, smoked his clay pipe, delivered some pious sentiments to the gentlemen of the press, and made his final exit. It had been quite an act.

14

A Bedroom in Pimlico

ADELAIDE BARTLETT, 1886

"THE PIMLICO MYSTERY," as the papers called it, was and was not a mystery. Everyone was pretty sure who had killed Edwin Bartlett, and to the normally cynical mind the Why was reasonably clear; but the How is unexplained to this day. As if this ambiguity were not enough to recommend it to our attention, the case is a rare blend of drama and sociological interest. From the very days when it commanded the headlines, it cried out for imaginative transferal to stage or novel, but certain of the crucial facts, without which the story would have much less meaning, could not be intelligibly dealt with except at the risk of grave offense to spectator or reader. Today, of course, there are no such taboos, and the strange history of the *ménage à trois* in a flat in Claverton Street, a story involving a tantalizing scientific puzzle, secrets of the bedchamber, and a Methodist preacher acting as a reserve husband, is available to anyone desiring to revive its unquestionable glories.

Adelaide Bartlett, a pretty, pixyish lady aged thirty, had been born at Orléans, the natural daughter of "an Englishman of good position" who was never named in the case. In 1875 her father married her to Edwin Bartlett, ten years her senior, whom, according to her story, she had seen but once before the wedding. Bartlett used her dowry to expand his holdings in a chain of six South London groceries, a business which evidently was flourishing at the time of his death. Instead of setting up a home, however, Edwin sent his twenty-year-old bride to school for two years at Stoke Newington and later, for a year, to a Belgian convent. They cohabited—using the term in its most innocent sense—only during her holidays.

It can be divined from this that Edwin Bartlett was a rather extraordinary husband. His father, a demanding, vindictive person who made an unfavorable impression at Adelaide's trial, testified, in all probability unaware that he was quoting Juliet's nurse's affectionate reminiscence of her late husband, that Edwin was "a very merry man." And to a certain extent this was true. Even in the last days of his life, when he was troubled by symptoms suggestive of necrosis of the jaw and mercurial poisoning, he had a robust appetite for good food. On the very eve of his death he enjoyed half a dozen oysters at tea, jugged hare at dinner, and more oysters, as well as a chutney dish, at supper; and, figuratively rubbing his hands and licking his chops in anticipation, he desired that a large haddock be served at tomorrow's breakfast. He did not live to eat it.

But the catholicity of his sensual appetites, as we shall see, later became a matter of dispute. Along with his merriness, Edwin Bartlett entertained peculiar ideas. He believed in animal magnetism, and on one occasion, when his doctor asked him how he had slept, he answered, "I could not sleep; I was nervous and restless when I saw my wife asleep in the easy chair, so I got up and went and stood over her like this [holding up his hands] . . . for two hours, and I felt the vital force being drawn from her to me. I felt it going into me through my finger tips, and after that I laid down and slept." (Adelaide's comment: "That is a nice story. Imagine him standing for two hours and doing anything.")

Much more pertinent to the issue at hand than his exercises in reverse hypnosis, however, were his opinions respecting marriage. Witnesses testified that he believed a man should have two wives, one for companionship, the other for "use." Adelaide told Dr. Leach, the aptly named physician who became desperately entangled in the fatal proceedings, that, from the outset, she and Edwin had lived by a compact of platonic marriage. This, she said, was violated on only one single, solitary occasion, at her request; and on that lone occasion she conceived a child, which, however, was born dead. Apart from this instance, they had been as continent as Adam and Eve before the Fall.

Into this queer but supposedly tranquil arrangement came, or more precisely slithered, the Reverend George Dyson, a Methodist clergyman—no relative, apparently, of Charley Peace's victim at Sheffield. This pious young man immediately won the hearts of both Adelaide and her husband; soon after their acquaintance began, Edwin wrote Dyson a letter overflowing with gratitude that they had become such great friends, and a short time later he made a will leaving everything to Adelaide and appointing Dyson co-executor. When Dyson ventured to confide to Edwin scruples that occasionally afflicted him in respect to his relationship to the agreeable Adelaide, Edwin told him, in effect, not to give it a second thought. And so it was doubtless with the purest of consciences that the Reverend Mr. Dyson addressed to her the following verses, a fragment of literature which in its way is surely unique in the annals of British jurisprudence.

> Who is it that hath burst the door
> Unclosed the heart that shut before
> And set her queenlike on its throne
> And made its homage all her own—My Birdie.

Perhaps this was part of Adelaide's education; for at Edwin's request, Dyson called on her almost every day to supplement her formal schooling with lessons in Latin, history, geography, and mathematics. Poetry was not specified in the curriculum, and if the above quatrain is any sign, it may well not have been included. Dyson had good educational credentials—he was B.A., Trinity College, Dublin—but it was odd that he never brought any books with him on this didactic mission, and the kind of book that was later discovered in the Claverton Street rooms was instructive only in a rather special sense.

Dyson, or "Georgius Rex" as he soon came to be known *chez* Bartlett, practically took up his daytime abode there, and when husband and wife went to Dover on holiday, he visited them at their expense. The Bartletts even bought him a season ticket from Putney, where he nominally resided, to Waterloo station, from which he could easily take a bus or even walk to Pimlico.

In the flat they kept an old serge jacket and carpet slippers into which he could slip from his inhibitive clerical garb. It is not pertinent to inquire what was happening to the souls of his Wesleyan flock meanwhile.

Edwin's psyche, it may be said at this point, would have been of much interest to the young Viennese neurologist who, in the very season of Edwin's death, was enjoying his fruitful collaboration with Charcot in Paris and would, in the following autumn, return to Vienna to begin to apply his emerging principles of psychoanalysis to live patients. If Freud, as firm a believer in mesmerism as Jean Martin Charcot on the one hand and Edwin Bartlett on the other, had exercised the art upon the latter, he might have learned much that remains obscure to us, confined as we are to the court record. Or, for that matter, nearer at home Havelock Ellis might have been professionally interested in the odd ways of this middle-aged Pimlico husband. With Edwin's enthusiastic blessing, Adelaide and Dyson indulged the pretty habit of kissing each other in his presence. Besides appointing Dyson co-executor of his will, Edwin designated their clerical friend to have reversionary rights to Adelaide after his death. Thus Dyson had the privilege of being Adelaide's fiancé even while her husband lived and relished his jugged hare. It was all very companionable. And although a servant testified that she had once entered the room to find Adelaide sitting on the floor with her head resting against the minister's knees, at no time in the trial was any allegation made that their relationship had exceeded what might be called, in a late Victorian context, the bounds of liberal propriety.

But this domestic idyll was interrupted in mid-December 1885 by Edwin's sickness. He showed signs of mercurial poisoning which were never explained, although it must be stressed that neither Adelaide nor their friend was shown to have had anything to do with it. He also had trouble with his teeth, the result of a botched job some time earlier when an incompetent dentist had sawed them off, not removed them, for the fitting of plates. He was currently in the unpleasant process of having his mouth renovated; in four visits to another dentist, eighteen badly diseased teeth were pulled. The last of these sessions occurred on the last day of the year and, as it proved, the last day of his life. In view of what happened that night, it is noteworthy that Edwin required longer than the usual dental patient to be put to sleep. He seems to have had a constitutional resistance to anesthesia.

Notwithstanding these physical trials, however, Edwin remained a merry man. According to Dr. Leach, Adelaide told him that "Edwin sits in his armchair and cries an hour at a time; and when I ask him about it, he says it was because he was so happy." It is hard, therefore, to understand why anyone should wish to upset the delicate balance of happiness with which all three were blessed at this moment. But on December 28, Adelaide had prevailed upon Dyson to buy, at three separate chemist's shops, considerable quantities of chloroform. Edwin, she said, had been suffering for the past half-dozen years from an unspecified "internal complaint" which sometimes caused him paroxysms of pain, and it was to relieve these that chloroform was needed. Dyson, however, told the chemists, two of whom attended his chapel, that he wanted it to remove some grease spots. However reprehensible we may find a reverend clergyman's cool infraction of the biblical law against telling fibs, it is to his credit that he disdained using the old arsenic-and-rat routine.

After his return from the dentist on New Year's Eve, Edwin was in excellent spirits and, as we have seen, looked forward to a large haddock for breakfast.

Ring out the old, ring in the new. That night Adelaide, watching by his bed as usual, dropped off to sleep. A week or two earlier, upon Dr. Leach's protesting that she might as well go to bed at night, since her sitting up added nothing to her husband's comfort, she had replied, "What is the use of my going to bed, doctor? He will walk about the room like a ghost. He will not sleep unless I sit and hold his toe." "The drollness of the expression," Dr. Leach commented, "fixed itself upon my mind." The drollness of the expression was matched by the drollness of the act itself; but Adelaide, who seems to have taken her husband's foibles seriously, persisted in this wifely ministration. When she awoke early New Year's morning, holding, if not his toe then at least his foot, he, and it, was cold. An autopsy was called for, and the chief examiner reported that the smell issuing from the stomach was that of a "freshly opened bottle of chloroform."

It was immediately after this revelation that Adelaide told Dr. Leach the remarkable story of her marital existence with Edwin, some aspects of which we have already noted. She averred in addition that in the last weeks of his life, Edwin had shown unmistakable signs of reneging on their compact. But this, she said she pointed out to him, would be unfair to her as a woman as well as to her intended. To accede to one's husband's desires would constitute unfaithfulness to one's fiancé. So, to quell Edwin's ardor whenever it arose, she kept some chloroform in a drawer near their bed, to sprinkle on a handkerchief which she would then gently wave before her lustful mate's nostrils, "thinking that thereby he would go peacefully to sleep." She did not attempt to explain how the liquid chloroform entered his system from the bottle on the mantelpiece (whither it had been transferred from the drawer). Defense counsel, however, completed the story by postulating that after a chat on the subject of their renunciation of platonism, that festive New Year's Eve, Edwin, after acknowledging the justice of her views, decided to speed her and George's happiness by removing himself from the scene via the chloroform. This hypothesis had a distinct air of desperation.

Still, the prosecution too was at a disadvantage, because this was the world's first case of alleged murder by chloroform. Medical witnesses, including Dr. Thomas Stevenson, who had succeeded Alfred Swaine Taylor in the chair of medical jurisprudence at Guy's Hospital and edited Taylor's standard works on the subject, agreed on cross-examination that liquid chloroform, whether taken intentionally or administered by someone else, would cause the recipient such pain as to force him to scream and would leave seared places in his mouth and throat. Yet nobody, including the landlord and his wife, who lived upstairs, had heard any sounds from the sickroom that night. The only way a murderer could hope to administer liquid chloroform without causing strenuous resistance would be to render the victim unconscious first. Yet here too was a seemingly insuperable difficulty, because unconsciousness also meant loss of the power to swallow. Dr. Stevenson allowed that theoretically there might be a brief interval during which "the patient might be so far insensible as not to feel the pain and yet sufficiently sensible to be able to swallow." But not even an expert could prove the existence of such a period, or when it might occur, or how long it would last. How, then, could a mere inexperienced woman succeed?

Despite the evidence against her, therefore, as the trial neared its end Adelaide probably was ahead on points. But her counsel, the great courtroom advocate Edward (later Sir Edward) Clarke, Q.C., M.P., almost undid his case by calling back to the stand, after the prosecution's closing speech, the nurse who had attended Adelaide when she gave birth to the stillborn child. Knowing how fantastic was Adelaide's story of her non-fleshly marriage, Clarke wished to prove that it had not been concocted, for Dr. Leach and thence for general distribution, *after* Edwin's death. Here was the great moment of the trial, one of the most sensationally dramatic moments in the history of English justice:

Q. At the time you nursed Mrs. Bartlett in her confinement, did you become aware from anything she said to you with regard to its having been the result of a single act?
A. Yes, sir.

Good. The defense was eminently satisfied. But then, to Clarke's horror, Mr. Justice Wills, who had often interposed peppery questions of his own during the examination of witnesses, spoke up:

Q. What was it [that is, what the nurse had been told]?
A. That it happened only once—on a Sunday afternoon.
Q. She said so?
A. Both of them; that there was always some preventive used.
Q. You say you had that from both of them?
A. Both of them.

So the elaborate tale of the platonic marriage was, at the very last moment, shaken; and it was toppled, during the judge's summing-up, by his recalling the testimony of a policeman who had found four or five French letters (contraceptives much favored by the Victorians) in Edwin's trousers pocket. Why, if Edwin had been as indifferent to a tumble with the ladies as he was alleged to have been, did he possess those surreptitious articles? Perhaps, of course, they had been for use outside the domestic establishment; but, as the judge said, the testimony of the nurse suggested that they might equally well have been called into requisition in connection with Adelaide. "And then," he continued as defense counsel blanched,

what becomes of this morbid romance about the non-sexual connection, and what becomes of the man with such exalted ideas about matrimony that he thought the wife whom he elected for his companion too sacred to be touched? The whole foundation for that baseless illusion is swept away by the one sentence which you heard in the witness-box today. . . . And if the one little grain of truth which is generally to be found in any romance, in any story of falsehood, be found in these articles and in the use habitually made of them between husband and wife, what becomes of the whole story of the use for which the chloroform was wanted?

It was a compelling argument, but in the end the eloquence of Clarke's closing speech, which has been called "a classic of forensic oratory," prevailed.* The jury returned the English equivalent of Not Proven by expressing grave doubts about Adelaide's innocence but concluding that the evidence was not strong enough to convict her.

The courtroom erupted in a joyous roar. Adelaide fainted and was removed from the dock. Giving way to his emotions for the first and only time in his fifty years at the bar, Clarke dropped his head on the desk before him and sobbed. The fashionable ladies who had sat through the trial, wearing seasonable primroses and, according to the *Pall Mall Gazette*, drinking "deep draughts from stimulating bottles," passed from the tumult within to an even greater one outside, where their carriages waited; "their limbs," commented the reporter, who seems to have used empathy where observation failed, were "still quivering from

* In her letter of thanks to her counsel, Adelaide wrote, "I have heard many eloquent Jesuits preach, but I never listened to anything finer than your speech." Presumably her extensive experience of Jesuit pulpit oratory was not acquired while she was in the company of the Wesleyan Mr. Dyson.

their pleasant excitement. 'It is all over now. When shall we drink such another draught?'" When Clarke emerged into the Old Bailey courtyard, the jurymen were gathered to shake his hand in congratulations, and a cheering crowd ran alongside his brougham as it made its way through the rainy streets. The evening papers came out with great headlines, and "as one walked along from Newgate to Charing Cross, almost everyone was bending over his paper, and one heard Mrs. Bartlett's name on every tongue." That night at the Lyceum Theatre, where Clarke went to see Henry Irving in *Faust*, the audience's cries were for Adelaide's triumphant lawyer, not for the actor on the stage. But it had been a near thing.

The subsequent fates of Adelaide and the Reverend Mr. Dyson seem not to be known. It is at least certain that they went their separate ways; for as the judge observed in a passage of his summing-up in which he excoriated Dyson as man and as man of God, if anything was clear in this shadowy case, it was Dyson's anxiety to save his own skin. On the whole, one may doubt that he resumed his Methodist ministry. As for Adelaide, whatever became of her, she had earned a permanent niche in the history of science. Sir James Paget, the eminent surgeon, is reported to have remarked, "Once it was over, she should have told us, in the interests of science, how she did it." No Victorian murderer could have wished a finer accolade.

Nor was it only her unprecedented and inexplicable feat of killing a man with liquid chloroform that testified to Adelaide's genius for invention. There was, in addition, that bizarre narrative of the connubial arrangements in Claverton Street. But its persuasiveness did not match its audacity. Mr. Justice Wills was right to call Dyson's story of Bartlett's pressing him to persevere in his intimacy with Adelaide, despite Dyson's doubts of the ethics involved, one of "almost revolting improbability"; and no less could be said for Adelaide's concomitant account. And the key that destroyed its plausibility was found in Edwin's trousers pocket. "I had a strong suspicion," the judge said, "that, before the case was over, they [the contraceptives] would throw some light upon the matter. I little anticipated what it would be. It

did occur to me that this story told to Dr. Leach was the poet-
icized version of the use of these French letters." It was difficult,
he continued, after the nurse's recall to the stand and her shat-
tering answer, "to elevate these people into the hero and heroine
of an extraordinary sensational romance. It looks much more as
if we had two persons to deal with abundantly vulgar and commonplace in their habits and ways of life."

Again he was right, of course. Adelaide's confidences to Dr.
Leach were worthy of the queens of the sensation fiction papers,
where she may have found her basic inspiration, though the
embellishments probably were suggested by an imagination
stimulated also by a book which played an important role in
the trial. It is here that the Bartlett case contributes most signally
to our knowledge of that most secretive aspect of the Victorians'
private lives, about which we have only lately begun to be a
little more accurately informed, namely their sexual habits. The
book in question, the only book possessed by the Bartletts of
which we hear anything, was *Esoteric Anthropology (The Mysteries of Man): A Comprehensive and Confidential Treatise on
the Structure, Functions, Passional Attractions and Perversions,
True and False Physical and Social Conditions, and the Most
Intimate Relations of Men and Women,* by Thomas Low Nichols,
M.D., F.A.S., an American doctor unlicensed to practice in
Britain, where he resided at the time of the trial. *Esoteric Anthropology* was one of a fair number of contemporary treatises,
some with grandiose and deliberately obscure titles, some plainly
and more or less honestly purporting to be works on physiology
and personal hygiene, which dealt in detail or glancingly with
"Malthusianism": that is, to continue the Victorian euphemism,
with practices and devices which would serve as prudential
checks to the production of offspring.

The history of birth control in Victorian times is very poorly
documented. Because it was not a subject for open discussion,
modern historians are handicapped by a paucity of dependable
and relatively plain-spoken contemporary material. But it is
known that following the Malthusian campaign of the journeyman breeches-maker and radical reformer Francis Place in the

1820s there were four decades in which little was written about birth control. The subject was resumed in the late sixties and early seventies, and in 1877 the famous case of *Regina* v. *Charles Bradlaugh and Annie Besant* gave it the most extensive publicity it had yet enjoyed. The case concerned the alleged obscenity of a work of the *Esoteric Anthropology* genre, *The Fruits of Philosophy*, by another American, Charles Knowlton, which had first been published in England, without any stir, in 1841. Thanks to the free advertising the trial afforded, 125,000 copies of this book were sold in three months, a sufficiently impressive index of the widespread public interest in birth control. Meanwhile, as testimony in the trial revealed, similar works sold steadily, year by year and without interference, in the most reputable bookshops and on railway stalls.

The sworn presence of *Esoteric Anthropology* and contraceptives in the Bartletts' rooms is a valuable, because rare, fragment of historical evidence. It suggests how extensively the knowledge and practice of birth control had been disseminated by the mid-eighties, and it supplies a documented example of one reason why the birth rate among the middle class declined in the latter half of the Victorian era. No historian of late Victorian morals and mores nor any student of population trends has, I think, used this trial to illustrate the prevalence of contraceptive information and practice at the time.

And although Adelaide was herself no bluestocking and no feminist, in her sexual role, if we read it aright, she may be regarded as an immediate precursor of the "New Woman" of the nineties, who claimed the right to free love and evasion of motherhood. The intimate policy and practices in Claverton Street obviously were the result of Edwin's idiosyncrasy rather than ideology, but it is interesting to note that the Bartletts' marital arrangements came into public view at the very time that the women's emancipation movement was gathering momentum. Two influential papers setting forth advanced ideas on women's rights, "The Woman Question" and "Socialism and Sex," by the socialist university lecturer and eugenicist Karl Pearson, appeared, respectively, in the year preceding the trial and the year following it. Whether or not Adelaide and Edwin were even aware of the currents of advanced thought in respect to love and marriage in the late 1880s—and nothing adduced at the trial suggested they were—their rejection of the strict ideal of monogamy in favor of a permissiveness governed by spontaneous emotional preference and their use of contraceptives in preference to the Malthusian "prudential continence" had the accidental effect of identifying them with the avant garde. Thus, in its own special way, the Bartlett case is closely linked to a particular moment in history.

Judge Wills, however, saw nothing of potential historical value in the revelations from the witness box. He was lengthily caustic about books like *Esoteric Anthropology*—"garbage" which "under the garb of ostentatious purity, obtains entrance, probably, into many a household from which it would be otherwise certain to be banished." It was undoubtedly the perusal of its evilly instructive and stimulating pages that "unsexed" countless women, who thereby were rendered willing, nay eager, to hear the minutest details of the sordid case now nearing completion; and in the special instance of Adelaide Bartlett, he said, "one has learnt today what is the natural and to be expected consequences of indulgence in literature of that kind."

Perhaps so, perhaps not. Adelaide's reading alone cannot account for her inventiveness. She was a magnificent natural improviser, and it is impossible not to believe that talents like hers were squandered both on the technique with which she disposed of her odd husband and on the extravagant coloration she gave to her purported relations with him. Her genius deserved a loftier arena, a wider scope.

Similarly, one feels that Mr. Justice Wills's moralizing was not worthy of the case or of the judge himself, who deserves a special word before we take leave of him and the fair Adelaide of whom he so obviously disapproved. Of all the judges whom we watch presiding over famous Victorian trials, he is among the most interesting—and the most complex. We have noted how his worldly wisdom, his cynical shrewdness, enabled him to see through the bogus romanticism of Adelaide's version of her love

life with Edwin and to deduce the significance of the French letters. He seems to have labored under few illusions as to the
moral strength, not to say the probity, of his fellow men. The
evidence of their weakness in the Bartlett case saddened him but
did not surprise him, and we sense that his denunciation of
printed "garbage" was more or less *pro forma,* the sort of thing
any Victorian judge would have felt obliged to say. Yet it was
this same judge who, ten years later, charging the jury in the
Oscar Wilde–Alfred Taylor trial, declared, "I would rather try
the most shocking murder case that it has ever fallen to my lot
to try than be engaged in a case of this description," and who,
addressing the defendants after the jury had found them guilty,
said: "It is no use for me to address you. People who can do
these things must be dead to all sense of shame, and one cannot
hope to produce any effect upon them. This is the worst case I
have ever tried. . . . That you, Wilde, have been the centre of a
circle of the most hideous kind among young men, it is equally
impossible to doubt." In contrast to the cheers of approval after
Adelaide Bartlett was acquitted, Mr. Justice Wills's sentence of
Wilde to two years at hard labor drew cries of "Oh! Oh!" and
"Shame!"

No contradiction is necessarily involved, of course. The
moral indignation evoked by each of the two cases was of very
different quality. At the turn of the century, sodomy was a
virtually unspeakable offense, while murder, with or without
adultery, was at least a fairly commonplace and comprehensible
transaction. Moreover, Wills, as the record of his interventions
and charge to the jury in the Bartlett trial makes clear, had a
divided nature. One side of him was experienced, unflappable;
the other side was puritanical, morally intolerant, in the gravest
Victorian tradition. His role in the Bartlett case is a study in
contrasts.

His moralizing, *in re* Bartlett no less than *in re* Wilde, has
not worn well. But no one could possibly fault one dictum of
his, in the course of his summing-up, which is as sage in the
ways of the world as it was on the day it was uttered from the
bench in the Old Bailey: "When a young wife and a younger
male friend get to discussing, whether in the presence of the hus-

band or out of his presence, the probability of his decease within a measurable time, and the possibility of the friend succeeding to that husband's place, according to all ordinary experience of human life that husband's life is not one that an insurance office would like to take at any premium."

15

Arsenic and the Lady from Alabama

FLORENCE MAYBRICK, 1889

THE CASE OF Florence Maybrick offers, if any-
body is disposed to look at it that way, a fortuitous conjunction
of Jack the Ripper and Henry James. The former's association
with Mrs. Maybrick is chronological: the sixth victim attributed
to him by some authorities, and, as it turned out, the last according to anyone's count, was found on July 18, 1889, and her
trial opened in Liverpool thirteen days later. Henry James's association is of a very different, much subtler sort, perhaps not really
demonstrable: but one thinks of him because Mrs. Maybrick
participated in that memorable exodus of marriageable young
women from America to Europe between the end of the Civil
War and the turn of the century which so often hovers in the
background of James's fiction. It is altogether too fanciful to see
her as a small-scale, bourgeois replica of a Jamesian heroine—
an Isabel Archer, a Milly Theale, a Maggie Verver—and yet . . .

Mrs. Maybrick was born Florence Elizabeth Chandler, the
daughter of a banker in Mobile, Alabama; her husband, twenty-
four years older than she, was a Liverpool cotton merchant temporarily resident in America, where they were married in 1881.
There is delicious reverse snobbery in the statement of James G.
Blaine, secretary of state in Benjamin Harrison's cabinet, when

he wrote in support of his countrywoman's reprieve: "That she may have been influenced by the foolish ambition of many American girls for a foreign marriage, and have descended from her own rank to that of her husband's family, which seems to have been somewhat vulgar, must be forgiven to her youth, since she was only eighteen at the time of her marriage."

The story of the Maybrick murder is a simple one, the complications in the trial record being almost exclusively due to the battle of the toxicologists being once more rejoined. On May 11, 1889, James Maybrick died "under mysterious circumstances" in his home, after an illness attended by many distressing symptoms. The principal evidence against his wife was the presumption of motive. In March she had spent a few nights in London with another man, and later the same month, after their return from the Grand National Steeplechase, where they had happened to meet him, she and her husband had had a violent argument in the course of which he had given her multiple bruises and a black eye. Only the pleas of a servant and the family doctor dissuaded her from leaving him. Moreover, a month later, a week or so before her husband's final illness began, she had bought flypaper at a chemist's, even though flies were not yet in season and there was some flypaper left in the kitchen from last year. A servant saw her soaking the paper in her bedroom basin to remove the arsenic coating. Her explanation, following in the hallowed steps of Madeleine Smith, was that she wanted to make a cosmetic solution to clear her complexion, as she was planning to accompany her husband to a ball. As at Madeleine's trial, some evidence was produced that arsenic was occasionally favored as a complexion aid or, alternatively, as a depilatory cream. Another chemist from whom Mrs. Maybrick had bought a dozen flypapers in April said, "I can speak to the fact that ladies came to buy fly-papers when no flies were about." But the line of inquiry this statement invited—the possibility that certain other ladies' husbands subsequently died of violent gastric disturbances—was not pursued.

Combined with this indisputable possession of arsenic was the fact that Maybrick's nurses reported some apparent sleight-of-hand on his wife's part with the beef juice that the doctor had ordered given to the patient. A search of the house after his death revealed the presence of arsenic in tiny or more significant amounts on a rag, in one of Mrs. Maybrick's handkerchiefs, in a bottle of aperient mixture, in a bottle of glycerine, in a packet marked "Poison for Cats" (*sic*—not "rats"), and elsewhere. All told, the analysts estimated that the arsenic found scattered about the house was enough to kill fifty people. But all this was circumstantial evidence, and in its totality it did not constitute a crushing case against the young woman.

A comparison of this trial with, say, those of Palmer, Pritchard, Smethurst, and Madeleine Smith in 1856–65 reveals how far the Age of Science had progressed since those remote days when the sciences of toxicology and of forensic medicine in general were in their hesitant, inexperienced infancy. The medical evidence which occupies by far the greater part of the Maybrick transcript—the scene of virtually the whole reconstructed drama is the victim's sickroom—has a much more scientific air about it, a greater assumption of authority. Home Office analysts were not forced to admit, as Dr. Taylor had, that the poison revealed by their analysis was derived from their analytic tools. But the trouble was that along with heightened authority should have come consensus; and no such consensus was reached. The doctors disagreed as violently as ever.

Was Maybrick's death really caused by arsenic? Some expert witnesses deposed that it was, while others, equally expert, deposed with equal assurance that it was not. The defense labored mightily to show that he suffered from gastro-enteritis. Certain it was that, despite a basically healthy constitution, he was a hypochondriac of long standing, addicted to taking all kinds of medicines. Medicines were a favorite topic of his in conversation, and he eagerly followed the tips of his friends, sometimes doubling the recommended dose to be sure of good results. Evidence was brought from Norfolk, Virginia, where he had lived for a time, and from Liverpool itself, to the effect that he had sampled virtually the whole pharmacopoeia, with special attention to substances normally deemed lethal in sufficient quantity but including also such relatively benign items as quinine compound, cardamom pills, and seidlitz powders. He was in the habit of dropping into a chemist's shop in downtown Liverpool from two to five times a day for a "pick me up" laced with liquor arsenicalis, the quantity of which was steadily increased over ten years. If this suggests sheer aberration on the part of the cotton broker, it must be noted that, as his chemist testified, many other level-headed businessmen he knew liked their daytime potations strengthened with arsenic. Whatever the practice says about Maybrick personally, it says a good deal more about the pressures of Liverpool business life.

By May 1889, one would therefore assume, Maybrick had built up a high tolerance for a wide range of chemicals, pharmaceutical and non-pharmaceutical, against those last days when, as a letter to *The Times* after the trial put it, his stomach served as "a druggists' waste-pipe." For his malady, whatever it was, his doctors prescribed, in addition to measured doses of arsenic, a variety of substances including strychnine, jaborandi, cascara, henbane, morphia, prussic acid, papaine, and iridin. It was a formidable intake for a patient of whom one physician testified, "He seemed to be suffering from nervous dyspepsia. I should say that he was hypochondriacal." But neither nervous dyspepsia nor hypochondria would seem adequate to account for the voluminous and disagreeable symptoms Maybrick suffered toward the end, except on the not unreasonable premise that the curative regimen was worse than the disease. In view of his well-attested appetite for those many drugs, one wonders why his wife should even have been suspected of doing away with him. If she was intelligent enough to soak flypaper in a basin, she was also surely intelligent enough to realize that nature or the doctors, or both, would eventually do her work for her. Still, considering how long and scathelessly he had been ingesting those potions and powders, she may be forgiven for doubting that in his case nature was to be much relied upon.

The technical and contradictory nature, repetitiveness, and often the repulsiveness of the medical testimony do not recommend the trial record to the layman's attentive reading. But it is lightened by occasional passages in which the atmosphere and action of the courtroom are vividly evoked. At one point, for example, an expert witness handed in as evidence a glass tube containing a "film" composed of arsenic crystals obtained from Maybrick's liver. The judge, James Fitzjames Stephen, tried two high-power magnifying glasses but was unable to see the film and asked defense counsel to point it out to him. Counsel very properly admonished, "You must look for it yourself, my lord." Stephen tried again, this time with the court chaplain's slate hat as background. "After a pause of some time, during which the court was silent, his lordship handed back the tube to the jury, with his two glasses, explaining that one was much more powerful than the other, but the more powerful one required to be so near to the eye on the one hand, and so close to the object on the other, that it was very difficult to manage. The jury then proceeded to use the glasses of his lordship, the black coats of their fellow-jurymen being used as a background."

That the judge had to be instructed by counsel as to his proper conduct when presented with an exhibit is a small indication of what was, in fact, a governing circumstance in the trial: his evident incompetence. James Fitzjames Stephen, a brilliant lawyer, legal historian, and man of letters, had become a judge of the high court in 1879. But by now it was obvious that his mental powers were no longer what they had been. H. B. Irving wrote of this disturbing state of affairs with exemplary delicacy:

It is impossible for the historian of the Maybrick case to ignore the statement, frequently made, that at the time of her trial the judge's mind was suffering from the early attacks of an insidious disease which, two years later, compelled Sir James to retire from the bench. The judge had had a slight stroke of paralysis at Derby in 1885, and been obliged to give up work for a time. Whether on his return to work his mind had entirely recovered its former vigour, or was suffering a gradual loss of strength, is a matter that need not be discussed. But those familiar with the judge's powers during his earlier years on the bench may well doubt, in reading the report of Mrs. Maybrick's trial, whether those powers were as conspicuous and effective in the trial of her case as they would have been had it taken place some few years before. Of the judge's scrupulous anxiety to be fair, just, and considerate towards the prisoner no impartial reader can doubt.

Perhaps it is unfair to cite the following excerpt from his summing-up as evidence of his failing intellect, but to most Englishmen it would be otherwise inexplicable: "The next date after that took place is the Grand National something. I don't know whether it is a race, or a steeplechase, or what it is—but it is something called the Grand National, as if everybody knew what the substantive was—but the Grand National took place on the 29th March." Counsel at the bar and spectators must have mentally shaken their heads at such ignorance. In any case, Stephen's conduct of the trial called forth much sharp comment in both the press and the legal profession and provided the chief basis for later action in Mrs. Maybrick's behalf. Stephen left the bench two years later, was created a baronet, and died in a private asylum in 1894.

Florence Maybrick was found guilty and was sentenced to death. But the case had aroused so much interest, and her plight so much sympathy, that almost half a million persons throughout the kingdom signed petitions to the Home Office urging her reprieve. Among those who circulated the petitions were members of the Liverpool Exchange (who obtained signatures over quick ones laced with arsenic at the corner chemist's?) and medical men, who argued that the quantity of arsenic found in Maybrick's body was too small to have caused death and that the symptoms observed during his last illness did not point to arsenic poisoning; some of the classic manifestations were not present. Some members of Parliament signed the petitions. Public meetings in Mrs. Maybrick's support were held in London and Liverpool, and, since Mrs. Maybrick was American by birth, leading officials and citizens of the United States also pleaded in her behalf. Among the names subscribed to the petitions were those of Cardinal Gibbons, Vice-President Levi P. Morton, members of the cabinet in addition to Secretary Blaine, and high army officers.

At length, as in the quite different case of Jessie M'Lachlan, public opinion had its way to the extent that the condemned woman's sentence was reduced to life imprisonment.* Mrs. May-

* One of the popular songs celebrating the commutation affords a good idea of the distance of time and social mood that separated Mrs. Maybrick's case from, say, Greenacre's. In the interval the flavor of the death-hunters'

brick was released after fifteen years and returned to the United States, living first in Highland Park, Illinois, then in Florida, and finally in South Kent, Connecticut, as an eccentric old woman in a shack overrun with cats. She died in 1941. The beginning of her story, in the fair promise of a transatlantic marriage—overlooking the "vulgar" origin of her husband—may have been fit for Henry James's pen, but the long unhappy sequel would have had to be written by another hand.

---

street ballad, studiously naïve and lugubrious, had given way to the facetious pseudo-sophistication of the music hall song:

> The Maybrick trial is over now, there's been a lot of jaw,
> Of doctors' contradiction, and expounding of the law;
> She had Sir Charles Russell to defend her as we know,
> But though he tried his very best it all turned out no go.
> CHORUS
> But Mrs. Maybrick will not have to climb the golden stairs;
> The Jury found her guilty so she nearly said her prayers;
> She's at another kind of mashing and at it she must stop,
> Old Berry is took down a peg with his big long drop.

James Berry had succeeded Calcraft and William Marwood as England's premier hangman.

16

Poison by Pill and Pen

THOMAS NEILL CREAM, 1892

ANOTHER import from America, though he was Scottish by birth, was Dr. Thomas Neill Cream, upon whose head was centered the storm of public indignation which would have been visited upon Jack the Ripper had he been caught, but which, in default of this, had been pent up to await the appearance of a suitable substitute. There is no question that Cream earned the honor.

Except for the American interludes, which are subsidiary to the main plot, the portion of Cream's story which engages us belongs to London, the night London of the unfashionable demimonde, the locale of Michael Sadleir's novel *Forlorn Sunset* now illuminated not by flaring gas jets but by Edison's incandescent lamps. Socially it is a cut, but only a cut, above the Whitechapel environment of Jack the Ripper with its festering, sinister slums and last-ditch drabs and their pimps. The setting is the promenades and bars of certain London theaters and music halls, for decades the notorious haunts of prostitutes on the prowl, and the pavements outside; and, most of all, the lodging houses and overnight "hotels" at the southern end of Waterloo Bridge where the women took their pickups. A far cry from the prim Richmond cottage of Mrs. Thomas and the Pimlico flat of the Bartletts, though Henry Wainwright would have found himself at home in these places of nocturnal dalliance, and probably did.

Into such a milieu, saturated with mercenary sex and at-

tendant forms of crime, came Dr. Cream, aged forty-one. Born
in Glasgow, he had emigrated with his family to Canada, where
he took his M.D. at McGill University. His first recorded crime
was that of arson, followed by a career as a professional abortionist; he did not, therefore, begin at the top. In 1880 he was
justifiably accused of murder in Chicago, but it was not until
the next year, in the same city, that he was convicted—in another case. McGill at this early point in his career foresightedly
washed its hands of him by striking his name from its alumni
roll. In addition to being deprived of his right to a medical title,
Cream paid for this murder by spending ten years of a life sentence in the Illinois State Prison.

Upon his release he went first to Canada and then to London, where one evening in October 1891 he fell in with a
"soiled dove" named Matilda Clover, went with her to her
squalid room in Lambeth Road, and in due course emerged and
disappeared. Not long afterward, Clover—to use the curtailed
terminology the Victorians adopted when speaking of members
of her degraded class—was discovered in agonized convulsions
from which she died the next morning. Attending her briefly
was a doctor's assistant who had responded to the call instead of
his chief. This well-meaning but unqualified practitioner, who
later told the court that he had "had fourteen years' experience
in this part of London, and a good deal of experience of drink
in its various forms," interpreted the woman's violent symptoms
as those of alcoholism, a reasonable guess in view of the fact
(which the assistant did not know at the time) that Matilda had
been undergoing treatment by another doctor for that very
malady. There is something chilling in his matter-of-fact description of the sub-Draconian measure he chose to deal with her
case:

Q. Are you acquainted with the symptoms of strychnine poisoning?
A. Yes. Nothing in her appearance suggested that to me. I should put
    the symptoms down to delirium tremens; from convulsions; that
    sometimes occurs. There was nothing to point out to me that she
    died from anything but delirium tremens.
Q. What medicine did you prescribe?
A. Carbonate of soda.

When the doctor whom Matilda had been consulting for her drink problem was apprised of her death, he unhesitatingly filled out the requisite certificate. Primary cause of death: delirium tremens. (*Q*. "In giving a certificate in this way, I suppose you were aware of a very grave dereliction of duty?" *A*. "I am not aware of it.") This easy disposition of the case seemed to obviate any necessity for looking into it more closely. If there had been, someone might have discovered that Matilda had died from tetanic convulsions caused by strychnine poisoning.

The tall gentleman with a heavy moustache and a pronounced squint, wearing a large caped coat and a high silk hat, who had been with Matilda that evening, could have made such a diagnosis with an authority no other doctor could have matched, because it was he who had personally administered the strychnine. And actually, he did communicate the correct diagnosis, though in a peculiar way. On November 28, signing himself "M. Malone," he wrote a letter to a prominent London physician, Dr. Broadbent, accusing him of poisoning Matilda Clover by strychnine. The evidence could be purchased for £2,500; otherwise it would be given to the police. Instead, Broadbent immediately gave the letter to Scotland Yard, which inserted in the *Daily Chronicle* the advertisement "M. Malone" had specified if the doctor was agreeable to meeting his conditions. A watch was then put on Broadbent's house, but no one appeared, and the matter was dropped.

This uninspired handling of the blackmail letter strikes us today as being as culpable as the negligence of the medical assistant who prescribed baking soda for Matilda's death throes and the doctor who signed the certificate without having attended the patient. And it struck the court at Cream's trial the same way. First, an inspector of L Division, which included Lambeth, testified that Scotland Yard had never forwarded the Broadbent letter to him for investigation; he had not, in fact, heard of Clover's death until after Cream's further exploits had brought him to the attention of the police generally. Then Inspector Tunbridge of the C.I.D. went into the box to testify that after the failure of the trap laid in the agony column of the

Daily Chronicle, nothing further was done. "The letter was
looked upon as a letter from an insane person." At this point the
judge took up the questioning. He could not believe that no detective had called at Clover's late lodgings.

A. Well, it was not done, my lord.
Q. My surprise remains.
Q. [By the Attorney-General] Nothing was done beyond watching
   Dr. Broadbent's house?
A. No.
Q. [By the Court] But my surprise remains. [To witness] I cannot
   see why it should have been thought of more importance to watch
   Dr. Broadbent's house than to make this inquiry?
A. It was thought from the tone of the letter that it was an attempt
   to extort money without any ground such as that stated in the
   letter.
Q. [Again by the Court] Suppose the man had been caught, would
   any inquiry of this kind have been made?
A. I presume so, my lord.
Q. I should presume not, from what happened.

So it was only late in May of the following year, after two more
streetwalkers had died by strychnine, that Tunbridge was instructed to look into the South Lambeth poisoning cases.

But we must go back to the preceding October. A week before Matilda Clover was killed, another South Bank prostitute,
Ellen Donworth, had died of strychnine, as the police knew.
(Their awareness of her death by poison makes all the more
incredible their failure to follow up the report of Clover's similar
death a few days later.) Six days after the Donworth crime, the
local coroner received a letter offering information about it for
a steep price; again, nothing was done. And a fortnight later
(November 5) a partner in the bookselling firm of W. H. Smith
and Son received a letter, signed "H. Bayne," informing him that
the writer possessed two incriminating letters proving that the
businessman had murdered Ellen Donworth. "My object in
writing you is to ask if you will retain me at once as your coun-
sellor and legal adviser. If you employ me at once to act for you
in this matter, I will save you from all exposure and shame in
the matter." Scotland Yard, upon being communicated with,
reacted as unimaginatively as it was to do at the end of the same

month when confronted with Dr. Broadbent's letter. It advised Smith to post in a designated window of his shop the notice of agreement "H. Bayne" specified, and he did so. But no one turned up.

The author of all these disturbing missives was Cream himself, of course. He was no novice at the fashioning of poison-pen letters. The penchant, it was later learned, had been evident as early as 1881, when he was arrested for sending scurrilous postcards to a Chicago furrier whom he had attended as a physician: "You had better learn that low, vulgar wife of yours to keep her foul mouth shut, with her second-hand silk dohlmans and second-hand silk dresses, and not talk about others. Two can play at that game. I heard on very good authority that you had to leave England on account of a bastard child you left behind. T.N.C." But when Cream resumed this unlovely practice in London, there was this significant difference: whereas he had had a demonstrable grudge against the Chicagoan, who he claimed owed him $20 on his bill, he either did not know his English addressees at all or, if he did in one later case, there still was no apparent reasonable motive behind the malevolence. He never attempted to follow up any of the blackmailing letters he wrote while in London. The pleasure his twisted, drug-excited mind derived from these sinister epistolary capers must have been of a piece with the pleasure he got from the poisoning episodes themselves—that of gloating, at a safe distance, over the mental or bodily suffering he caused.

Cream now returned to Canada and the United States for a short visit. A traveler for a wholesale grocery firm who made his acquaintance in Quebec later gave the London court a fair description of Dr. Cream's character and habits. He carried around dirty pictures which he was eager to exhibit to whoever wished to look upon them; he made no secret of the fact that he was himself in the wholesale line—as an abortionist; and he prided himself, above all, on his knowledge of street women. "He told me that he had had lots of fun in London with the women. He mentioned Waterloo Road, Westminster Bridge Road, London Road, and Victoria Road, and said he had met as many as three women on one night, between the hours of 10 P.M.

and 3 A.M., and had been in their company, and had used them, and had paid no more than one shilling to each." Which tells us as much about a certain aspect of London life in the nineties as it does about Cream.

Shortly after his return to London in early April 1892, two other "unfortunates," Alice Marsh and Emma Shrivell, died dreadful convulsive deaths in the same vicinity. More attentive work on the part of the coroner and the police resulted in the finding that these women had died by poison; and now it was recalled that the strychnine death of Ellen Donworth had never been solved. One further, somewhat overdue insight on the part of the police—that is, recollection of the Broadbent letter—led to the exhumation of Matilda Clover's body. Ample traces of poison were discovered there also. Past events were falling together in an ominous pattern.

At this juncture, as if to fill out the pattern, the threatening letters resumed. One, addressed to a respected Barnstaple physician, Dr. Joseph Harper, and another, to the foreman of the coroner's jury looking into the recent deaths of Alice Marsh and Emma Shrivell, declared that the writer—"W. H. Murray" this time—had proof that Dr. Harper's son, a medical student at St. Thomas's Hospital who had lived in the same lodging house with Cream during Cream's earlier stay in London, had killed both women. The price of silence to young Harper's father was £1,500.

The strangest of these exercises, however, was his having printed in Canada five hundred copies of a handbill warning guests of the Metropole Hotel, London, "that the person who poisoned Ellen Donworth on the 13th last October is to day in the employ of the Metropole Hotel and that your lives are in danger as long as you remain in this hotel. Yours respectfully, W. H. Murray." These were not distributed but were found among Cream's belongings after his arrest.

Cream, it is evident, liked to live on the dangerous edge of things. As occurs so often in criminal careers, this audacity was accompanied by what can only be called stupidity; for Cream also liked to talk too much, and he picked the wrong people to talk to. One of his acquaintances was Police Sergeant M'Intyre,

to whom he exhibited an unduly intimate knowledge of the unsolved poisoning cases, including one of which the police had not
even heard, that of a girl named Louisa Harris or Harvey.

Even worse, a fellow-lodger at his new address in the Westminster Bridge Road, Lambeth—an area that plainly held him
in thrall—was a man named John Haynes, whose role in the case
remains tantalizingly undefined, insofar as the official record, at
least, is concerned. Ostensibly an unemployed engineer, Haynes
seems to have been a private investigator working for the Home
Office. According to the judge presiding at Cream's trial, he "had
been employed by the Government as a secret agent very often
in important affairs," the most recent being in connection with
"a certain class of suspected persons," which we may interpret
as the dynamiting Fenians. He had been an associate of "Major
Le Caron," otherwise Thomas Miller Beach, one of the greatest
of nineteenth-century spies, who in the 1880s had worked inside
the Fenian organization in America on behalf of the British government. Haynes himself, testified a friend of his who was a
sergeant in the C.I.D., had returned from America only six
months earlier.

Beyond these statements, the trial record does not go; but it
seems remarkable that an undercover agent for the British government should happen to have been a fellow-lodger of Cream.
Was it merely a coincidence? Or was Cream, with his background in Canada and the United States, suspected of being a
Fenian? The Home Office archives may contain the answer if
anyone is disposed to search for it. However this may be, Cream
confided to Haynes a large amount of inside information concerning the deaths of Donworth, Clover, and Lou Harvey, noting that one villain was responsible for all three.

As a result of this loose talk, the police began to shadow
Cream, and through his solicitors he wrote to the Chief Com-
missioner of Police complaining of this annoyance, saying it was
hurting his business. Actually, this proved to be an understate-
ment, because a week later, Cream's business was shut down
entirely, on the occasion of his being arrested for blackmail: the
handwriting of the poison-pen letter to Dr. Harper had given the
police the break they needed and possibly did not deserve. The

results of the belated analysis of Matilda Clover's body enabled them to raise the ante to a charge of murder.

The newspapers, exploiting this new development in the frail flower murders for all it was worth, mentioned that Cream had spoken of the as-yet-unreported death by poisoning of one Lou Harvey. Immediately it transpired that there was a very good reason for this omission, because the young woman in question was still alive and in tolerable health, and she wrote the authorities to tell them so. She had had a narrow escape from Cream. Only a night or two after Matilda Clover's murder, Cream, once again prospecting for victims, had encountered Louisa, a suitable candidate, at the Alhambra and later the St. James's music halls. They had spent the night at a hotel in Berwick Street. The next morning, critically examining his recent bedfellow with the fond solicitude of a lover, he told her she had a few spots on her forehead and would bring her some pills to eradicate them.

Met him same night opposite Charing X. Underground R. Station. Walked with him to the Northumberland Public house, had glass of wine, and then walked back to the Embankment. Were he gave me two capsules. But not liking the look of the thing, I pretended to put them in my mouth. But kept them in my hand. And when he happened to look away I threw them over the Embankment.

That Louisa had a head on her shoulders is proved not only by her prudent deception of her medical benefactor as they strolled in the night shadows on the Embankment; she had also brought with her the man she was living with at St. John's Wood, one Charles Harvey, who watched the proceedings from a distance.

Satisfied that she had taken her capsules—"pink pills for pale prostitutes," as William Roughead called them—Cream pleaded another engagement which would prevent his escorting her to the Oxford Music Hall as they had earlier planned, but gave her five shillings for her seat. "I met Harvey at the corner," she concluded when she recounted her adventure before the court, "and told him what had happened, and then I went to the Oxford Music Hall"—whether to see the show or pick up another client she did not make clear.

Thanks to her self-protective shrewdness (never take pills

from a stranger, even—or particularly—if you have slept with him), Louisa's name appeared only in a subsidiary position in the indictment under which Cream was tried at the Old Bailey: ". . . for the wilful murder of Alice Marsh, Ellen Donworth, Emma Shrivell, and Matilda Clover; also for sending to Joseph Harper a letter demanding money with menaces, without any reasonable or probable cause; for sending a similar letter to William Henry Broadbent; and for attempting to administer to Louisa Harris a large quantity of strychnine with intent to murder her." One wonders, though, how the last charge could have been proved, in the absence of the strychnine.

The Crown proceeded with that portion of the indictment referring to Matilda Clover only, relying upon the corroborative effect of evidence relating to the other murders to prove Cream's guilt in the Clover case. This tactic (allowed by the judge, who admitted evidence which would have been excluded from most of the other trials we have been looking at) was successful. No witnesses were called in Cream's behalf, and the jury was out of the room only ten minutes. Exactly a year and a day after he killed Matilda Clover he was sentenced to hang.

Even in Lambeth, where life was as cheap as the sexual favors of some of its women, the case had a depressing effect. Matilda Clover's landlady had a complaint reminiscent of that associated, years earlier, with the Richmond cottage where Kate Webster had done her bloody work: "Her rooms were not let again for months after her death. . . . My rooms used not to be long empty, but since her death I have not let so well. I don't remember how long it was after her death before a lodger came; it was a long time."

17

The Deaths at
George's American Bar

GEORGE CHAPMAN, 1903

THIS CASE, like the following one, owes its admissibility into our brief chronicle of Victorian murder to the circumstance that, while the wheels of justice began to mesh after the Queen's death—Chapman was arrested on the very day of her son's coronation, October 25, 1902—a goodly portion of the criminal career under review had occurred within her reign. Strict chronology, therefore, happily enables us to regard as *echt* Victorian crimes several murders which it would be a pity to be forced by some pettifogging technicality to omit.

George Chapman could not have claimed descent from his namesake, the Elizabethan dramatist and translator of Homer. On the contrary, he was as Polish as Teodor Josef Konrad Korzeniowski, who had lately abandoned a seafaring career to devote all his time to writing fiction in English.* Chapman's name

---

* Conrad, like Henry James, was an admirer of Roughead's connoisseur-like approach to true crime. Roughead dedicated his *The Riddle of the Ruthvens* to Conrad, and in another book printed an interesting essay on "Conrad's attitude towards crime and the criminal, and . . . the extent to which he made use of these elements in the alembic of his art." "Crime *qua* crime," wrote Roughead, "had for him no artistic significance; it was always 'the psychological interest' that mattered." That was why Conrad, though admiring his Edinburgh friend's scholarly edition of the Burke and Hare

in the old country had been Severin Klosowski; in time he changed it to something more discernibly English by the simple expedient of borrowing the family name of the first of his several mistresses, Annie Chapman. Like his fellow Pole, but in a quite different sphere of life, Klosowski/Chapman had vacillated in his occupation. Claiming to have had some surgical training in Poland, on his arrival in Britain he first practiced the historically associated profession of barbering. Despite this early experience in blood-letting, however, he preferred poison to the knife or razor when, in later years, drastic solutions were required for incommodious situations. For a time he was a floating barber in the East End and elsewhere in London, and for another period he operated a gentlemen's hairdressing shop at Hastings, where he was assisted by his current female companion, who lathered the customers. It is also said that she sometimes ventured to shave them, but owing to the frequent unsteadiness of her hand, the customers did not encourage her, preferring instead that while her husband performed the operation she supply a musical background from the piano he had installed in the shop.

This, however, is to anticipate. In May 1890, Chapman went to America, accompanied by his recently acquired wife, one Lucy Baderski,* and settled in Jersey City. A coincidence of dates, along with other circumstantial evidence, has inclined some students to the theory that Chapman was Jack the Ripper. One point in its favor is that Jack's mutilative methods suggested the hand of someone with surgical training. However, there are several serious objections to the supposition, including the fact that in all the known cases attributed to him, Chapman was consistently faithful to the poison technique. In any event, he accumulated enough demonstrable demerits to qualify him for the gallows, whether or not he also committed the Whitechapel murders.

---

trial, found the case itself repellent. "The callousness of these wretches," he told him, "is so completely perfect that it reduces the psychological interest to [the] vanishing point."

* Some sources allege that when he "married" Lucy, he already had a legal wife in Poland who subsequently, to his embarrassment, turned up in London. But in view of his habits in such matters, the issue of who was, in fact, his first and legal spouse is utterly pedantic.

On his return to England in 1892, he became a publican, keeping a succession of houses both in and outside of London. His most absorbing interest outside business hours was in a series of females whom he took informally to wife, Lucy Baderski Klosowski being still extant but not present. The standard procedure was for the happy couple to announce to the social circle headquartered at the pub that they intended to marry that day, then to drive off in a cab and come back a reasonable time later proclaiming that they were now husband and wife. If they stopped anywhere during the ride, it was not at a church or a registry office.

The first casualty among these extra-legal wives (Annie Chapman, who had been his mistress in 1893 and whose name he assumed, survived her relationship with him and therefore failed to make the list) was the bottle-addicted, estranged wife of a railway porter memorably named Shadrach Spink.* Two years after they announced themselves as married, Mrs. Spink died after a lingering illness. It later developed that she had been fed tartar emetic on a regular schedule, but at the time there was no suspicion of untoward behavior on the part of her consort, and the doctor who signed the death certificate attributed Mrs. Spink's demise to "phthisis." This was at Christmas 1897. The next year, Chapman acquired another companion, Bessie Taylor, who departed this life, again not suddenly, in February 1901, the month after Queen Victoria died. Bessie's death entered the statistics as being the result of "exhaustion from vomiting and diarrhoea." Before the funeral baked meats had grown cold, she was succeeded, as "bar maid," by one Maud Marsh, who went the way of the others in October 1902.

There was this crucial difference, however: Maud's working-class parents, unconvinced that she was dying a natural death, called in their own physician, Dr. Francis G. Grapel, who, as the judge at Chapman's trial was to remark, was the first medical man to bring "some originality and some intelligence" to bear on

---

* Shadrach's only close rival in the *index nominorum* of Victorian crime is a Greenwich printer whose son Edmund was accused in 1871 of butchering a seventeen-year-old girl in a lover's lane near Eltham. Father was named Ebenezer Pook.

the cases of George Chapman's death-prone women. Driving back to Croydon after examining Maud Marsh in her sickroom at the Monument Tavern, Borough, Dr. Grapel thought; and the more he thought, the less he liked the look of things. Unlike Glasgow's Dr. Paterson in similar circumstances, he took positive action: he telegraphed back to Maud's regular attendant, Dr. Stoker, suggesting the possibility that she was being poisoned. The message arrived too late to save Maud, for Chapman, alarmed by the visit of the Croydon doctor, had given her quietus with an especially strong dose of antimony. When the question of the death certificate arose, Chapman, remembering Dr. Stoker's convenient diagnosis on a former occasion, proposed that Maud had died from "inflammation of the bowels caused by continual vomiting and diarrhoea." But this time Stoker, rendered tardily mistrustful by the intervention of Dr. Grapel, countered with the obvious question: "What caused the vomiting and diarrhoea?" Chapman had no answer.

Maud was analyzed, and her predecessors, whose remains, despite the lapse of years, had been well preserved by Chapman's choice of chemical, were exhumed; they all contained antimony. Chapman was arrested, and from his prison cell he arranged for an expensive wreath of lilies, tuberoses, camellias, and pink chrysanthemums to be sent to Maud's funeral, with a printed card reading "In Memorium" and signed "From a devoted friend, G.C." This thoughtful gesture did not, however, mitigate the case against him, which was so overwhelming that his counsel did not even bother to call any witnesses. He was duly convicted and hanged.

One of the principal values of the Chapman case is its revelation that the incompetence of the medical profession, which had been lamentably illustrated in several celebrated trials over the years, was still flourishing in some quarters when the Queen breathed her last. Making allowance for the probability that the *élite* of English doctorhood were not in residence in the decrepit neighborhoods where Chapman operated his successive places of male beautification and refreshment, still the various physicians who were called in to treat his ailing pseudo-brides should not uniformly have failed to suspect some irregularity. True, Chapman no doubt selected them particularly for their dependability from his point of view; but he seems to have had a deplorably large pool to choose from. In Bessie Taylor's case, four different doctors offered, with some confidence, four different diagnoses of her malady: "a severe form of hysteria," "womb trouble," "cancer of the stomach or intestines," and "constipation." None of these approached the truth, as Chapman, who willingly paid the consultants' fees, could have told them. Yet despite this lack of unanimity, no post mortem was thought necessary when Bessie died.

The record of the hospital to which Maud Marsh was sent for observation and treatment was equally deplorable. Guy's was, as the judge said, "one of the finest institutions in the world." But such observation as Maud received there did not go far toward clarifying what was the matter with her. An obstetric surgeon, who seems to have spoken with her only casually and depended, instead, on notes supplied by a clerk, first thought she was suffering from peritonitis but later opted for tuberculosis. The treatment at Guy's was of greater benefit, consisting, as it did, of a diet from which antimony was routinely omitted. But as soon as she returned to the Monument Tavern, Maud's symptoms recurred, as was only natural now that her diet was again being enriched by the hand of George Chapman.

It was with much reason, therefore, that the judge delivered himself at some length on the lamentable state of medical practice at the turn of the century. "It is a very sad thing," he said, "that a person who has up to now occupied only the position of a hairdresser has been able to defy the doctors [evidently he did not consider that pub-keeping qualified one in this respect], and who for years, if the evidence is true, has been carrying on practices of this kind perfectly irrespective of the doctors and without the slightest fear of their being able to discover it."

As in the Maybrick case in a markedly different social environment, the evidence in Chapman's trial centered mainly around the distressing symptoms that attended the final illnesses of the several victims; it too is damnably repetitious. But there is the saving presence of a genuine Sairey Gamp among the witnesses, a charwoman-cum-practical nurse who testified at delightful length. Her Gampishness probably would be more pronounced in the printed record had not (as always) the testimony been "normalized" and to a certain extent synthesized.* She may well have talked pure Dickensian; one would like to think she did. But her membership in the tribe of Sairey is sufficiently attested by her indignation that Chapman, following the death of Maud Marsh, whom she—Jessie Toon—had nursed, refused to treat her to a spot of spirits, "although I deserved the best in the house, because when I had spirits I talked." She seems to have been inclined, in the best tradition of her breed, to put her lips to the bottle on the mantelpiece when she was so dispoged.

Chapman was a ruthless dispatcher of outworn or outmoded mistresses: of that there can be no doubt. But he was no fool, as his intelligent selection of incompetent and suggestible doctors to attend them in their agonies proves. And it was very likely a disposition to cultivate a sympathetic relationship which might serve him in time of need that led him, when he was running the Prince of Wales pub in Bartholomew Square, to join the local police cycling club in its outings. Less easily explained, though—one would wish to know what advantage it was supposed to bring a keeper of licensed premises seventy years ago— was his tendency to insist that he was an American. In his successive public houses he prominently displayed the Stars and Stripes behind the bar. There is a photograph of it (a sadly tattered ensign which looks as if it had gone through the whole Civil War) in the published record of his trial. But the effect is somewhat marred by the fact that, as the editor of that volume fails to point out, it was placed upside down. At least Chapman played no favorites. Balancing it was a Union Jack—and it too was upside down.

---

* With such occasionally diverting results as the improbably forthright avowal attributed to one Mrs. Barbara Kay, who was called to the witness box in the Chantrelle case (1878): "I am a widow, and reside in Clyde Street, Edinburgh. I am the keeper of a brothel." It is regrettable that after this promising introduction Mrs. Kay was not allowed to proceed with her testimony.

18

The Man Who Trained
Nude Bicyclists

SAMUEL DOUGAL, 1903

WHILE George Chapman briefly operated the Grapes public house at Bishop's Stortford, Essex, early in 1899, it is conceivable that one of his customers was Samuel Herbert Dougal. This gentleman, who was about to face the unpleasant necessity of shooting and burying Miss Camille Holland, might profitably have consulted the landlord, who had already had initiatory experience in this general line although for results he relied on the more subtle method of poison and the incompetence of the attending physicians. Nor did he object to letting his victims have public burials.

It is appropriate that this, the last of our selected cases, should be especially rich in period charm. The charm, however, is—again appropriately—that of a changing world. Dougal introduced into Essex one of its first motor cars, referred to in his diary as the "loco" or the "locomobile." Like Chapman, he was also, in the best turn-of-the-century fashion, when the invention of the pneumatic tire had changed the whole English way of life, a bicycling enthusiast, and he liked to give lessons in the wholesome art to the girls of the neighborhood. In this, however, he had a tendency to confuse his innocent impulses—to share his zest for outdoor recreation—with others that were less credit-

able, because when the girls were on their bikes, they were "in
a state of nature." "What a picture," comments the editor of his
trial, Miss F. Tennyson Jesse, "—in that clayey, lumpy field, the
clayey, lumpy girls, naked, astride that unromantic object, a bi-
cycle, and Dougal, gross and vital, cheering on these bucolic im-
proprieties . . . !"

Bicycles or not, Dougal was certainly "gross and vital." During his four years at Moat Farm, he seduced ("if," again second-
ing Miss Jesse, "that term is applicable to those who were, for
the most part, such willing victims") a really impressive number
of servant girls and others. "In one case it is known that he had
relations with three sisters and with their mother." In fact, a
more suitable name for Dougal's rustic establishment would
have been Stud Farm; he hired the girls, put them in the family
way, and then discharged them, though continuing to maintain
friendly relations with them, as we shall see. None of this side
of Dougal's conduct, of course, was brought out in court, because it was irrelevant to the main issue. But his proclivities were
notorious in the region. He seems, in fact, to have repopulated
a large portion of rural Essex.

With good reason had Sherlock Holmes remarked to Dr.
Watson, as reported in the *Strand Magazine* for June 1892: "It
is my belief, Watson, founded upon my experience, that the lowest and vilest alleys of London do not present a more dreadful
record of sin than does the smiling and beautiful countryside."
Moat Farm, standing neighborless at the end of a series of country lanes, was the scene of a crime far more sinister than routine
fornication. The cold-blooded murder it witnessed amply justified the "only thought" a criminologist like Holmes had when he
beheld these lonely farmsteads—"a feeling of their isolation and
of the impunity with which crime may be committed there."

Dougal, aged fifty-two when he met his prospective victim
in 1898, had been an enlisted man in the Royal Engineers, and
upon his retirement after twenty-one years' service he received
the golden commendations of his superiors; as a soldier his conduct had been impeccable, irrespective of the number of girls
he had seduced off post across the years. After leaving the army,
he had launched upon a criminal career which on the whole was

more diversified even than Charles Peace's; arson, larceny, and forgery all were in his repertory. His concomitant marital arrangements—there were at least three formal Mrs. Dougals as well as informal company of indeterminate number—probably could not stand careful scrutiny. As an adventurer, however, he lacked Peace's picturesqueness; Dougal was nothing if not slick and unprincipled. In 1898 his affairs had come to a crisis. He had lost his army pension long since because of his criminal convictions, his less shady projects for making money had not panned out any better than the others, and now he looked once more to exerting his accustomed powerful influence on a woman, for the sake of the money she possessed. He found her in a lodging house in Bayswater.

Miss Camille Holland, born in India and a lady of comfortable inherited means, was then aged about fifty-six. The landlady with whom she and Dougal stayed at Saffron Walden testified that "when dressed [she] looked about fifty years of age, but when in bed ten or fifteen years older." In other words, she was precisely the archetypal lady described by the judge in *Trial by Jury:* she may very well have passed for forty-three, in the dusk with a light behind her. The toilette that knocked a decade or more off her age no doubt consisted of the system of elaborate artifices employed by Mrs. Skewton, the berouged and corseted "fatal Cleopatra" in *Dombey and Son.** She was a perfect mark for a calculating and avaricious man like Dougal—a spinster of blameless life who had managed to make her material circumstances additionally comfortable by being fairly close with the income from her invested money.

In January 1899, some four months after they met, they bought Coldhams Farm, between Saffron Walden and Audley End. She supplied the money and he supplied the new name by which it eventually would achieve notoriety: Moat Farm.

* Dickens does not confide the details of what Mrs. Skewton wore, but we have the word of the Saffron Walden landlady, who was a dressmaker, as to Miss Holland's customary attire: "a pair of 'natural' woollen combinations, a pair of white linen combinations, a pair of steel-framed corsets, two pink woollen underbodices, black cashmere stockings, a pair of bloomers, and two petticoats"—formidable accouterment, one thinks, for a spinster lady out to meet the world.

One thinks irresistibly of "Mariana in the Moated Grange." Miss Jesse, whose great-uncle wrote that hauntingly atmospheric poem, describes Moat Farm well in her own prose:

The house itself is a building that on a sunny day holds something sinister and dreary, a look as of a house in some wild Brontë tale, and that on a wet, grey day might stand for the epitome of everything that is lonely and grim. . . . Surrounded by dark fir trees and gnarled apple trees in a very ecstacy of contortion, it is a small, neat, almost prim house, its deeply sloping roof patterned in diamond shapes with lighter tiles; its famous moat circles it so completely that it is only possible to enter it at one point, where a bridge spans the water. . . . The soil is heavy clay that clings about the feet, and the inhabitants seem to hold in their slouching walk and heaviness of mien some recognition of this fact, as though the perpetual drag of the clay pulled them always downwards, both body and soul.

After staying awhile in lodgings at Saffron Walden, "Mr. and Mrs. Dougal," as they now called themselves without warrant, took possession of this depressing retreat, amply furnished with seven rooms' worth of her furniture which was transferred from storage in London.

Two weeks later a maidservant arrived; another week, and Dougal tried to break into her room, allegedly to wind the clock. The girl had hysterics, Miss Holland—as, in the interests of accuracy, we shall continue to call her—intervened, and took the frightened girl into her own bed. Dougal was faced with a heavy decision. His irresistible urge to meddle with toothsome servants obviously did not recommend him to the decorous lady upon whose largess he was completely dependent. He could not do without either the girls or the money; he could, however, do without Miss Holland, and three days after his attempt upon the servant's virtue, Miss Holland disappeared.

To the girl, whose mother promptly removed her, *virgo intacta*, the next day, Dougal explained that Miss Holland had gone up to London for a day or two. But the days lengthened into weeks, and then into months, and then into years, four of them. Dougal continued to live at Moat Farm, comfortably furnished as it was with Miss Holland's belongings (oddly, she had also left all her clothing behind). He improved his time by giving bicycling lessons in the mire, fathering bucolic brats, and

for three of the four years giving shelter to a genuine Mrs. Dougal—his third—whom he had invited down to Moat Farm the
very day after Miss Holland was last seen. In April 1902, however, this lady eloped with a laborer and the injured husband
promptly filed for divorce. She did not contest the suit and he
was awarded a decree *nisi* in August.

Meanwhile, by frequent correspondence with Miss Holland's
bankers, using her signature, of course, Dougal methodically
collected all the cash he needed for a gracious way of life, liqui-
dating an investment or two when current income proved insufficient. This could have continued indefinitely, as long as the
money held out, had not one of his seducees, with less forbear-
ance than her several predecessors, sworn out an affiliation order
against him. This had the effect of reviving and bringing to official attention the disquieting rumors that had hung in the damp
Essex air for several years. The fruits of the police investigation
were indications that Dougal had been guilty of extensive and
high-handed forgery. The Essex and London police got into
communication, and a representative paid him a friendly visit
for the sake of obtaining information. The next day, reading the
signs aright, Dougal closed out his accounts in two banks and
took the outstanding balances in cash. A few days later, appearing at the Bank of England itself, he attempted to cash some
ten-pound notes. But the bank had been alerted to watch for
those serial numbers, Dougal was arrested, and, after an abortive
attempt to escape—he had the ill luck to pick a dead-end street—
he was returned, handcuffed, to Saffron Walden.

The question naturally arose, Where was the lady whose
bank accounts and broker's portfolio he had been steadily de-
pleting? The Essex constabulary got to work. Failing to find an
inch of space inside the house where anything could be concealed, they began to dig up the garden, then the moat. At
length someone recalled that shortly after Dougal and Miss
Holland had moved in, he had ordered workmen to fill in a
drainage ditch leading from the farmyard to a pond. The ex-
cavation site therefore was shifted once again. For five weeks the
policemen slaved, "often working up to their waists in slime,"
slithering in liquid manure, falling into the mess, spraining

ankles, finding bones—of animals—, receiving advice from manipulators of divining rods and other specialists in the occult, and eventually, just four years after Miss Holland's arrival at the farm, retrieving what remained of her. It had been the most protracted, and certainly the filthiest, bit of police spade work (in the strictest sense) on record. But it was worth the trouble. The body was identified by its clothing, and the philanderer-forger-cycling instructor was charged with murder, to the applause of a rapt press and public which had watched the marathon digging operations with mounting excitement.

In Chelmsford prison, Dougal passed the time conducting chatty correspondences with acquaintances from the past. Not the least striking of these letters was one he wrote to a girl who had borne one of his more recent by-blows. Always the practical man of affairs, he offered advice on arrangements for a peculiar *ad hoc* journey—the pilgrimage of her numerous peers to bear witness against him:

I daresay the girls have received their notices, etc., to attend next Monday at Chelmsford, have they not? There will be several from about there, and it would be a good idea to club together and hire a trap and drive all the way. It is a delightful drive through undulating country, and at this time of year it would be a veritable treat for them all.

The notion of a whole sisterhood of young unwed mothers, bound together in common debt to Dougal, chartering a conveyance for a comradely excursion to his trial on a capital charge, is one to occupy the imagination.

What they witnessed, if they all arrived, pink-cheeked after their ride through blossomy Essex, was a trial in which the prosecution held all the cards. The lack of doubt as to the result drained it of drama. But its fundamentally anticlimactic nature was relieved—or perhaps enhanced—by a spot of comedy provided by a flustered witness, the proprietress of the Bayswater boarding house where Dougal met Miss Holland. She was asked to identify Dougal.

Q. Do you see him in the Court?
A. [Looking straight at the jury box] Yes, I see him among those gentlemen over there.

Q. Will you kindly remove your veil, madam?
A. Yes. Oh, yes, now I can see him. [Pointing to the same gentle-man.]
Q. Will you kindly listen to me for a moment, madam. Look slowly round the Court again?
A. Yes, there is the gentleman. [Pointing to the Shire Hall keeper.]
Q. [By defense counsel] I don't know if I ought to interfere, but I understand this lady has identified a gentleman on the other side of the Court.
Q. [By the prosecution] Will you do what I ask, madam, and look around the Court slowly, please.
A. [Pointing to the prisoner in the dock] That is the man sitting there.

The rows of Dougal's erstwhile girlfriends must have got a hearty giggle out of the scene. Dougal's reaction at this point is not on record. His counsel, having called no witnesses, made a gallant but futile address to the jury, which somewhat surprisingly required an hour and a half to come to the foreordained verdict. After sentence was pronounced, the Chief Constable of Essex obtained leave to read a statement bringing to public notice the "dogged perseverance and unwavering cheerfulness" with which the police of Essex and London, from inspectors to mire-covered constables, had discharged their "most laborious and unsavoury task." The practice of ending a murder trial with credit lines was not usual (one rare instance would be the citation of Stokes, in the Wainwright case, for his footwork), but in this instance it was fully justified.

We began this garland of great Victorian cases with the Norfolk police floundering in the muck of James Blomfield Rush's farm; we end it with the constabulary of another eastern county emerging in triumph from the muck of Samuel Dougal's drainage ditch. Even though the latter force, in their deepest and muddiest moments of despair, may not have conceded it, police work, and its appreciative public, had come a long way in half a century. A great novelist had—unfairly, as we now know—derided the Norfolk force for their inability to find what they were looking for; now a Chief Constable gave public praise to his men for persevering to success. To adapt the words of the late Laureate, they strove, they sought, and they found.

19

Murder and the Victorian Mind

WHO CAN ACCOUNT FOR the prevalence of murder in Victorian England? Or—more to the point—was murder really as prevalent as our emphasis upon it in these chapters has implied? By concentrating upon one strand in the complicated web of Victorian social life we have necessarily attributed an excessive degree of importance to it. But this is merely to emulate the Victorians themselves, for to them also murder had a part in their imaginative lives that was far out of proportion to its actual incidence.

It is true that we do not know exactly how many murders were committed in Britain in these years, nor how, or even whether, the rate was affected by changing social conditions. In the eighteenth century the low incidence of homicide in England as compared with that in continental countries was the constant subject of remark by foreign visitors. But no useful figures survive from that period, and although there are various collections of criminal statistics dating from the first half of the nineteenth century, they are all erratic and unreliable. Only in 1856–57 did the Home Office begin to keep systematic records of murder and other crimes. These annual volumes of "Judicial Statistics," though they represented a great advance in that they were compiled on a uniform basis, were sharply criticized on various grounds. There was, for example, a wide discrepancy between the number of murders reported to the police and those returned at coroners' inquests. (Part of the difference may have been due to the latter's practice of including infanticides in the total: in 964 cases of murder that were the subjects of inquests in 1862–65, seventy per cent of the victims were less than a year old.) In their passage through the courts, furthermore, many cases of what had initially been classified as murder were reduced to manslaughter. And so, although from the middle of the century onward criminal statistics abound, modern experts on the history of nineteenth-century crime, police, and other subjects reject them as almost useless. They are fully as unreliable as those for twentieth-century American crime, which is saying a good deal.

All we can be sure of is that the number of known murders was small in proportion to the population and that it varied greatly from year to year. It seems probable, also, that the rate fell behind the increase of population (for England and Wales, about 15 million in the year of the Queen's accession, and more than double that—32.5 million—in the year of her death). For whatever the figures may be worth, it may be said that for England and Wales the annual murder total, as given in some reference books, ranged between 272 (in 1866) and 142 (in 1899); and this is not to take account of Scotland, which was healthily competitive. But these statistics, besides having the deficiencies just noted, fall short of representing the homicides *actually committed,* for an untold number of murder and manslaughter cases never came to the attention of the police. And even when the police received strong intimations that a certain death was worth looking into, they sometimes failed to respond as positively as they might be expected to have done: compare their easy dismissal of Cream's letter to Dr. Broadbent as the work of just one more crank. How many murders to which they were tipped off in one way or another went uninvestigated?

It was not only the occasional inadequacy of the police in London and the provinces which made it far easier for a murder to go undetected then than it is today. The conditions under which people lived—in the teeming yet socially isolated slums of the cities on the one hand, and in the remotenesses of the countryside on the other—made the sudden, unexplained death or disappearance of a human being an event that would by no means automatically come to the attention of the police.

That ordinary doctors could not always be relied upon to recognize suspicious cases of death when they saw them has been adequately shown in our chapters on Cream and Chapman, among others. No laws requiring the accurate certification of cause of death and the notification of the coroner or the police in cases of what appeared to be death from other than natural causes could ensure the punctilious observance thereof by incompetent, over-busy, incurious, or just plain dishonest practitioners.

The most knowledgeable and conscientious Victorian doctors, furthermore, were aware of many suspicious cases. Unlike the overscrupulous (or self-protecting) Dr. Paterson in the Pritchard affair, however, they had insufficient grounds to warrant bringing these cases to the attention of the proper authorities. That perceptive and readable informal historian of late Victorian society, E. E. Kellett, recorded: "A doctor once told me that he did not believe there was a single medical practitioner in London, of twenty years' standing, who had not serious reason to believe that wives in his practice had poisoned their husbands and husbands their wives; but in the vast majority of cases the doctors could not utter their suspicions." For every Adelaide Bartlett, Edward Pritchard, and Madeleine Smith who got caught, there may well have been hundreds of wives, husbands, and lovers who discreetly found their illegal way out of an inconvenient situation and, for all we know to the contrary, lived happily ever after. After all, to those privy to the nominal secret, there was the example of Madeleine Wardle, *née* Smith, placidly pouring tea for members of the William Morris socialism-and-art circle. Admittedly, she had been caught; but she had also been spared, to provide living proof that a poisoning episode in one's past need not interfere with one's subsequent enjoyment of life or detract from one's social graces.

The widespread assumption, dating perhaps from the sensational sixties, that in ordinary social intercourse one was quite likely to see and even chat with undetected murderers added an undeniable piquancy to life in Victorian drawing rooms. The matter, as H. B. Irving observed, could "only be referred to clandestinely; they are gazed at with awe and curiosity, mute witnesses to their own achievement. Some years ago James Payn, the novelist, hazarded the reckoning that one person in every five hundred was an undiscovered murderer. This gives us all hope, almost a certainty, that we may reckon one such person at least among our acquaintances." In a footnote Irving added, "The author was one of three men discussing this subject in a London club. They were able to name six persons of their various acquaintance who were, or had been suspected of being successful murderers."

The act of murder, Leslie Stephen wrote in 1869, "has been so refined that it escapes observation. . . . Go to insurance offices . . . and you will be told that there are more things going on between earth and heaven than are dreamt of by the students of the police-reports." The companies, as we have seen, took a long time to acquire this wisdom; having failed to be rendered permanently wise by Thomas Griffiths Wainewright's fraud, they continued to issue policies on such bad risks as Palmer's wife and brother.

Again, the institution of baby-farming accounted for an undetermined but unquestionably large number of deaths which under the law may not have been due to anything more than criminal negligence but which for all moral purposes were nothing short of murders. The grim plight of unwanted children among the Victorian poor led, in the first instance, to abortion and infanticide, and the unlucky children who escaped this fate were often thrust upon the stony charity of the authorities. In 1849 occurred the dreadful case of Drouet's baby farm at Tooting, which stirred Dickens's ever-available indignation to produce four caustic articles for the *Examiner* newspaper. Drouet was one of the numerous men and women who contracted with parishes to care for homeless infants and small children at 4s. 6d. a head per week. Early in 1849 it was learned that 150 of these, out of a total of 1,372 then at the farm, had died of cholera within three weeks—while in the outside world of Lower Tooting (population 10,000) not a single case of the disease had occurred. An investigation of the place revealed appalling conditions—starvation, brutal treatment, inadequate clothing, revolting sanitary provisions, total lack of medical care, gross overcrowding—which made Squeers's middle-class boarding school at Dotheboys Hall seem a luxury establishment by contrast. Drouet was tried for the death of one of the hapless victims—and acquitted.

Despite the wide publicity given to cases like this, baby-farming continued to flourish, and what had hitherto been an institution intended to solve a problem among the masses recommended itself to the middle class, which had its own broken homes and its own undesired children to commit to someone else's care. In the best-remembered allusion to baby-farming in Victorian literature—Little Buttercup's former profession as revealed in the dénouement of *H.M.S. Pinafore*—there is no hint of the evil side of the practice. But throughout the sixties, seventies, and eighties, cases of culpable or even intentional maltreatment and negligence leading to death were periodically aired in court, and for every one that happened to be exposed, hundreds of others went undetected. In 1868 the *British Medical Journal* remarked that "there is not the slightest difficulty in disposing of any number of children, so that they may give no further trouble, and never be heard of, at £10 a head."

To the toll taken in these "centres of infanticide" must be added the similarly incalculable number of working-class children who perished, either by deliberate neglect or by actual murder, in order that their desperate parents could collect a small sum of burial money which they could devote to keeping themselves alive—and, in many instances, dead drunk—for a brief period. All in all, there was much substance behind the Hogarthian vision of life among the masses expressed by the speaker—himself to become a murderer later in the narrative—in Tennyson's *Maud* (1855):

And the vitriol madness flushes up in the ruffian's head,*
Till the filthy by-lane rings to the yell of the trampled wife,

* "At the Chester Assizes [April 8, 1853], Honor Gibbons, aged 21, and Bridget Gerratz, 40, were placed at the bar on an indictment and inquisition, charging them with the wilful murder of Mary Gibbons, by the administra-

And chalk and alum and plaster are sold to the poor for bread,
And the spirit of murder works in the very means of life.

And sleep must lie down arm'd, for the villainous centre-bits *
Grind on the wakeful ear in the hush of moonless nights,
While another is cheating the sick of a few last gasps, as he sits
To pestle a poison'd poison behind his crimson lights.

When a Mammonite mother kills her babe for a burial fee,
And Timour-Mammon grins on a pile of children's bones . . .

It is plain, then, that the yearly statistics, whatever form
they take, reflect but a fraction of the total number of men,
women, and children who died by another's hand, whether or
not the act was legally describable as murder. Confining ourselves to clear cases of intentional, unlawful, and malicious killing, we may well ask: Why did these people die? The reasons
were as many and complex as are the moral complications of
human life. The greatest single class of murders was domestic.
The Victorian veneration of family and fireside certainly did
not have the effect of making the home a safer place. In a sampling which includes approximately 480 cases that resulted in
the execution of the murderer, 1837–1901, no fewer than 127 involved the killing of a wife (as against only five in which the
husband was the victim!). Twenty-five individual cases involved
the murder of one or more of the children of the accused, and
close relatives, including sisters, brothers, uncles, aunts, and
grandparents, were victims in the same number of instances.
Some thirty women listed as "concubines," "paramours," and
"sweethearts"—the elasticity of Victorian terminology does not
encourage the making of firm distinctions here—also were victims.

This sampling is, of course, a small one, but it is probably
quite representative. As to the actual motives lying behind this
slaughter of relatives, it is possible only to say that while well
tinged by sexual considerations (e.g. a husband's knowledge or

---

tion of oil of vitriol, at Stockport, on the 12th of March last. The motive to
this murder was reported to be the fees which would be payable on the
death of the child." (*Annual Register* for 1853.) See the ninth line of the
quotation.

* Burglar's tools. The allusion three lines later on to "poison'd poison"
recalls that the notorious adulteration of food and drink in Tennyson's
time extended, by bitter irony, to poison.

suspicion of his wife's unfaithfulness), motives of gain played an important part as well. Nearly all the killings of "concubines, sweethearts," etc. naturally can be enrolled in the category of sexually motivated crimes, whether arising from jealousy, a desire to dissolve an old and now discommoding liaison, or, as was true in many cases, the woman's pregnancy.

After this most numerous class (domestic murders), the next largest class involved homicide committed for the purpose or in the act of robbery. And at the very bottom of the list come murders committed for political reasons, which were virtually unknown in Britain (to which our study is limited) although they were common enough in perennially troubled Ireland. Vendettas too were virtually unknown, unless a crime such as Rush's against Jermy is eligible for that category. A methodical analysis of the circumstances and motives behind a large number of Victorian murders is possible. Although it would require much more detailed information than is accessible in statistical tables, all the necessary data are preserved in the newspaper files. Such an analysis would be worth the labor it would entail, because it would throw valuable light—much more light than our selection of a few cases could possibly provide—on Victorian social conditions and (shall we say?) the "interpersonal relationships" which characterized Victorian society.

To these motives might be added one which I have not actually found in the records, but which the more doctrinaire political economists, at least, might have thought of: namely, that murder was a providential device by which human nature unintentionally helped Nature to control the population—a kind of mini-Malthusianism. Poverty, disease, drink, and other social evils, including such freshly devised institutions as the inhumane workhouses or "Poor Law Bastilles," gave the most assistance in keeping the population more or less in balance with the food supply, but, as the more philosophical among Victorian murderers may have meditated while they sought to lay a flattering unction to their uneasy souls, every little bit helped.

Speculations like these, grave or gay, are the province of the social psychologist rather than the historian, who may doubt whether much genuine instruction is to be had from subjecting any past society to the posthumous inquisition of the couch. Nor can one be more confident as he tries to account for the extraordinary hold murder had upon the imagination of the period. Theories are available, and some may even point the way to truth. Was the passion for beholding murder a necessary accompaniment to the long *Pax Victoriana*, a stretch of English history when the domestic scene, after a turbulent start, became relatively tranquil and such wars as the British army fought were conducted far away? Did the lengthy series of sensational murders which we have sampled supply the excitement, or in more strictly psychological terms the alternative outlet for innate aggressive impulses, which in other eras were provided by fierce political-religious controversy or by wars like the Napoleonic conflict? The Victorian psyche may have found murder to be a kind of immoral equivalent to war.*

We can speak with assurance, in any event, of some of the results produced by the Victorian delight in murder. It is not an exaggeration to say that the spread of reading habit through the Victorian populace, with all its profound political, social, and cultural consequences, was signally assisted by the presence of murder as a topic of perennial interest. Engaging as it did the minds of uncounted hundreds of thousands of the illiterate or barely literate masses, it invited them to a mastery of the printed word sufficient for their needs—a goal which the existing agencies for formal elementary education all too often failed to achieve. It provided an inexhaustible source of material for the mass-circulation journalism which developed in the course of the Victorian era. By revealing that there was an untapped and ever-growing audience for easy-to-read sensationalism (and its accompanying illustrations), it had a main hand in turning the newspaper, magazine, and cheap book publishing trades into big business, making the printed word a commodity infinitely more profitable, if shrewdly handled, than it had ever been in the days of a restricted market of the educated few. The distance

---

* I am aware of the theory that it was also a substitute for sex. But in view of the recent belated realization that the Victorians had more outlets for their sexuality than used to be admitted, this idea has even less to recommend it than it formerly did.

from Thurtell, Greenacre, and the Mannings to, say, the enlarged electorate and eventually the democratic politics fostered by the Second Reform Act of 1867, the establishment of a nationally financed and controlled school system after 1870, and the momentous burgeoning of a popular culture shaped and fed by cheap papers and books is a long one; but the connection is easily traced. If it would be too much to say that the England which existed at Queen Victoria's death was the product of murder—and it would—it can at least be affirmed that without the presence and extravagant publicizing of murder that had occurred over the preceding eighty years, the England of 1901 would have been a quite different society.

ii

At the beginning of the century, murder served moralists in the old familiar ways. Like great fires, epidemics, lightning strikes, terrible storms, and all other dramatic visitations of evil, it was interpreted as carrying a stern message to the errant and the downright ungodly. The lesson of Mary Ashford's violent fate was inscribed on her very tombstone by the Rev. Luke Booker, LL.D., Vicar of Dudley: "As a warning to female virtue, and a humble monument of female chastity, this stone marks the grave of Mary Ashford, who, in the 20th year of her age, having incautiously repaired to a scene of public amusement without proper protection, was brutally violated and murdered on the 27th May, 1817." The Reverend Dr. Booker elaborated upon this solemn theme in a pamphlet published the same year, "a disquisition on the evils of promiscuous dancing assemblies, and the perils to which female virtue is subjected."

Such moralizing pamphlets and tracts had, of course, a long tradition behind them, as did the custom of basing Sunday sermons on current events. But in Victorian times the growing public zest for murder and the expansion of the means by which it was gratified broadened, likewise, the opportunities available to the custodians of the nation's conscience and the critics of society. Thanks to the broadside and newspaper press, the preachers' and critics' audience could be relied upon to be fully briefed in the background facts which gave point to the moralizing and particularly disposed the audience to be attentive. The sermon on Ezekiel 33:11 which the Methodist minister from London preached to thousands of people gathered in the shadow of Corder's Red Barn exemplified the countless sermons inspired by current murder, including those delivered by venerable custom to mark the opening of the county assizes as well as those before the convicted murderer and his fellow prisoners, on the eve of his execution.

Some public executions, most notably those which concluded notorious cases and hence could be depended on to attract enormous audiences, had side shows in the form of revival meetings. At Stafford in 1856, the night before Palmer was hanged, several dissenting chapels held all-night services on behalf of his imperiled soul, and as day broke a corps of preachers held forth from impromptu platforms within sight of the gallows. One "religious gentleman from Liverpool and his helpers" passed out eighty thousand tracts suitable to the occasion. Nine years later, when Dr. Pritchard was about to mount the scaffold in Glasgow, the crowd, estimated at one hundred thousand, was infiltrated by a number of persons bearing sandwich boards inscribed with scriptural texts, and an informal corps of preachers, including, in addition to local talent, the secretary of the London Open Air Mission and a revivalist from Dublin, worked to bring home the awful lesson of Pritchard's fate. Evangelists undoubtedly addressed the crowds at other hangings as well, but it is odd, and it may be significant, that the main records of their presence which I have encountered are in connection with the execution of doctors.*

---

* Religious men and women played other roles in the stories of great Victorian murders. In the record of Jessie M'Lachlan's ordeal we meet a female straight out of Dickens, one Miss Hislop, who visited the wretched woman, as she said, "in my official capacity" as "Scripture Reader in the General Prison." She spoke to Jessie "as I do to other prisoners, as being a lost sinner in the sight of God" and informed her that "I believe you to be the guilty person throughout. You have been guilty of a deed for which you ought to have been hanged, as God has never repealed that law He gave, that blood should answer for blood, but by a very mysterious providence your life has been spared, and I would beseech you to make early and earnest application to Him whose blood cleanseth from all sin." This

Religious activity was far from limited to the actual scenes of the murder, trial, and execution. Throughout the country, from Church of England pulpit and the plainer rostrum of Dissent, parsons took their texts from the headlines whenever they contained news of murders from which wholesome morals could be drawn. At least three of the Corder-inspired sermons found their way into print and thus into the library of the British Museum: *A Sermon on the Power of Conscience, with an Application to the Recent Trial and Condemnation of W. Corder,* by the Rev. George Hughes; *The Sinner Detected: A Sermon . . . on the Occasion of the Execution of William Corder . . . Including Particulars of His Life Never Before Published,* by Charles Hyatt; and *An Address to My Parishioners and Neighbours on the Subject of the Murder Lately Committed at Polstead,* by "A Suffolk Clergyman." The Rush case produced, in addition to Parson Andrew's well-received discourse, S. Hobson's *The Root of All Evil: A Sermon Preached . . . on the Sunday before the Execution of J. B. Rush,* and H. Squire's *On Behaviour to the Sinful,* a sermon based on Galatians 6:1.

Once in a while a particular circumstance in a murder case seemed delivered from the hands of the Lord, for the numerous devout Christians of the Victorian age regarded Providence as an agency as awesome as it had ever been in Old Testament days. The Queen was the special favorite of Providence, because, as was widely known, the weather smiled upon her whenever she made public appearances; and it was Providence, not faulty or non-existent sanitation, which visited typhoid and cholera upon a sinful England. Similarly, the hand of Providence could easily be detected in the dreams by which Maria Marten's stepmother divined that her body lay beneath the floor of the Red Barn. Thus murder came to the aid of the pious in their ceaseless struggle with Victorian doubt: if (as no one denied) Mrs. Marten had had prophetic dreams in 1828, who then could challenge the Scriptural report of Pharaoh's?

---

sanctimonious officiousness drew a well-merited rebuke from some portions of the press, which found a new target two years later in the Lutheran minister who, as he accompanied Franz Müller to the scaffold, practically browbeat him into a last-minute confession.

This was the argument used by the heroic self-taught Biblical scholar John Kitto in his *Daily Bible Illustrations,* a popular theological work of the middle of the century.

The supposed increase in crime and the wholly demonstrable increase in popular interest in the subject was an ever-handy case in point for those who deplored the trend of the times. If one chose to believe that English society was going to the demnition bow-wows, for whatever reasons, there was murder to prove it. When, for example, in the late 1820s there was a flurry of excitement over the campaign to educate working-class adults through mechanics' institutes and cheap books and papers laden with useful information, Burke and Hare were available to attest the foolhardiness of any such enterprise. "It is singular," observed the *Edinburgh Weekly Chronicle* after the trial, "that the only symptom we have yet discovered of the 'march of intellect' among the lower orders, is certain recent discoveries in the art or science of crime. The most important of these is the poisoning of people, for the sake of the money to be found upon them, and the strangling of them for the sake of the money to be obtained from the sale of their carcasses; with both of which our simple ancestors were perfectly unacquainted." There was not the slightest evidence that the body snatchers had been educated in their trade, or been beckoned to it, by any instrument of "the march of intellect"; greed and ruthlessness need no encouragement from the classroom or the printed word. But throughout the ensuing Victorian period, opponents of popular education seized upon the spread of crime and the avidity with which the great public consumed the news thereof as evidence—depending on whether one was a reformer or a pessimist—of "the deficiency of sound and religious education for the great mass of the people most exposed to vicious influences," as the *Law Magazine* put it in 1845, or of the masses' innate and insuperable resistance to the redeeming powers of education once it was provided.

The general satisfaction with the progress of the nation in respect to wealth, education, morality, refinement of manners—a leading theme in the continuous Victorian process of self-examination—was constantly being challenged by the lurid evidence of the police reports. In 1849, a bumper year for murder, *Chambers's Edinburgh Journal* struck a note that rang familiar throughout the period:

Growing up in the very midst of this kindliness of spirit, fastidious delicacy, and romantic refinement, there is a tendency to crime more wild, more brutal, more abominable, than the darkest ages of the world ever heard of. In former times, a truly "terrific murder" was the opprobrium of the epoch, and a landmark of history: now, one succeeds another with such rapidity, that the mind becomes deadened to the sense of horror. Wives destroy their husbands by means of the long agonies of days or weeks—watching in the meantime, like Gouls [*sic*] by their bedside, and gloating on the struggles of their despair; mothers poison their infants when sucking at their breasts; and husbands and wives, conspiring at their firesides to assassinate, prepare the details of the deed a month before, and receive daily the intended victim as a friend and guest till the moment of murder arrives. This horrible taint in the national mind occurs in the midst of social, moral, and religious soundness. It is the attendant of our civilisation, the shadow of our refinement.

The *Chambers's* writer believed therefore that the "taint" was not universal; rather, society simply was cursed with the presence of "great numbers of individuals with ill-regulated minds, . . . whose mental imperfections induce a fatal imitative tendency towards evil actions."

But other writers and speakers were more sweeping, as they were even more vehement, in their indictment of society or a broad portion of it. Carlyle's bleak estimate of the spiritual condition of England at mid-century and his sardonic interest in the headlines led him often to apply the one to the other; it was among his most characteristic rhetorical habits. In the second of his *Latter-Day Pamphlets,* dated March 1, 1850, he drew specifically on what was obviously his and his wife's favorite murder. His lament here, as recurrently through his social criticism, was that while "the materials of human virtue are everywhere abundant as the light of the sun . . . they lie yet unelaborated, and stagnant in the souls of wide-spread dreary millions, fermenting, festering; and issue at last as energetic vice instead of strong practical virtue." The instance Carlyle chose was the former lady's maid who kept her nerve to the end: "A Mrs. Manning 'dying game,'—alas, is not that the foiled potentiality of a kind of heroine too? Not a heroic Judith, not a mother of the Gracchi now, but a hideous murderess, fit to be the mother of hyaenas! To such an extent can potentialities be foiled."

Nine months later, in the short-lived journal *The Christian Socialist*, Charles Kingsley, signing himself "Parson Lot," used the murder of his colleague at Frimley as a peg upon which to hang a series of polemics. Although the men arrested for the murder actually belonged to a gang of professional thieves based at Guildford, the crime had brought into belated notoriety the presence at Frimley and elsewhere in the vicinity of permanent nests of "ruffian squatters," "a deposit of human slime," as Kingsley uncharitably called them. It was upon the society which made possible and then tolerated these "Rogues' Harbours" that Kingsley focused the ire of his Christian conscience:

Along miles of moorland-border, parish beyond parish, similar nests of corruption are dotted, each bringing back from the yearly hop-picking a fresh taint of Cockney iniquity, till the disease reaches its climax; almost every gentleman's house for miles is either robbed or attempted; and, at last, under circumstances too notorious and too hideous to dwell on, an innocent and pious man, beloved and respected by his parishioners, is brutally and cowardly murdered in his wife's presence, a martyr to the sins of society—the real accomplices of Smith, Trower, and the rest, being *the whole enlightened and civilized British Public*. I say this advisedly and deliberately. The blood of good Mr. Hollest cries from the ground, not merely against these three poor untaught barbarians, but against the conceited and boastful society which allows the possibility of such men's existence.

By social critics like Kingsley, the prevalence of murder could be read as an indictment of the complacency and blindness of a society which engendered the conditions in which murderers were bred; by others, less anxious for comprehensive social reform, it was interpreted more simply—and fatalistically—as revealing the spirit of a people at its ugliest. In Liverpool in 1874 there was a sordid trial of two members of a group of young colliers charged with the gang rape of a tramp woman they found lying dead drunk in a ditch; she had died of her injuries. Their companions testified that "they did not think the tramp-woman was ill used, nor what was done was wrong. . . . She never said nothing."

The *Daily Telegraph* burst out in execration:

Nothing in the supposed nature of "Englishmen" can be expected to make our assizes maiden, and our gaol deliveries blank. But there was thought to be something in the blood of our race which would somehow serve to keep us from seeing . . . a gang of Lancashire lads making a ring to see a woman outraged to death. A hundred cases nowadays tell us to discard that idle belief; if it ever was true, it is true no longer. The most brutal, the most cowardly, the most pitiless, the most barbarous deeds done in the world, are being perpetrated by the lower classes of the English people—once held to be by their birth, however lowly, generous, brave, merciful, and civilized. In all the pages of Dr. Livingstone's experience among the negroes of Africa, there is no single instance approaching this Liverpool story, in savagery of mind and body, in bestiality of heart and act. Nay, we wrong the lower animals by using that last word; the foulest among the beasts which perish is clean, the most ferocious gentle, matched with these Lancashire pitmen, who make sport of the shame and slaying of a woman, and blaspheme nature in their deeds, without even any plea whatever to excuse their cruelty.

Though the indignation at the deficiencies of contemporary social morality and culture which murder illustrated spoke in many voices, in literary terms it has proved most durable when expressed with irony. Matthew Arnold's application is probably the most famous: the "Wragg is in custody" passage in "The Function of Criticism at the Present Time" (1864). Arnold quotes two examples of fatuous mid-Victorian complacency from the speeches of the day's politicians:

. . . Mr. Adderley says to the Warwickshire farmers:—"Talk of the improvement of breed! Why, the race we ourselves represent, the men and women, the old Anglo-Saxon race, are the best breed in the whole world. . . . The absence of a too enervating climate, too unclouded skies, and a too luxurious nature, has produced so vigorous a race of people, and has rendered us so superior to all the world."

Mr. Roebuck says to the Sheffield cutlers:—"I look around me and ask what is the state of England? Is not property safe? Is not every man able to say what he likes? Can you not walk from one end of England to the other in perfect security? I ask you whether, the world over or in past history, there is anything like it? Nothing. I pray that our unrivalled happiness may last."

Arnold proceeds, in his own words, to "confront with our dithyramb this paragraph on which I stumbled in a newspaper soon after reading Mr. Roebuck:—"

"A shocking child murder has just been committed at Nottingham. A girl named Wragg left the workhouse there on Saturday morning with her young illegitimate child. The child was soon afterwards found dead on Mapperly Hills, having been strangled. Wragg is in custody."

Nothing but that [continues Arnold]; but, in juxtaposition with the absolute eulogies of Mr. Adderley and Mr. Roebuck, how eloquent, how suggestive are those few lines! "Our old Anglo-Saxon breed, the best in the whole world!"—how much that is harsh and ill-favoured there is in this best! *Wragg!* If we are to talk of ideal perfection, of "the best in the whole world," has any one reflected what a touch of grossness in our race, what an original shortcoming in the more delicate spiritual perceptions, is shown by the natural growth amongst us of such hideous names,—Higginbottom, Stiggins, Bugg! In Ionia and Attica they were luckier in this respect than "the best race in the world;" by the Ilissus there was no Wragg, poor thing! And "our unrivalled happiness;"—what an element of grimness, bareness, and hideousness mixes with it and blurs it; the workhouse, the dismal Mapperly Hills,—how dismal those who have seen them will remember;—the gloom, the smoke, the cold, the strangled illegitimate child! "I ask you whether the world over or in past history, there is anything like it?" Perhaps not, one is inclined to answer; but at any rate, in that case, the world is very much to be pitied. And the final touch,— short, bleak, and inhuman: *Wragg is in custody.* The sex lost in the confusion of our unrivalled happiness; or (shall I say?) the superfluous Christian name lopped off by the straightforward vigour of our old Anglo-Saxon breed! There is profit for the spirit in such contrasts as this. . . .

The year of Wragg, 1864, was also the year of Müller, whose case Arnold used in his attempt to reconcile his fellow-passengers on the Woodford branch of the Great Eastern Railway to their tragic destiny. The "Wragg is in custody" passage appears, indeed, in the same *Essays in Criticism* volume whose preface includes Arnold on Müller.

John Ruskin, too, found the railway carriage crime full of ironic social significance. The manner in which he employed it to drive home a Ruskinian "truth" provides an interesting measure of the difference between his angle of vision and Arnold's. Delivering at Manchester the first of the lectures subsequently published as *Sesame and Lilies,* he commented on the contrast between the nation's absorption in the Müller case and its simultaneous response to the infinitely more urgent fact of the American Civil War:

A great nation, for instance, does not spend its entire national wits for a couple of months in weighing evidence of a single ruffian's having done a single murder; and for a couple of years see its own children murder each other by their thousands or tens of thousands a day, considering only what the effect is likely to be on the price of cotton, and caring no wise to determine which side of battle is in the wrong.

iii

The unconcealed pleasure with which the Victorians welcomed a new murder sensation was, of course, one of the most disturbing facts in the whole situation. "There seems," observed the judge in the Thurtell trial as early as 1824, "to be a pruriency and an appetite for news among the people of this country, such as characterized the Athenians of old. . . . In fact, they seem to be never satisfied unless they are absolutely glutted with things of this sort"—in this case, Thurtell's purported confession, which had been published in the newspapers before the trial began.

"Pruriency" was a strong and useful word: it occurs often in the copious editorializing which the public appetite for crime evoked throughout the century. And in all this complaint there was one invariable motif, the responsibility of the press. It was virtually axiomatic that, as the *Law Magazine* said in the article quoted earlier, "The publication, in all their prurient and debasing details, of the foulest and bloodiest outrages . . . is invariably followed by a fresh crop of crime." The attack on sensational press coverage of murder and other felonies was one phase, and a prominent one, of the larger campaign against "poisonous literature" in all forms, notably the penny bloods that were the favorite pabulum of the barely literate masses. It assumed that crime in print catered to the naturally evil propensities and suggestibility of the uneducated mind.

Substantiation of the charge that murder when extravagantly publicized bred more murder seemed well supplied by events of the 1850s and '60s. Although the two physicians were brought to trial eleven years apart, it has always been assumed that Dr. Pritchard took a leaf, so to speak, out of Dr. Palmer's prescription book. While Pritchard may have developed his technique independently of his celebrated predecessor, such incidental touches as his writing pious sentiments in his diary even as his latest victim expired in agony seem to indicate a specific indebtedness. And it is on record that the extensive publicity attending Palmer's adoption of strychnia for John Parsons Cook's fatal dose lighted the way for William Dove, the alcoholic thirty-year-old son of a Leeds leather manufacturer. Dove, who had a long record of sadism (his recreations included chasing his sisters with a red-hot poker, burning cats' eyes out with vitriol, and hoisting a cow's leg over a beam), had it in mind to rid himself of his wife, preferably by a means that would cause her the greatest possible pain. In January 1856, the newspapers providentially were filled with reports of the Palmer case and especially with evidence that strychnia caused exquisite pain and, moreover, could not be detected in a corpse. Dove, it was later proved, read every word he could about Palmer's feats and was forever talking about the sterling virtues of strychnia. Late in the next month he accomplished his purpose and, although Dove was duly hanged for the crime, Palmer should have received part of the credit. It was ironic that while Dove was awaiting trial, the physician and nurse who had attended his wife testified at the trial of the man who had assisted from afar.

Less than two years later, in December 1857, a journeyman tailor named John Thomson was tried in Glasgow for administering prussic acid—a Scottish "first"—to a girl who had, in the then-familiar phrase, rejected his addresses. At the trial it was shown that in the preceding July Thomson had evinced an interest even stronger, if possible, than that of the public at large in the revelations of the Madeleine Smith case as they unfolded in the newspapers. It was from this source, as well as subsequent conversations with a photographer and a painter, that Thomson acquired his useful knowledge of such matters as the ease with which both arsenic and prussic acid could be obtained and the most practicable quantity to be given to one's victim. Witnesses also reported that Thomson, having absorbed the newspaper accounts day by day, expressed his frank opinion that Madeleine

should have been hanged; "which, in view of the benefit he derived from her experience," as Roughead rightly observes, "was
not only ungallant but savoured of ingratitude."

These well-documented cases of murder by emulation gave
color to the claim that newspapers were "accessories before
the fact to three-fourths of the more extravagant murders that
occur in England. . . . A murder occurs; the journalist does his
work; and the poison he gives forth floats over the country like
a pestilence." Like many such generalizations, however, this one
was not consistently supported by the facts. A speaker before the
Statistical Society in 1875 sought to test it by comparing the
number of murder cases brought to trial in the year of a highly
publicized one with the number tried in the following year. In
the year of Greenacre (1837) there were forty-three such cases;
in the following one, seventy-five—a startling increase of
seventy-five per cent. In the year after Good (1842) the number
rose from sixty-seven to eighty-five. But, alas for the theory,
whereas in the *annus mirabilis* of Gleeson Wilson, the Mannings,
Rush, *et al.* (1849) there were eighty-four murder trials, in the
next year there were but fifty-two. And, to crown the conflict of
evidence, in the year following the very case—Palmer's in 1856
—which was proved to have inspired certain others, there were
twelve fewer murder trials (seventy as against eighty-two in
1856). Whether murder did in fact feed on itself was, therefore,
a moot question, not unconnected with the familiar *post hoc ergo
propter hoc* fallacy. But, statistics aside, it was an enduring assumption, and assumptions, not facts, usually control opinion.

Although the periodical quoted above happened not to
admit crime news to its columns, many such blasts were printed
in the very papers which on other pages were replete with police
intelligence. If one seeks abundant illustration of the hypocrisy
which has so long been assumed to be among the unlovelier attributes of Victorianism, he can do no better than examine a file
of a daily or weekly newspaper which saw no incongruity in
describing the minutiae of the latest murder on one page and
censuring the prurience of the press on another—a close relative
of the technique of leading off a crime report with the usual deploring clichés and then getting down to the real business of the

gory details. The moralizing hand did not want to know how
the reportorial hand offended, nor did it care. They were two
separate journalistic departments, both of which sought to give
the public what it wanted, an initial brief surge of decent outrage and then a wholesome wallow in blood. And when the editorialist assailed the public avidity for crime news, it was always
with an implied *tua culpa*. The beam was always in the other
papers' eye.

It was possible, of course, to report crime without excessive
sensationalism, and this was the reasonable premise upon which
the *Illustrated London News* sought, in its second issue, to justify
its promised coverage. The editors began by assuring their
readers that "coroners' inquests, and civil and criminal trials,
will command no small share of our attention"—an interesting
indication that in 1842 the promoters of a weekly paper specifically meant for the middle-class audience knew that a certain
amount of police intelligence was indispensable. But, they
went on, "we will seek to infuse a healthier tone of morality upon
the subject of such dismal atrocities—to diminish the wild and
dreadful excitement which at such moments agitate the public
frame, and to cleanse that bad and brutal spirit which is fond of
revelling in execration, and makes a holiday spectacle of the
crisis that sends the murderer before his God." This moderate
approach to the problem of crime coverage may well have contributed to the paper's great success.

The vogue of the sensation novel in the sixties evoked, not
surprisingly, much indignation. If the faintest suggestion of im-
propriety was likely to bring a blush to the cheek of the Young
Person, what, then, must be the effect of melodramatic fiction
like Mrs. Wood's and Miss Braddon's? In a now utterly forgotten
novel, Emma Jane Worboise's *Thornycroft Hall* (1864), Miss
Arabella Ward expresses her satisfaction at her current reading:

"There are no less than five murders in this book," said Arabella,
taking up the volume before her; "five murders, very interesting cases
of slow poisoning, and two elopements, and several faithless wives;
and everybody gets into a predicament—into the most awful situations you can conceive; but the hero and the heroine—they are both
of them poisoned, only they get well again somehow—are married at

last, and have a castle left them, and ever so much a year. O, it is so exciting and beautifully written!"

But her killjoy cousin Ellen reproves her:

"You must know—your instincts ought to tell you—that such stories are unfit for our reading. What has a young girl to do with such shameful wickedness? I wish all such books were burnt, for they can do nothing but harm; their very cleverness and piquancy makes them the more dangerous. I suppose we must know of the evil that is in the world some day, but let us keep our minds pure as long as we can. What have we to do with poisoning, and elopements, and other things —things that are shame to us young girls to speak of at all?"

These were sentiments to which the Bishop of York, for one, would have murmured a heartfelt Amen. In November of the same year, addressing the Huddersfield Church Institute, he denounced sensation novels as "tales which aimed at this effect simply—of exciting in the mind some deep feeling of overwrought interest by the means of some terrible passion or crime." The writer in the *North British Review* who quoted him was both more vigorous and more explicit:

According to Miss Braddon, crime is not an accident, but it is the business of life. She would lead us to conclude that the chief end of man is to commit a murder, and his highest merit to escape punishment; that women are born to attempt to commit murders, and to succeed in committing bigamy. If she teaches us anything new, it is that we should sympathize with murderers and reverence detectives. Her principles appear to us to resemble very strikingly those by which the Thugs used to regulate their lives.

Not all commentators, however, saw the mania for reading about murder as proof of human depravity. In 1833 Bulwer (who, it must be admitted, as a practitioner of the Newgate novel may have had his reasons for taking this optimistic stand) had contended:

The superficial jest against our partiality to a newspaper tale of murder, or our passion for the *spectacle* of the gibbet, proves exactly the reverse of what it asserts. It is the tender who are the most susceptible to the excitation of terror. It is the women who hang with the deepest interest over a tale or a play of gloomy and tragic interest. . . . If you observe a ballad-vender hawking his wares, it is the bloodiest murders that the women purchase. It is exactly from our unacquaintance with crime, viz. from the restless and mysterious curiosity it excites, that we feel a dread pleasure in marvelling at its details. This principle will suffice to prove that the avidity with which we purchase accounts of atrocity, is the reverse of a proof of our own cruelty of disposition. . . .

Soothing words indeed for the murder-loving man in the street whose conscience faintly reproached him, and welcome comfort for the newspaper or cheap magazine proprietor troubled by the accusations of social irresponsibility which the guardians of public morality were forever leveling against him!

iv

But if there is one truth these chapters have made clear, it is that the Victorians were far from habitually viewing murder with a grim and solemn mien. Shudder they did when they read of a fresh outrage; but it was an appreciative response, a form of pleasure. Let social psychologists make of it what they will, the fact is that murder was above all a popular entertainment.

Entertainment takes many forms and has as many nuances, which in the case of Victorian murder-as-spectacle ranged from the crude thrills of the Grand Guignol as anglicized in stage melodramas and penny dreadfuls to the higher and elegantly subtle delights that appealed to a sensibility like Henry James's. Tragi-comedy? Black humor? Facetiousness? The half-hysterical laughter that comes to the rescue of one's sanity when the horror is too immense for the normal constitution to contemplate with equanimity? Or simply the mechanism which firmly divorces the moral sense from the aesthetic, and allows us, protected by this convention, to discover the beautiful—or at least the craftsman-like—in the macabre? All these explanations, and more, could be invoked to account for the perennial Victorian delight in murder.

Readers who delve into the still lively volumes of early Victorian humor cannot fail to be impressed by the painless violence, the sunny indulgence of the grisly, which is a characteristic of the genre. Sudden death and grievous injury are accepted as lightheartedly as similar events are in nursery tales and fairy lore. The expected mode of response is implicit in Mr. Jingle's affecting anecdote in *The Pickwick Papers,* relative to the low

archway of a coach yard: "Terrible place—dangerous work—
other day—five children—mother—tall lady, eating sandwiches
—forgot the arch—crash—knock—children look round—mother's
head off—sandwich in her hand—no mouth to put it in—head
of a family off—shocking, shocking!" The jaunty spirit in which
such episodes were received by the contemporary public undoubtedly was related to that same public's response to gory
incidents in real life as reported in the broadsides and newspapers. At the very least, it modified, softened, the reaction
which otherwise would presumably have been one of unqualified
horror.

Once in a while, a comic poet alluded to real murders.
Thomas Hood, in his "Ode to the Great Unknown," had:

> Thou nameless captain of the nameless gang
> That do—and inquests cannot say who did it!
> Wert thou at Mrs. Donatty's death pang? *
> Hast thou made gravy of Weare's watch—or hid it?

Richard Harris Barham, in his "Lay of St. Gengulphus," included
an equally topical reference:

> They contrived to pack up the trunk in a sack,
>   Which they hid in an osier-bed outside the town,
> The clerk bearing arms, legs, and all on his back,
>   As that vile Mr. Greenacre served Mrs. Brown.†

And in "The Lay of the Lovelorn," an amusing parody of Tennyson's "Locksley Hall" (later collected in the *Bon Gaultier Bal-*

---

* In March 1822 a well-to-do elderly widow, Mrs. Donatty, was murdered
in her ten-room house in Bloomsbury under what were called "circumstances
of peculiar atrocity and cruelty." This was one case—Wainewright's was
another, in a quite different way—in which murder touched the world of
art. The victim's fortune derived from her husband, a sheriff's officer who
frequently had had custody of the animal- and genre-painter and chronic
debtor, George Morland. He is said to have "amassed a considerable sum of
money . . . by the sale of pictures painted by Morland."

† Oddly—or perhaps not so oddly—Barham seems not to have referred
in humorous terms to a case in which he was personally involved. When
Mrs. Donatty's body was found, a gag in her mouth and her throat cut from
ear to ear, Barham, then a minor canon of St. Paul's Cathedral, went to
the scene with his friend, the police magistrate Sir Richard Birnie, and
George Ruthven, a Bow Street detective. Reconstructing the murderer's actions, Ruthven accused the victim's dissolute nephew of the deed. The
nephew's protestations of grief so convinced the magistrates that he was

lads), William Edmonstoune Aytoun had his distraught hero cry:

> Better thou wert dead before me,—better, better that I stood
> Looking on thy murdered body, like the injured Daniel Good!

The Victorians obviously loved hangman's humor, and they continued to revel in it in the generation following that of Hood and Barham. The frivolity of Ko-Ko in *The Mikado* is a case in point, though a mild one, since the grimness of the Lord High Executioner's role is totally obscured by the surrounding satiric comedy. But earlier, W. S. Gilbert had written, as one of his *Bab Ballads*, "Annie Protheroe: A Legend of Stratford-le-Bowe." Annie, the local postmistress, "loved a skilled mechanic, who was famous in his day— / A gentle executioner whose name was Gilbert Clay." He entertains her with technical discussions during their courtship, and she delights in reading his "favourable [press] notices, all pasted in a book." But, in the course of his occupation, he is called upon to execute her former lover, Peter Gray. Annie watches Gilbert as he takes a cheap hatchet, chips and chops its blade, and anoints it with sulphuric acid "until / This terrible Avenger of the Majesty of Law / Was far less like a hatchet than a dissipated saw." She protests, but to no avail. The next day, just when the murderously serrated instrument is being raised over the prospective decapitee, she cries "Stay!" and produces a reprieve from the Home Secretary, which had arrived in the post office many weeks ago but which she had suppressed because "I thought it might be awkward if he came and claimed my hand." Conclusion:

> In anger at my secret (which I could not tell before)
> To lacerate poor Peter Gray vindictively you swore;
> I told you if you used that blunted axe you'd rue the day,
> And so you will, you monster, for I'll marry Peter Gray!

The old and new conventions governing the treatment of murderous violence in humorous literature, then, lightened the mood in which the public received real-life murders. And among

---

freed, but years later, in America, he confessed that he had killed his aunt just as Ruthven had hypothesized. His object had been to destroy her will in which he was cut off without a penny.

the especially well educated and artistically aware, there was another kind of convention which affected their response. The attitude of connoisseurship had been classically exemplified by De Quincey's two papers on murder as a fine art, the first appearing in *Blackwood's Magazine* for February 1827, the second (much inferior) in the same periodical for November 1839. The delicacy and discrimination of this pioneer aesthetic approach to murder are too well known to linger over here, but there can be little doubt that it influenced many a Victorian who was prepared to accept, appreciate, and evaluate artistic achievement wherever he found it. Like the poetical character described by Keats, his was the temperament which "lives in gusto, be it foul or fair, high or low, rich or poor, mean or elevated—It has as much delight in conceiving an Iago as an Imogen. What shocks the virtuous philosopher, delights the camelion Poet. It does no harm from its relish of the dark side of things any more than from its taste for the bright one. . . ."

Precisely in the middle of the Victorian era, De Quincey's point of view was restated for a new generation by a little-known essay (it has never, I think, been reprinted) in the *Cornhill Magazine*. It is wholly faithful to the spirit of what might be called the higher criticism of murder, in that it assumes the achievement of the ideal distance, moral as well as aesthetic, from the object. And, inseparable from this, it also faithfully represents the educated Victorian's attitude toward murder at its most humane—as a creative activity in which there are infinite gradations of value and success. For these reasons it will serve as a fitting conclusion to this book. "The Decay of Murder" appeared in the December 1869 issue of the *Cornhill* (by sheer coincidence, only a few months after the last volumes of Browning's *The Ring and the Book*, his great "Roman murder story," had been published), and it was signed "A Cynic": the pen name of Leslie Stephen.*
Stephen began by lamenting the disappearance of virtuoso murderers:

* By a singular exercise of prescience, this article had been anticipated by De Quincey as long before as 1827, in the first of his "Murder as One of the Fine Arts" papers. There he spoke of the dissatisfaction felt over the Thurtell case by "the old cynical amateur, L. S——, that *laudator temporis acti:*" who grumbled, "Not an original idea in the whole piece—mere plagiarism!"

. . . the style of the act is in a state of perceptible decline. Murders are not only immoral—an objection to which they have long been liable—but they are becoming simply gross, stupid, and brutal. They are in the style of the novelists or painters who are incapable of reproducing the beautiful, and try to stun us by sheer undiluted horrors.

Where now are the Eugene Arams, cultivated men whose ventures into homicide were accomplished with a certain agreeable panache?

Though his [Aram's] actions were decidedly wrong, one can follow his course without the uncomfortable sense that comes from plunging into the back-slums and loathsome hiding-places of plebeian vice. Morally, the difference may not be in his favour; he may have been really as vile as the first brutal ruffian who kicks his wife into a jelly, or beats out her brains with a poker. But, artistically speaking, he was far more fit to be the central figure in a drama or a novel. His intellect was not altogether rudimentary nor his sentiments entirely free from any suspicion of nobility. . . . In short, the style of our murderous artists has wofully degenerated since their trade became less fashionable in polite society.

(Stephen could not have foreseen Florence Maybrick, for example, or John Selby Watson, a member of Eugene Aram's own academic profession.)

Like Carlyle, Ruskin, Arnold, and other critics, Stephen used murder to illustrate the present unsatisfactory state of society; but he did so with a difference. His thesis was that the whole climate of the age militates against artistic murder. "The picturesque elements of life" have disappeared.

We are fallen . . . upon the days of petty passions and commonplace characters. Our modern heroes are marked by an absence of the ancient energy. One man is more and more like his neighbour. . . . That we do not commit great crimes is owing less to any positive advance in virtue than to a general desire to conform to the average standard. . . . The tyranny of the majority, of which we have so much, has entered into our souls as well as our laws, and is insidiously transforming us into a very dull, highly respectable, and intensely monotonous collection of insignificant units. If manners have grown softer, we suffer from a stifling atmosphere of public opinion, in which any vigorous development of peculiar idiosyncrasies is fast becoming impossible. . . . We are in such a dread of being blamed as crotchety or eccentric, that we dare not make a move a hand's-breadth from the prescribed path, in which millions of fellow-travellers will keep us in countenance. Originality is growing to be a term of abuse; and ridicule is becoming a more terrible instrument of oppression than was ever wielded by oppressors in the old days of persecution with fire and sword. We have ceased to grow forest-trees, and are content with a vast growth of carefully clipped and preserved garden-shrubs.

This was exactly what John Stuart Mill had been arguing, without reference to murder, just ten years earlier, in his essay *On Liberty*. The curse of conformity was everywhere in English society, leaving no room for originality or eccentricity, in fact refusing to tolerate it.

Under these circumstances it is hardly to be expected that we should get up good murders. The disposition to take such a decided line of action is confined to those ruder classes who retain something of the vices and virtues of a more barbarous state of society. We have amongst us large masses of a population who have escaped the enervating polish of civilization. To them we may still look occasionally for vigorous passions and decided actions. They have the rude energy along with the brutal propensities of a more animal existence.

(Ten years later, Kate Webster would prove brimming with the requisite vigorous passions, decided actions, rude energy, and brutal propensities, almost to a fault.)

Stephen's elegiac piece continued: "revenge," once a dependable stimulus to murder, "may be said to have become almost obsolete. It gives too much trouble. We don't hate anybody enough, or love any one enough, to make it worth our while. . . . You and your intended victim must be alone in the world before his pursuit can become an absorbing occupation. When you are distracted at every step by a thousand causes of excitement, it is impossible to be bothered by a single absorbing passion." It was, in fact, just as Matthew Arnold (whom Stephen omitted to quote) had been saying: "the sick fatigue, the languid doubt," the "strange disease of modern life, / With its sick hurry, its divided aims" distracted the would-be artist in vengeful murder from his "*one* aim, *one* business, *one* desire," just as it prevented men from becoming martyrs or heroes. "If we have not time or energy to spare for vengeance, we lose the great motive for murders of the heroic caste, and can have no more Iagos or Hamlets. Hamlet would now apply to a detective instead of a ghost; and Iago would confine himself to writing spiteful despatches to the War Office at Venice."

As is often the case with men who sigh over the degeneracy of the present, the facts by no means substantiate the lament. The murderous record of the 1860s was in reality a distinguished one. In all probability Leslie Stephen's expectations were unfairly enlarged by the fashion of the sensation novel at the time. "If there were many murders of the romantic character generally described in fictions—murders which form the catastrophe of a long and exciting drama in real life—they would probably come to the surface occasionally. The absence of startling revelations may not prove the non-existence of crime, but it raises a very strong presumption that such crime as exists is of a commonplace and unambitious order. If it often formed the climax of a thrilling story in real life, it would produce a greater explosion, and force its way, somehow or other, into upper air." (How could Stephen possibly have forgotten the bizarre Northumberland Street business, stranger than any fiction, only eight years before?)

Despite the close association between real-life murders and the murders in contemporary sensation fiction, art was not then, any more than at any other time, a slavish imitation of life. The business of artists, even the monarchs of the circulating library and the popular magazines, is to refine and heighten reality. It is not often, even in the best of times, that the dénouements of dramas such as Miss Braddon and Mrs. Henry Wood concocted for their great public have their full-fledged counterparts in the police reports. To expect that they should, as Leslie Stephen did, was to demand more of life than it could reasonably be expected to provide.

His regret over the decline of the English murder actually was as premature as the one George Orwell pronounced in 1946. The English institution of murder, like the Broadway theater, has been an inveterate fabulous invalid. Fortunately, a long life was before Stephen—he would outlive the Queen by three years —and as he read the papers over the next three decades he must have appreciated how unfounded his pessimism had been. As Browning, that fine connoisseur of murder, had remarked in a different connection only five years before "The Decay of Murder" was solemnized, the best, or some of it anyway, was yet to be.

Notes on Sources

Epigraph (*page 15*)

The Journal of Sir Walter Scott (Edinburgh, 1950), p. 583.

1. Early Murders for the Million

i (*pages 18–28*)

Scott on the Gill's Hill tragedy: *Journal*, pp. 203–4, 553–54.

Material on the Thurtell case, not otherwise attributed, is from *Trial of Thurtell and Hunt*, ed. Eric R. Watson (Edinburgh, 1920).

Hazlitt's "The Fight" is found in many collections of his essays, e.g. the Everyman edition of his *Lectures on the English Comic Writers and Fugitive Writings*, pp. 171–85.

Borrow on Thurtell: *Lavengro* (Everyman ed.), pp. 151–52; *The Romany Rye* (Everyman ed.), p. 276.

De Quincey on Thurtell: "On Murder, Considered as One of the Fine Arts," *Blackwood's Magazine*, XXI (1827), 211–12.

Scott's severe judgment of Thurtell: *Journal*, p. 553.

The pamphlets referred to are *Pierce Egan's Account of the Trial of John Thurtell and Joseph Hunt* (London, 1824) and *Recollections of John Thurtell* (London, 1824). Alexander Woollcott's copies, from which I have quoted, are in the Hamilton College Library.

Bulwer and Thurtell's caul: Keith Hollingsworth, *The Newgate Novel* (Detroit, 1963), p. 92.

William Webb: *Notes and Queries*, 11th ser. IV (1911), 244. Browning's recitation of the quatrain is recorded in C. Kegan Paul, *Memories* (London, 1899), p. 338.

ii (*pages 28–31*)

There is no modern edition of Corder's trial. Unless otherwise attributed, the material in this section is derived from the book by J. Curtis mentioned in the text, *An Authentic and Faithful History of the Mysterious Murder of Maria Marten* (London, 1828; reprinted London, 1928).

J. Curtis is described in James Grant, *The Great Metropolis,* 2nd ser. (London, 1837), II, 199–212.

Cordell's behavior at his trial and the Bury workmen's holiday: [Walter Thornbury,] "Old Stories Retold," *All the Year Round,* XVIII (1867), 401–2.

iii (*pages 31–37*)

The definitive work on Burke and Hare, from which all data otherwise unascribed in this section have been drawn, is *Burke and Hare,* ed. William Roughead (new and enlarged ed., Edinburgh, 1948).

The Ettrick Shepherd: *Blackwood's Magazine,* XXV (1829), 382. This number of the "Noctes Ambrosianae" (pp. 371–400) has the Burke-Hare atrocities as its main subject; it provides a good notion of the impact they had on a certain portion of the Edinburgh literati.

The story of Mary Ann Cotton is told by Richard S. Lambert, *When Justice Faltered: A Study of Nine Peculiar Murder Trials* (London, 1935), chapter 5.

The bibliography alluded to is in Roughead, as above, pp. 397–412.

Scott's indignation: *Journal,* p. 618.

iv (*pages 37–40*)

I do not know of any single full account of the Greenacre murder. My brief narrative is taken from two contemporary sources: the *Annual Register* for 1837, Chronicle pp. 12–13, 37–42, 45–46; and *The Chronicles of Crime, or the New Newgate Calendar,* ed. "Camden Pelham" (London, 1886; originally published 1841), II, 428–53.

The children's song and "By right he ought to pay for two passengers": *The Life and Adventures of George Augustus Sala, Written by Himself* (London, 1895), I, 82–83.

"Sixpence a head": *Edmund Yates: His Recollections and Experiences* (London, 1884), I, 42–43.

The attempts on Queen Victoria's life: Elizabeth Longford, *Victoria R. I.* (London, 1964), pp. 151, 169–70, 390, 446. One assault which Lady Longford omits, but which is necessary to account for her figure of seven, is the affair of 1850, when a "ruffian" went at the Queen with a stick. See the *Annual Register* for 1850, Chronicle pp. 73–74, Law Cases pp. 331–39.

2. *"A Highly Popular Murder Had Been Committed"*

(*pages 41–43*)

Footmen buying broadsides: Henry Mayhew, *London Labour and the London Poor* (London, 1861–62; facsimile reprint, New York, 1968), I, 223.

Women at the Staunton trial: *The Trial of the Stauntons,* ed. J. B. Atlay (Edinburgh, 1911), p. 26.

Notes on Sources (pages 42–54)   311

"It is a noteworthy fact . . .": Mrs. Eliza Stephenson, *Janita's Cross*, quoted in Myron F. Brightfield, *Victorian England in Its Novels* (Los Angeles, 1968), I, 18. The succeeding quotations from Emily Eden and Julia Kavanagh are from the same place.

i (pages 43–54)

The chief sources of material on Catnach and his productions are two books by Charles Hindley, *The Life and Times of James Catnach* (London, 1878) and *The History of the Catnach Press* (London, 1887). Whatever these lack in biographical detail and reliability is compensated for by the copious reprints of ballad and broadside texts and facsimiles of their illustrations.

There seems to be no full-length modern account of the Mannings. The *Annual Register* for 1849, Law Cases pp. 429–47, provides a good summary.

The description of the street hawker's board on the Mannings is from Mayhew, I, 301–2.

The sales figures on Catnach's Thurtell productions are from Hindley, *Life and Times of Catnach*, pp. 142–43; those on later murders from Mayhew, I, 284.

"Greenacre didn't sell so well as might have been expected": Mayhew, I, 223.

Pegsworth: *Annual Register* for 1837, Chronicle pp. 7–8, 23–24. Wilson: *Annual Register* for 1849, Law Cases pp. 424–29. Sarah Thomas: *Annual Register* for 1849, Law Cases pp. 417–24. Good: *Annual Register* for 1842, Chronicle pp. 64–68.

" 'Then,' said one Death-hunter, 'we has our fling' ": Mayhew, I, 283.

On the "Waterloo Road mystery": *Annual Register* for 1838, Chronicle pp. 81–83; Belton Cobb, *The First Detectives* (London, 1957), chapter 9.

The contents of "gallows literature" are described by Mayhew, I, 281–84.

"There wasn't no time for a Lamentation . . .": Mayhew, I, 283.

"There's so long to wait . . .": *ibid.*, I, 225.

George Cruikshank's early contributions to the iconography of murder are listed in Albert M. Cohn, *A Bibliographical Catalogue of the Printed Works Illustrated by George Cruikshank* (London, 1914).

The title pages of the street books on Mary Ashford and Greenacre are reproduced from Ted Peterson, "British Crime Pamphleteers," *Journalism Quarterly*, XXII (1945), unpaged.

On the Thornton case, see *Trial of Abraham Thornton*, ed. Sir John Hall (Edinburgh, 1926).

The apocryphal details of the Rush case: Mayhew, I, 284.

The paragraph on pre-printed "last dying speeches" is based on Mayhew, I, 229, 234.

Sale of broadsheets on Müller and Constance Kent: Charles Hindley, *Curiosities of Street Literature* (London, 1871), p. 159. On the Pritchard literature see *The Trial of Dr. Pritchard*, ed. William Roughead (Edinburgh, 1906), p. 304.

The 1903 ballad on Dougal and Moat House: *The Trial of Samuel Herbert Dougal*, ed. F. Tennyson Jesse (Edinburgh, 1928), p. 225.

ii (pages 54–66)

Joseph Hatton's comment is in his *The Talents of Barton* (1867), quoted by Brightfield, *Victorian England in Its Novels*, II, 281.

The newspaper coverage of Mary Blandy: R. M. Wiles, *Freshest Advices: Early Provincial Newspapers in England* (Columbus, Ohio, 1965), pp. 244–46, 265.

Material on the background of early nineteenth-century English journalism is from Richard D. Altick, *The English Common Reader* (Chicago, 1957), chapter 14.

Scott's observation on the journalistic value of a bloody murder: *Letters of Sir Walter Scott*, ed. H. J. C. Grierson (Edinburgh, 1932–37), VIII, 160.

Circulation of the London Sunday papers: Altick, p. 329.

Journalistic coverage of the Thurtell case: introduction to Watson's edition of the trial, cited in notes to chapter 1; the "contemporary writer" quoted on the penny-a-liners is Grant, *The Great Metropolis*, 2nd ser., II, 285–86.

The *Observer*, the *Weekly Chronicle*, the *Illustrated London News*, and contemporary crime: Mayhew, I, 229; Mason Jackson, *The Pictorial Press* (London, 1885), pp. 223, 241–43, 265–66, 291; Clement K. Shorter, "Illustrated Journalism: Its Past and Future," *Contemporary Review*, LXXV (1899), 483–86.

The demand for Norwich papers during the Rush trial: *Notes and Queries*, 4th ser. III (1869), 170.

Coverage of the Constance Kent case: John Rhode, *The Case of Constance Kent* (London, 1928), pp. 223–24; of the "Ardlamont Mystery," William Roughead, *Rogues Walk Here* (London, 1934), p. 4.

The press at Dr. Adams's trial: Sybille Bedford, *The Trial of Dr. Adams* (New York, 1959), p. 51.

"Lord love you . . . ": Mayhew, I, 225.

"Reporters dogged the footsteps . . . ": *The Trial of Mrs. M'Lachlan*, ed. William Roughead (Edinburgh, 1911), pp. xxvi-xxvii.

Combe and Hazlitt: *Complete Works of William Hazlitt*, ed. P. P. Howe (London, 1930–34), XX, 200–4.

The exhibition of Corder's head at Bartholomew Fair is reported by Thomas Frost, *The Old Showmen and the London Fairs* (London, 1874), pp. 302–3; the phrenological diagnosis is in *All the Year Round*, XVIII (1867), 403.

3. Literature with a Sanguinary Cast

i (pages 67–72)

The quotation from *Gideon Giles the Roper* is by way of Brightfield, *Victorian England in Its Novels*, I, 66.

Montague Summers's remark is in his *A Gothic Bibliography* (London, 1941), p. 132.

Sweeney Todd's stage career is described by H. Chance Newton, *Crime and the Drama* (London, 1927), pp. 251–58. The indictment in the libel suit against Catnach is quoted *in extenso* by Hindley, *Life and Times of Catnach,* pp. 85–87.

Dickens on the *Terrific Register:* John Forster, *The Life of Charles Dickens* (London, n.d.), I, 48 note.

ii (pages 72–74)

The standard study of the Newgate novel, from which some of my facts are drawn, is Keith Hollingsworth, *The Newgate Novel* (Detroit, 1963).

Bulwer-Lytton and the Eagle Insurance Company: Jonathan Curling, *Janus Weathercock: The Life of Thomas Griffiths Wainewright* (London, 1938), pp. 313–14, 374.

There is a good contemporary account of Courvoisier in *The Chronicles of Crime,* ed. Pelham, II, 563–83. See also the *Annual Register* for 1842, Law Cases pp. 229–45.

iii (pages 74–85)

The pioneer study of some aspects of the sensation novel is Walter C. Phillips, *Dickens, Reade, and Collins, Sensation Novelists* (New York, 1919). Although it remains valuable, there is room for a more comprehensive and searching book on the subject. The suggestive germ of such a book is Kathleen Tillotson's essay "The Lighter Reading of the Eighteen-Sixties," prefixed to her edition of Collins's *The Woman in White* (Boston, 1969).

T. A. Trollope's mention of *A Siren* is in his *What I Remember* (London, 1887–89), II, 290.

Charles Reade's declaration is quoted by John Coleman, *Charles Reade As I Knew Him* (London, 1904), pp. 263–64.

Henry James's remark on Collins is quoted by Tillotson, p. xvi.

The passage by Mansell is in the *Quarterly Review,* CXIII (1863), 489.

Albany Fonblanque's *Cut Adrift* (1869) is quoted in Brightfield, I, 66.

Thackeray on the Northumberland Street affair: "On Two Roundabout Papers Which I Intended to Write," *Cornhill Magazine,* IV (1861), 379–80. The curious may find a more circumstantial account in the *Annual Register* for 1861, Chronicle pp. 119–27.

"From vice to crime . . . ": Mansell again, p. 501.

The quotation from Paget's *Lucretia* is derived from Robert A. Colby, *Fiction with a Purpose* (Bloomington, Indiana, 1967), p. 275.

The Bravo case: see William Roughead's "Malice Domestic" in his volume of that name (Edinburgh, 1928).

Ainsworth's letter is quoted in S. M. Ellis, *William Harrison Ainsworth and His Friends* (London, 1911), II, 301.

The *Saturday Review* passage is in XCI (1901), 295.

4. The Blood-Stained Stage and Other Entertainments

i (pages 86–97)

Allardyce Nicoll's catalogue of English plays is in his *History of English Drama, 1600–1900* (Cambridge, 1952–59), volume VI. Three useful general studies of melodrama are M. Wilson Disher, *Blood and Thunder* (London, 1949), Frank Rahill, *The World of Melodrama* (University Park, Pa., 1961), and Michael Booth, *English Melodrama* (London, 1965).

On *Jonathan Bradford:* S. M. Ellis, *Wilkie Collins, Le Fanu, and Others* (London, 1931), pp. 169–71; Newton, *Crime and the Drama*, pp. 259–60; Rahill, p. 172. Fitzball's statement on the run of the play is in his *Thirty-Five Years of a Dramatic Author's Life* (London, 1859), I, 241–56.

The Thurtell play Fitzball did not write: *Thirty-Five Years*, II, 402–3.

The story of Boiled Beef Williams is in *Rogue's Progress: the Autobiography of "Lord Chief Baron" Nicholson*, ed. John L. Bradley (Boston, 1965), pp. 149–50. Hindley, *Life and Times of Catnach*, pp. 146–47, quotes the action against Williams in the Court of King's Bench.

The *Oliver Twist* quotation is from chapter 17.

"No theatre with a reputation to lose . . . ": Disher, *Blood and Thunder*, p. 128.

Material on the penny gaffs is from Mayhew, I, 40–42, and James Grant, *Sketches in London* (London, 1838), a chapter reprinted in the Society for Theatre Research Pamphlet series, No. 1 (London, 1952).

Dramas at the London fairs: Frost, *The Old Showmen*, pp. 230, 264–67. The strolling company with the all-purpose wardrobe is mentioned in Mayhew, III, 140.

Material on Punch and Judy and puppet shows is from George Speaight, *The History of the English Puppet Theatre* (London, 1955), pp. 194–95, 246–47, 334–37.

Henry Arthur Jones's remarks are in the *Nineteenth Century*, XIV (1883), 445–46.

The harrowing story of Dickens's later career as a platform reader is told by (among many others) Edgar Johnson, *Charles Dickens: His Tragedy and Triumph* (New York, 1952), II, parts 9 and 10. Dickens's mention of the faintings at Clifton is at II, 1106.

ii (*pages 97–108*)

The pages on Madame Tussaud's waxworks are based on John Theodore Tussaud, *The Romance of Madame Tussaud's* (London, 1920) and Leonard Cottrell, *Madame Tussaud* (London, 1951).

John Holloway's crime is described in detail in *The Chronicles of Crime*, ed. Pelham, II, 262–74.

"And every one of these here has been hung . . . ": "Our Eye-Witness in Great Company," *All the Year Round*, II (1860), 252–53.

V. I. St. John's *Undercurrents* is quoted by way of Brightfield, *Victorian England in Its Novels*, III, 28.

Tawell's case is in the *Annual Register* for 1845, Chronicle pp. 1–2, 42–44; Law Cases pp. 365–78.

The standing patterer's tribute to Madame Tussaud is in Mayhew, I, 233.

The cot withheld from the Road House sale: Rhode, *The Case of Constance Kent*, p. 212.

"Daniel Good . . . was a first-rater": Mayhew, I, 223.

The *Monson v. Tussaud* lawsuits: Roughead, *Rogues Walk Here*, pp. 49–56.

The Bartholomew Fair exhibition is mentioned in Samuel McKechnie, *Popular Entertainments through the Ages* (London, n.d.), p. 48.

"Lord" George Sanger's autobiography is *Seventy Years a Showman* (London, 1910). The quotation is from the New York, 1926, edition, pp. 23–24; Jack Kelly appears on p. 97.

The testimony of the one-handed peep showman: Mayhew, III, 88–89. The range of subjects is described by Frost, *The Old Showmen*, pp. 289, 305–7.

Children playing at Greenacre: Sala, *Life and Adventures*, I, 84.

The repertory of the toy theater: A. E. Wilson, *Penny Plain Two Pence Coloured* (London, 1932) and George Speaight, *Juvenile Drama: A History of the English Toy Theatre* (London, 1946). Archer's theory is quoted by Wilson, p. 37.

Material on the Staffordshire figurines is from Bryan Latham, *Victorian Staffordshire Portrait Figures* (London, 1953), pp. 15–16, and Thomas Balston, *Staffordshire Portrait Figures of the Victorian Age* (London, 1958), pp. 79–81.

iii (*pages 108–114*)

The attendance at Wilson's hanging: *Annual Register* for 1849, Law Cases p. 429; at Brighton when Holloway's body was on view, Hindley, *Life and Times of Catnach*, pp. 242–43.

The Norfolk police intercepting the "Swell Mob": R. H. Mottram, "Town Life and London," *Early Victorian England*, ed. G. M. Young (London, 1934), I, 184.

The Blakesley murder is in the *Annual Register* for 1841, Chronicle pp. 83–84, Law Cases pp. 337–41. The Mayhew locus is I, 223.

The scenes at Barrett's hanging are described in the *Annual Register* for 1868, Chronicle pp. 63–65.

5. Murder and the Literary Life

(*pages 115–134*)

There is a copy of the Palmer item in classical Greek in the British Museum.

The murder of Scott's great-aunt is mentioned in John Gibson Lockhart, *Memoirs of the Life of Sir Walter Scott*, chapter 3. The section of his library devoted to malefactors is listed in the Abbotsford Library Catalogue, published in the *Maitland Club Publications*, XLV (1838), 126–32, 295–98. His letter to Maria Edgeworth is in *Letters*, ed. Grierson, VIII, 91.

Lamb's involvement with murder: *Letters of Charles Lamb*, ed. E. V. Lucas (New Haven, 1935), II, 413–14 (on Thurtell's execution), III, 202 (on Burke and Hare), III, 345, 348–49, 356 (on Danby's murder). Additional details of the Danby affair are in Hindley, *Life and Times of Catnach*, pp. 251–58, and the *Annual Register* for 1833, Chronicle pp. 1–9.

A full account of John Selby Watson's murder of his wife is in Lambert, *When Justice Faltered* (cited in notes to chapter 1), chapter 1.

Material on Thomas Griffiths Wainewright is from Curling, *Janus Weathercock*, cited in notes to chapter 3.

Jane Carlyle on Dalmas: *Jane Welsh Carlyle: Letters to Her Family*, ed. Leonard Huxley (London, 1924), p. 202. Thomas Carlyle to his brother: *Letters of Thomas Carlyle to His Brother Alexander*, ed. Edwin L. Marrs, Jr. (Cambridge, Mass., 1968), p. 591. See also the *Annual Register* for 1844, Chronicle pp. 51–52, and for 1845, Chronicle pp. 31–32.

Jane on "Greenacre-Carlyle": *Letters to Her Family*, p. 84; on Lady Ashburton and Maria Manning, *ibid.*, p. 336.

"What a bore that we cannot get done with the Mannings": *New Letters and Memorials of Jane Welsh Carlyle*, ed. Sir James Crichton-Browne (London, 1904), II, 6; the visit of George Rennie: *ibid.*, 103; her journal entry: *ibid.*, 101.

Mrs. Gaskell and *Mary Barton: Letters of Mrs. Gaskell*, ed. J. A. V. Chapple and Arthur Pollard (Cambridge, Mass., 1967), p. 196. The Ashton murder is in the *Annual Register* for 1831, Chronicle pp. 7–8, and the trial in the volume for 1834, Law Cases pp. 290–96.

Mrs. Gaskell and the Novelli murder: *Letters*, p. 101. The case is briefly described in the *Annual Register* for 1850, Chronicle p. 10.

Kingsley and the Hollest murder: Margaret Farrand Thorp, *Charles Kingsley* (Princeton, 1937), pp. 67–69. For the murder itself, see the *Annual Register* for 1850, Chronicle pp. 122–26.

Monckton Milnes's collection of criminalia is mentioned by James Pope-Hennessy, *Monckton Milnes: The Years of Promise* (New York, 1955), p. 130.

Thackeray's adopting the name of a murderer: Gordon N. Ray, *Thackeray: The Age of Wisdom* (New York, 1958), p. 72.

Lewis Carroll on Tennyson's interest in murder: Florence Becker Lennon, *Lewis Carroll* (London, 1947), p. 73.

Jowett's testimony: H. B. Irving, *A Book of Remarkable Criminals* (New York, 1918), p. 11.

FitzGerald on his delight in trials: *Letters and Literary Remains of Edward FitzGerald*, ed. Aldis Wright (London, 1902–3), II, 201; on Thurtell, *ibid.*, IV, 63. Thomas Wright's comment is in his *Life of Edward FitzGerald* (London, 1904), I, 51.

The senior Browning's letter on the Constance Kent case is mentioned in *The Browning Collections* (catalogue of Sotheby's sale), (London, 1913), p. 28. Kegan Paul's statement is in his *Memories* (cited in notes to chapter 1) p. 338.

The scholarly study by Philip Collins is *Dickens and Crime* (London, 1962); see especially chapter 11, "Murder: From Bill Sikes to Bradley Headstone."

Dickens's description of his visit to the scene of the Parkman-Webster murder is in the Nonesuch edition of his *Letters* (Bloomsbury, 1938), III, 599–600. He refers to the trial of Müller in the same volume, p. 402, and to "the latest piece of poisoning ingenuity in Pritchard's case" on p. 432. The story of the pilgrimage to the scene of the Dadd murder is told in *Edmund Yates: His Recollections and Experiences*, II, 104–5. The case is described in the *Annual Register* for 1843, Chronicle pp. 119–20.

The fullest accounts of the Constance Kent case are Rhode, *The Case of Constance Kent*, and Yseult Bridges, *The Tragedy at Road-Hill House* (New York, 1955). See also William Roughead's "Constance Kent's Conscience" in his *The Rebel Earl and Other Studies* (Edinburgh, 1926), pp. 49–86. The superintendent's pleasantry concerning the locked-in security force is in the same work by Roughead, p. 69. Dickens's theory, quoted by Bridges, is in a letter of October 24, 1860; I am indebted to Mrs. Madeline House, co-editor of the Pilgrim edition of Dickens's letters, for the information that the holograph is in the Pierpont Morgan Library.

W. L. Burn's comment is in his *The Age of Equipoise: A Study of the Mid-Victorian Generation* (London, 1964), p. 37. Also published New York, 1964, reissued 1965.

Reade and the Staunton case: *The Trial of the Stauntons,* ed. Atlay, pp. 308–15, where two of his letters are reproduced; the rest are in the Uniform Library Edition of his works (1895), volume XVII.

Spilsbury's findings are reported in Edgar Lustgarten, *The Murder and the Trial* (New York, 1958), p. 176.

Pater's interest in the "Waterloo Bridge mystery": Thomas Wright, *The Life of Walter Pater* (London, 1907), I, 134–35. The mystery itself is in the *Annual Register* for 1857, Chronicle pp. 194–97.

Stevenson and Gosse: *Letters of Robert Louis Stevenson,* ed. Sidney Colvin (London, 1911), I, 267; II, 75.

All fourteen of Henry James's letters to Roughead are printed in the latter's *Tales of the Criminous,* ed. W. N. Roughead (London, 1956), pp. 251–66. The first quotation is from p. 254, the second from p. 266.

NOTE. *Chapters 6–18 are based chiefly on the appropriate volumes of the Notable British Trials series as cited at the head of the notes for each chapter. Unless otherwise specified, all material is from these volumes.*

6. The Tragedy at Stanfield Hall

RUSH

(pages 135–145)

The standard source is *The Trial of James Blomfield Rush,* ed. W. Teignmouth Shore (Edinburgh, 1928).

The Tussaud handbill is reproduced in *Early Victorian England,* ed. Young, I, facing p. 186. The passage from the Tussaud catalogue is quoted by Cottrell, *Madame Tussaud,* pp. 173–74.

"He formed an intimacy with Cobbett": quoted in the *Trial,* p. 3.

Dickens's observations in the field: Nonesuch edition of his *Letters,* II, 141–42.

The article in the *Examiner* was attributed to Dickens by Alec W. Brice and K. J. Fielding, "On Murder and Detection—New Articles by Dickens," *Dickens Studies,* V (1969), 45–61.

Wordsworth on Rush: *Letters of William and Dorothy Wordsworth: The Later Years 1821–1850,* ed. Ernest de Selincourt (Oxford, 1939), III, 1323.

Dickens's availing himself of the book by the Pentonville chaplain: Collins, *Dickens and Crime,* pp. 148–49, 155–59.

Smith's *The Chronicles of Stanfield Hall* is discussed by W. Roberts, "Lloyd's Penny Bloods," *Book-Collector's Quarterly*, XVII (April–June 1935), 11.

Chadwick's *Victorian Miniature* was published in London, 1960; the Rush case figures on pp. 106–20.

7. *"Trust Not the Physician"*

(*pages 146–152*)

Background material on the Victorian medical profession is from Richard H. Shryock, *The Development of Modern Medicine* (Philadelphia, 1936), especially pp. 241–62.

St. John Long's notoriety is canvassed in, for example, *The Chronicles of Crime*, ed. Pelham, II, 217–28.

The two cases of death by Morison's pill are reported in the *Annual Register* for 1834, Chronicle pp. 305–9, and the volume for 1836, Chronicle pp. 38–45.

The Lady Flora Hastings affair is described in Longford, *Victoria R. I.*, pp. 95–99, 122–23.

The excerpts from *Martin Chuzzlewit* are from chapter 41.

"Fie on these dealers in poison . . . ": De Quincey in *Blackwood's Magazine*, XXI (1827), 209.

The case of Dr. William Smith is narrated by William Roughead, *Knave's Looking Glass* (London, 1935), pp. 265–88.

i PALMER

(*pages 152–160*)

The standard source is *The Trial of William Palmer*, 3rd ed. by Eric R. Watson (Edinburgh, 1952). A novelized account, from which I have taken a few additional details, is Robert Graves, *They Hanged My Saintly Billy* (Garden City, N.Y., 1957).

George Augustus Sala is quoted from his *Life and Adventures*, I, 271–72.

ii SMETHURST

(*pages 160–169*)

The standard source is *The Trial of Dr. Smethurst*, ed. Leonard A. Parry (Edinburgh, 1931).

The passage from Collins's *Armadale* is found in Book 3, chapter 15.

Material on the multiplicity of agencies granting medical degrees is chiefly from Shryock, pp. 252–53, and A. M. Carr-Saunders and P. A. Wilson, *The Professions* (Oxford, 1933), pp. 76–83.

The 1855 Sabbatarian disturbances are described in the *Annual Register* for that year, Chronicle pp. 106–9.

iii PRITCHARD

(*pages 169–174*)

The standard source is *The Trial of Dr. Pritchard*, ed. William Roughead (Edinburgh, 1906).
The trial of Dr. Lamson was edited by Hargrave L. Adam (Edinburgh, 1913).

8. Henry James's Perfect Case

MADELEINE SMITH

(*pages 175–190*)

The standard source is *The Trial of Madeleine Smith*, new ed. by F. Tennyson Jesse (Edinburgh, 1927). A later treatment, bearing Roughead's imprimatur, is Peter Hunt, *The Madeleine Smith Affair* (London, 1950), which incorporates research material gathered for the motion picture *Madeleine*—most notably some of the heroine's letters which were not offered in evidence at the trial.

"The papers of the time . . . ": J. B. Atlay, *Famous Trials of the Century* (London, 1899), pp. 104–5.

The "Murder-mania" article appeared in *Chambers's Edinburgh Journal*, new ser. XII (1849), 204–6. The quotation is from p. 204.

"The Poison-Eaters": *ibid.*, XVI (1851), 389–91.

The *Blackwood's* passage on arsenic, in a larger article on "The Beverages We Infuse," is in LXXIV (1853), 687–9.

The vexed question of Madeleine's career after her acquittal is most thoroughly examined by Hunt, pp. 194–200. *Violet* Hunt's assertion is in her *The Wife of Rossetti* (New York, 1932), p. 229 note.

Hawthorne's comments on the Smith trial: *English Notebooks*, ed. Randall Stewart (New York, 1941), pp. 517, 534.

The letters exchanged by John Blackwood, George Eliot, and George Henry Lewes: *The George Eliot Letters*, ed. Gordon S. Haight (New Haven, 1954–56), II, 360–63.

Jane Carlyle's observations: *Letters and Memorials of Jane Welsh Carlyle.* ed. James Anthony Froude (London, 1883), II, 319–21.

Henry James's tribute: Roughead, *Tales of the Criminous*, pp. 260–61 (and in *Letters of Henry James*, ed. Percy Lubbock [New York, 1920], II, 373–74).

The review of *Such Things Are: Quarterly Review*, CXIII (1863), 501–2.

9. A Deed of Dreadful Note

M'LACHLAN

(*pages 191–198*)

The standard source is *The Trial of Mrs. M'Lachlan*, ed. William Roughead (Edinburgh, 1911). I have added a few details from Christianna Brand, *Heaven Knows Who* (London, 1960).

10. The Murder That Thackeray Foretold

MÜLLER

(pages 199–209)

The standard source is *The Trial of Franz Muller,* ed. H. B. Irving (Edinburgh, 1911).

The French railway murders are described by Major Arthur Griffiths, *Mysteries of the Police and Crime* (London, 1901), II, 276–77, and in the *Annual Register* for 1860, Chronicle pp. 181–84.

C. Willett and Phillis Cunnington describe the "Muller-cut-down" in their *Handbook of English Costume in the Nineteenth Century* (2nd ed., London, 1966), p. 282.

"Fatal accidents were more than fifteen times as frequent": G. M. Young in *Early Victorian England,* II, 460 note.

11. A Spin Across London Bridge

WAINWRIGHT

(pages 210–219)

The standard source is *The Trial of the Wainwrights,* ed. H. B. Irving (Edinburgh, 1920).

FitzGerald's complaint to Fanny Kemble is in his *Letters and Literary Remains,* III, 190. Swinburne's is in *The Swinburne Letters,* ed. Cecil Y. Lang (New Haven, 1959–62), III, 73.

12. The Trouble with Servants

WEBSTER

(pages 220–230)

The standard source is *The Trial of Kate Webster,* ed. Elliot O'Donnell (Edinburgh, 1925).

Greville's comment on the Courvoisier excitement: *Memoirs,* ed. Lytton Strachey and Roger Fulford (London, 1938), IV, 261.

The Norwich dismemberment case is described in Jack Smith-Hughes, *Unfair Comment upon Some Victorian Murder Trials* (London, 1951), chapter 9.

The murder of Catherine Bacon is in the *Annual Register* for 1855, Chronicle pp. 17–23.

On Madame Riel, see Smith-Hughes as just cited, chapter 7.

13. Charley's Music Hall Turn

PEACE

(pages 231–237)

The standard source is *The Trial of Charles Frederick Peace,* ed. W. Teignmouth Shore (Edinburgh, 1926). A notable appreciation of Peace's personality and talents, discovered too late to be utilized in this chapter, is in Charles Whibley, *A Book of Scoundrels* (new ed., New York, 1912), pp. 253–62. The long chapter on Peace in H. B. Irving's *A Book of Remarkable Criminals* supplies a much fuller account of his earlier career and his housebreaking exploits in South London than is pertinent here.

14. A Bedroom in Pimlico

BARTLETT

(*pages 238–251*)

The standard source is *The Trial of Adelaide Bartlett*, ed. Sir John Hall (Edinburgh, 1927).

The scenes after Adelaide's acquittal were described by Sir Edward Clarke himself in "Leaves from a Lawyer's Case-book: the Pimlico Mystery," *Cornhill Magazine*, new ser. XLIX (1920), 663–66. The *Pall Mall Gazette* is quoted there. Other details are found in William Roughead's "The Luck of Adelaide Bartlett: A Fireside Tale," in his *The Rebel Earl and Other Studies*. Adelaide's note of thanks is quoted by Clarke in the article cited.

Material on Victorian "Malthusianism" is chiefly from J. A. Banks, *Prosperity and Parenthood: A Study of Family Planning among the Victorian Middle Classes* (London, 1954), and on feminism from Lloyd Fernando, "The Radical Ideology of 'the New Woman,'" *Southern Review* (Adelaide, Australia), II (1967), 206–22.

Wills at the Wilde trial: *The Trial of Oscar Wilde*, ed. H. Montgomery Hyde (London, 1958), pp. 329, 339.

15. Arsenic and the Lady from Alabama

MAYBRICK

(*pages 252–258*)

The standard source is *The Trial of Mrs. Maybrick*, ed. H. B. Irving (Edinburgh, 1912). A more recent treatment of the case is Trevor L. Christie, *Etched in Arsenic* (Philadelphia, 1968), which presents much new information, particularly on Mrs. Maybrick's family antecedents, the uproar after her conviction, and her later life.

The popular song about Mrs. Maybrick is reproduced—all six stanzas—in *Victorian Street Ballads,* ed. W. Henderson (London, 1937), pp. 48–49. Whatever its original title, it is there captioned "Penal Servitude for Mrs. Maybrick: She will not have to climb Golden Stairs."

16. Poison by Pill and Pen

CREAM

(*pages 259–267*)

The standard source is *The Trial of Thomas Neill Cream*, ed. W. Teignmouth Shore (Edinburgh, 1923).

17. The Deaths at George's American Bar

CHAPMAN

(pages 268–273)

The standard source is *The Trial of George Chapman,* ed. Hargrave L. Adam (Edinburgh, 1930).

Roughead's essay "Conrad and Crime: A Note of Admiration" is in his *Malice Domestic,* pp. 263–78.

On the involved story of Edmund Pook, see Smith-Hughes, *Unfair Comment* (cited in notes to chapter 12), chapters 1 and 2.

18. The Man Who Trained Nude Bicyclists

DOUGAL

(pages 274–280)

The standard source is *The Trial of Samuel Herbert Dougal,* ed. F. Tennyson Jesse (Edinburgh, 1928).

19. Murder and the Victorian Mind

i *(pages 281–289)*

Visitors' impressions of the low incidence of murder in eighteenth-century England are documented in Leon Radzinowicz, *The History of the English Criminal Law and Administration from 1750,* I (London, 1948), appendix 3. On the inadequacy of Victorian crime statistics, see J. J. Tobias, *Crime and Industrial Society in the Nineteenth Century* (New York, 1967), chapter 2; James T. Hammick, "On the Judicial Statistics of England and Wales," *Journal of the Statistical Society,* XXX (1867), 375–426 (especially pp. 376–78, 384); and George Grosvenor, "Statistics of the Abatement of Crime in England and Wales, during the Twenty Years Ended 1887–88," *ibid.,* LIII (1890), 377–413 (especially pp. 378–79). The incidence of infanticide in murder statistics is discussed by Hammick, p. 399, and the reduction of murder charges to lesser offenses by Grosvenor, p. 384. The year-by-year record of persons committed to trial for murder, 1836–74, is given by William A. Guy, "On the Executions for Murder That Have Taken Place in England and Wales During the Last Seventy Years," *ibid.,* XXXVIII (1875), 480.

E. E. Kellett's testimony is in his *As I Remember* (London, 1936), pp. 232–33.

H. B. Irving on undetected murderers: *A Book of Remarkable Criminals,* p. 16.

Leslie Stephen's comment is in "The Decay of Murder," *Cornhill Magazine,* XX (1869), 731.

A. W. C. Brice and K. J. Fielding discuss "Dickens and the Tooting Disaster" in *Victorian Studies,* XII (1968), 227–44.

The *British Medical Journal*'s statement on the disposition of unwanted children is quoted in J. A. and Olive Banks, *Feminism and Family Planning in Victorian England* (Liverpool, 1964), p. 86.

The sampling of 480 cases to classify the kinship of victim to murderer is my own, based on the list of executions in Joseph T. Haydn's *Dictionary of Dates* (25th ed., 1910). A similar breakdown of victims by relationship is found in Guy's article cited above, pp. 484–85.

ii (pages 289–297)

Mary Ashford's epitaph is quoted in *Notes and Queries*, 2nd ser. XI (1861), 431–32.

Religious exercises at Palmer's execution: Graves, *They Hanged My Saintly Billy*, p. 308; at Pritchard's, *Trial of Dr. Pritchard*, p. 338. The insufferable Miss Hislop is mentioned in the *Trial of Mrs. M'Lachlan*, p. xciii.

The *Edinburgh Weekly Chronicle*'s statement is quoted in Roughead's *Burke and Hare*, p. 383; the *Law Magazine*'s in *Littell's Living Age*, V (1845), 515.

"Growing up in the very midst . . .": *Chambers's Edinburgh Journal*, new ser. XII (1849), 209.

The *Daily Telegraph*'s excoriation of the colliers, December 17, 1874, was quoted by Ruskin in a note to *Fors Clavigera*, letter 49 (*Works of John Ruskin*, ed. E. T. Cook and Alexander D. O. Wedderburn [London, 1902–12], XXVIII, 251–52).

iii (pages 297–302)

The case of William Dove is in the *Annual Register* for 1856, Law Cases pp. 529–39.

The case of John Thomson is in William Roughead, *Glengarry's Way* (Edinburgh, 1922), chapter 3.

Newspapers as "accessories before the fact": *Chambers's Journal* as cited above.

The supposed propagative effect of a highly publicized murder: *Journal of the Statistical Society*, XXXVIII (1875), 472–73, 483.

Miss Worboise's novel is quoted in Brightfield, *Victorian England in Its Novels*, I, 19. The *North British Review* article is in XLIII (1865), quotations on pp. 202–3.

Bulwer's argument is in his *England and the English* (2nd ed., London, 1833), I, 68–69.

iv (pages 302–308)

The murder of Mrs. Donatty is recorded in the *Annual Register* for 1822, Chronicle pp. 43–45. Barham's involvement is mentioned in *Personal Reminiscences by Barham, Harness, and Hodder*, ed. Richard Henry Stoddard (New York, 1875), pp. 68–71.

Keats's description of the poetical character is in his letter of October 27, 1818, to Richard Woodhouse.

Orwell's lament over the decline of the English murder: *Shooting an Elephant* (London, 1950), p. 197.

Index

The principal discussion of a given murder is indicated by boldface numerals.